Will Davies spent 37 years working as an independent producer of mainly historical documentaries and series for the ABC and SBS. He retired in 2010. He began writing books with the first published in 2004, and to date has had 10 books published, including *Somme Mud: The War Experiences of an Australian Infantryman in France 1916–1919*, *In the Footsteps of Private Lynch* and *Beneath Hill 60*.

He was a member of the NSW Anzac Council, leads battlefield tours to the Western Front and has served on a number of boards. In 2018 he was awarded a PhD from the ANU and, among other projects, is working to build a war memorial school in the French village of Pozières.

Also by Will Davies

Somme Mud (editor)
In The Footsteps of Private Lynch
Beneath Hill 60
The Youngest Battalion Commander in the AIF
The Last 100 Days

Will Davies

SECRET & SPECIAL

The untold story of Z Special Unit in the Second World War

VINTAGE BOOKS

Australia

VINTAGE

UK | USA | Canada | Ireland | Australia
India | New Zealand | South Africa | China

Vintage is part of the Penguin Random House group of companies whose addresses can be found at global.penguinrandomhouse.com

Penguin
Random House
Australia

First published by Vintage in 2021

Cover design by James Rendall © Penguin Random House Australia Pty Ltd
Front cover: (top left) A small party of men on a boat near Berhala Island (AWM 121749); (top right) Supply dropping (National Archives of Australia); (bottom left) Members of the 2/2nd Australian Independent Company in New Guinea (AWM 030389/03); (bottom right) Soldiers on patrol in New Britain (AWM 018320)
Back cover: The *Krait* (AWM 044211)
Maps by Ice Cold Publishing
Typeset in 13/17.5 Adobe Garamond Pro by Midland Typesetters, Australia

Printed and bound in Australia by Griffin Press, part of Ovato, an accredited ISO AS/NZS 14001 Environmental Management Systems printer

A catalogue record for this book is available from the National Library of Australia

ISBN 978 0 14378 498 2

penguin.com.au

*To the forgotten men and women of SRD and the Z Special Unit,
in particular Roland Griffiths-Marsh and Edgar 'Mick' Dennis,
and to the memory of Maayken Griffiths-Marsh for her
dedication and love of a brave warrior.*

Contents

Foreword

By Major General Paul Kenny, DSC, DSM

Whether it be from films, television, comics, or even – as Dr Davies gamely admits in his preface to this vital work – from books reread and cherished as a child, many of us have formed a view of the quintessential Australian soldier. This soldier is unassuming and willing to accomplish the most impossible of tasks with a minimum of fuss, against all odds.

The stories contained within *Secret and Special* are of talented but ordinary men who were thrust into the most extraordinary of circumstances. Each of their journeys is unique, representing the best of all of us.

It is hard not to be moved by the audacity and determination of Bill Reynolds, commandeering an abandoned Japanese fishing vessel and piloting it through the Rhio Strait, rescuing anyone he could find as he went. Nor that of Lieutenants Page and Jones, paddling as silently as possible through enemy waters and attaching limpet mines with a terrifying *clang* to the sides of warships, while hoping for a clean escape. Likewise the diligent and level-headed Sergeant Ellwood, soldiering on with an increasingly doomed mission on the outskirts of Dili, digging a pit to bury his diary and sensitive plans while hoping to evade the next patrol.

Those who served in the Services Reconnaissance Department and Z Special Unit from 1942 until 1945 operated in environments of extreme peril. They did so with feelings of fear, apprehension, the thrill of adventure, and ultimately a slow dawning of hope that they would see their secret missions through. When their country called upon them to do something extraordinary, they did. Often it was at the cost of their own lives.

In the finest traditions of what would become Special Operations Command of the Australian Defence Force we know today, they embodied our values – of service, courage, respect, integrity and excellence – and we are forever indebted to them.

The keen and carefully researched narrative that Dr Davies paints within these pages is, ultimately, one of heroism. Often heroism performed with the hard knowledge that few would ever hear about it, or understand, the secret work these men performed. Dr Davies also places these deeds in the context of centuries of warfare, highlighting that while the character of war may change constantly, its dark truth and nature never does. Dr Davies' research allows us to share the private lives of these men, of whom so much was asked, and their families at home who shared the burdens of their service. I was deeply moved by the aftermath of the tragic Operation Copper, when Sapper Dennis honoured his commitment to his lost mates and visited their families to tell them what he could of their loved one's last moments.

As the Special Operations Commander – Australia, who is humbled and privileged to serve in the Australian Defence Force, it is a striking reminder of why I serve. I'm inspired by the Australian Defence Force values these men embodied. They were certainly different times, and yet our values remain the same. It is also a reminder that all of us in uniform ultimately serve to protect our families, our friends and the people we are fortunate to call fellow Australians. These men served to keep us safe, prosperous and free.

Dr Davies does us a significant service in bringing their stories, and the stories of their families and colleagues, to light.

Preface

This book had its origins in the mid-1960s, when, as a schoolboy, I read Ronald McKie's book *The Heroes*, the story of the audacious Operation Jaywick raid on Singapore. This had been undertaken in late 1943 when a captured Japanese fishing boat, the *Kofuku Maru*, renamed *Krait* after the deadly snake, sailed from Australia to near Singapore where a group of operatives in kayaks paddled into Singapore Harbour and blew up Japanese ships. They then rejoined the waiting *Krait* and returned to Australia.

At the time, little was known; the files were still embargoed and the men who'd taken part in the raid were bound to silence by the Official Secrets Act. But while some information had been made public about Jaywick and *Krait*, only the vaguest details had been revealed of the disaster of a similar operation in 1944, again on Singapore Harbour: Operation Rimau and the final execution of ten operatives just six weeks before the end of the war.

In 1988, I began working as the series producer on a four-part documentary series titled *When the War Came to Australia* for the ABC. Knowing a little of the Jaywick and Rimau stories, I decided to follow up with research at both the Australian War Memorial (AWM) and the National Archives of Australia (NAA) in Canberra. Armed with some file numbers provided to me by the Research Centre at the AWM, I put in an order to read some selected files at the NAA's Mitchell repository. Of the five or six

I ordered, in the end two were withheld for some reason unknown to me at the time, but those I did see gave me a glimpse of the wealth of information, the rich history and the untold stories, that resided there.

As part of my research at the NAA, I also met and talked with a wonderful group of veterans who were clearing files from the Second World War. One area of interest I wanted to include, and something I was able to ask them about, were the mysterious 'beadles' – the men of the Volunteer Air Observers Corps – but as they told me, the files of their service had vanished. I was able to confirm, however, that most of the operational files of the highly secret Services Reconnaissance Department (SRD) and Z Special Unit had been cleared and would be available at the NAA in due course. These organisations were the forerunner of today's Special Air Service and operated from 1942 until 1945 in the Japanese-held areas to the north of Australia. And as such, their actions and the danger of their missions has always fascinated me.

I put the idea of a book about this largely unknown and secret war on hold, and got on with life, at that time as a documentary producer mainly for the ABC and SBS. Now, some 30 years on, I have had the time to research and write this long-dormant book.

As with all my books, here I approach the subject and the history in my own particular way. First and foremost, this book is rich in details and facts, yet entertaining enough to immerse yourself in. Where necessary, I backfill and contextualise the story to give readers a fuller grasp of the time in which this played out. For research, I rarely read secondary sources, relying instead on official accounts, documents and files from the time and, in this case, the SRD-Z Special files held by the NAA.

I have been fortunate to also have had access to some oral-history interviews recorded by both Zed Films in Queensland and through a programme at the Australian Defence Force Academy in Canberra. Quotations, be they from interviews or documents, breathe life and passion into a story, and better inject historical accounts with a wonderful sense of sharing and inclusion.

While the men and women of Special Operations Australia (SOA) and the operatives of the Z Special Unit made up only a tiny proportion of the three Australian armed services in the Second World War, and while their contribution is difficult to quantify, it is worthy of the highest praise and recognition, something not afforded them over the intervening years. To date, although a number of books have been written about these events – mostly by the men themselves of their particular operation – there has not been a popular history published of the range of operations undertaken by SRD in the war. Now, with very few still left alive, their incredible exploits and escapades must be shared with a wider readership.

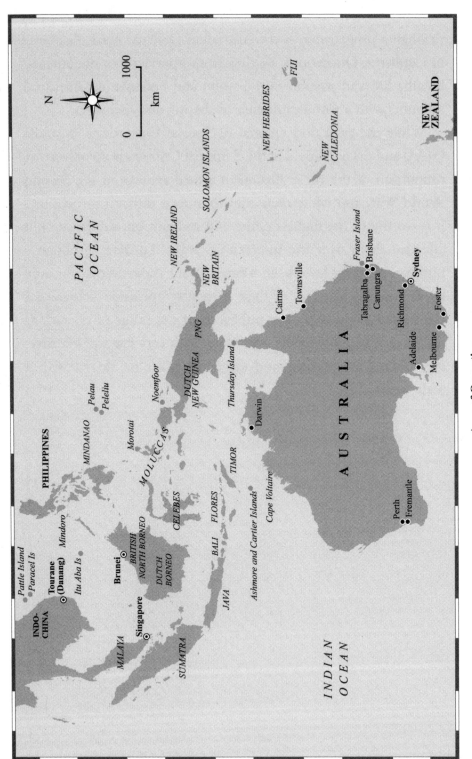

Area of Operations

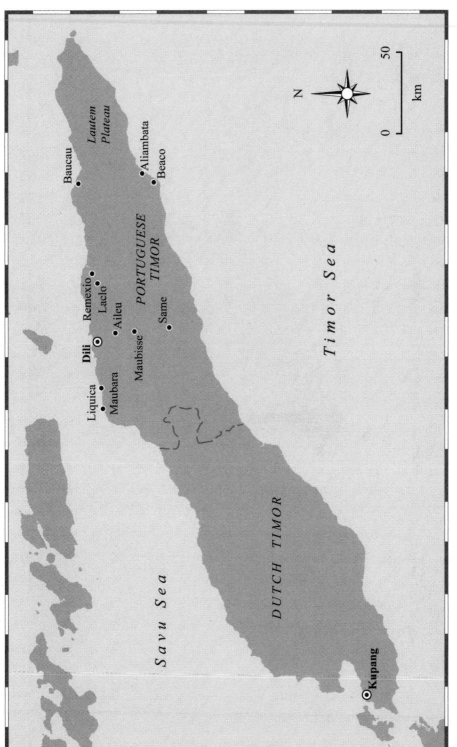

Timor

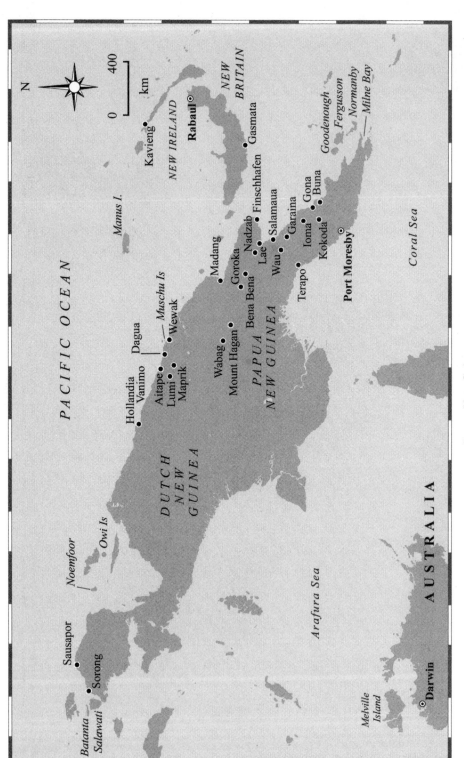

Papua New Guinea

MINDANAO

Celebes Sea

Tawi Tawi
• Bongao

Jambongan Is.
Sandakan •

Semporna •

Banggi Is.

Pensiangan
• Djoeata
Pitas • Ranau
Brantian Estate
Tarakan

BRITISH NORTH BORNEO

Balikpapan ◎

Sambodjalama •
Samarinda •
Semoi •
Riko ◎

Jesselton •

Kalabakan •

Labuan

Belait •
BRUNEI
Beluru •
Long Akah •

Moeara •

Seria •
Miri •
Marudi •
Belaga •
Song •

SARAWAK
Sibu •
Kanowit •

DUTCH BORNEO

Banjarmasin •

South China Sea

Santubong River

Kuching •

Pontianak •

Ketapang •

CELEBES

N

500

km

0

Borneo

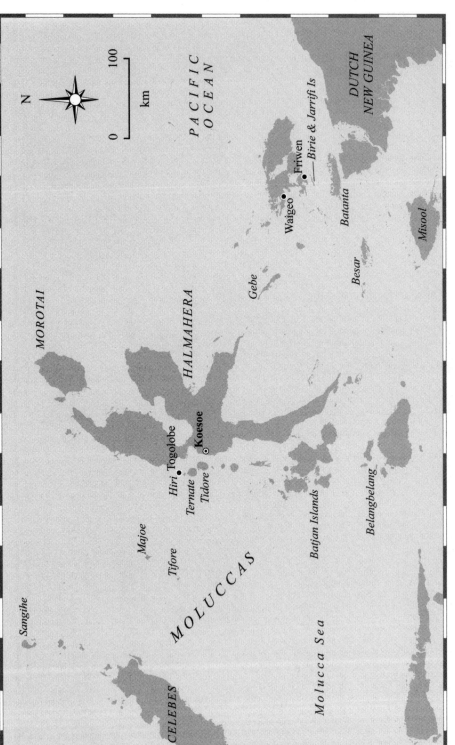

Morotai and Moluccas

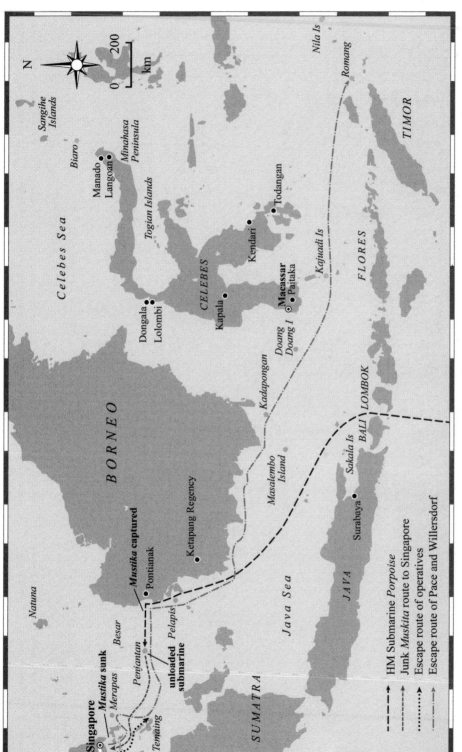

Operation Rimau

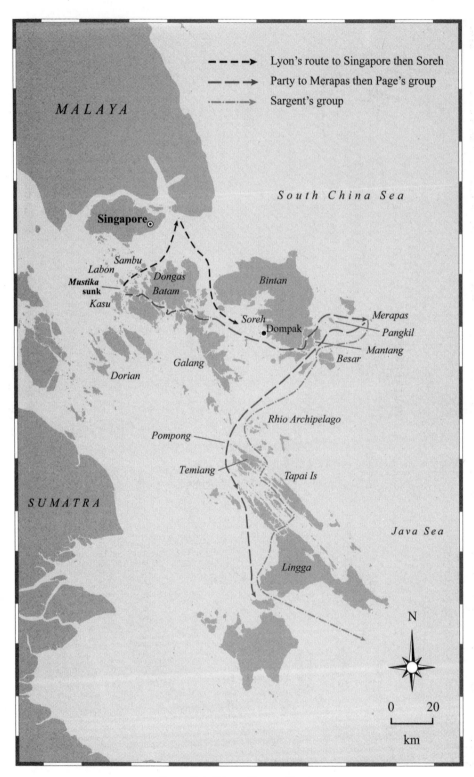

Operation Rimau Escape Route

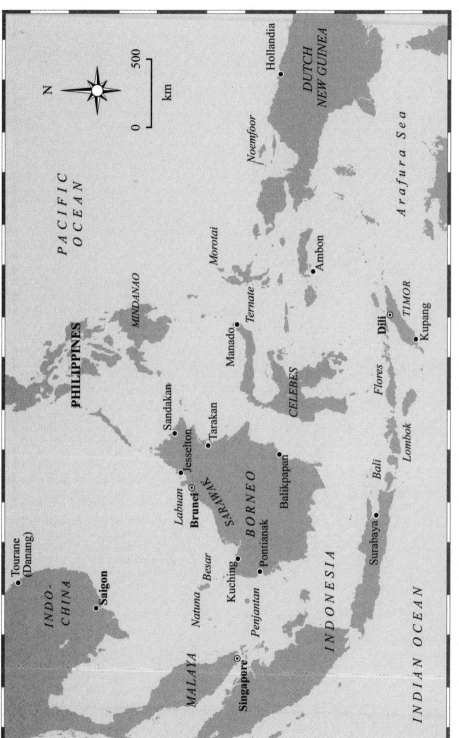

Philippines

Introduction

War has always created new problems and new answers, be they tactics, equipment, weaponry or defensive works. The requirements of war have seen difficult or dangerous tasks allocated to men with special skills or capabilities to deal with them. The 300 Spartans who held the pass at Thermopylae against the might of Xerxes' Persian army and died there were the best and the bravest, as was Pheidippides, the legendary runner who, we are told by Herodotus in *The Persian Wars*, was 'a trained runner'.[1] These specialists were given a range of missions and tasks that drew on skills such as sabotage, assassination, reconnaissance, communication or guard duties. Sun Tzu in *The Art of War* writes about 'crack armies', while the Chinese military strategist Jiang Ziya writes in his *Six Teachings* of tactics that included specialists and elite fighting units.

In the 1200s, as castles rose higher, as walls became thicker with the need for more secure defensive works, this in turn forced the development of siege tactics, and the evolution of specialist engineers known as sappers. These men were required to 'sap' forward: that is, dig a trench towards the castle they were attacking and then begin a series of enveloping, circular trenches, each one closer to the walls. But the sapper would eventually come within range of weapons and projectiles such as arrows or musket balls, and this danger increased as they sapped forward, particularly

1

when they were in the exposed trench that needed to be dug directly towards the wall to begin the next circular trench. These sappers were, in their time, special forces, but the history of such men, their tactics and their particular style of warfare goes back thousands of years.

In more recent times, the Confederate Army in the American Civil War used skilled reconnaissance and raiding parties, as did the French armies of Napoleon, who developed skirmishing tactics away from the formal battlelines and defensive squares. In 1846, the Corps of Guides were formed as part of the British Army to hold strategically important outposts on the Indian frontier and quickly became a trusted elite unit, as did the Gurkha Guides, formed in 1857. Similarly, in the Boer War, there were unconventional units like the Bushveldt Carbineers, the irregular mounted unit containing a large proportion of Australians, men like Harry 'Breaker' Morant and his mate Peter Hancock.

In the Great War after 1914, the German Army developed specialist assault units known as *Sturmtruppen* or stormtroopers. These were small, mobile groups who were heavily armed, not with rifles but large quantities of hand grenades, often held in special bags around their necks, along with pistols, trench knives and, later in the war, the first real submachine gun, known as a Bergmann. While the British did not develop separate elite units, their armies were graded in terms of their efficiency and fighting abilities. The five Australian divisions of the Australian Imperial Force (AIF) plus the Canadians and the New Zealanders were considered among the most reliable and competent in the British Army, and perhaps the closest to the German stormtrooper units.

Despite this long history of related tactics, the military designation of 'special forces' as such is relatively new. During the Second World War, both the Allies and the Axis powers developed specialist elite units. In 1940, the British formed what was then known as the Special Service Brigade, which soon after evolved into the commandos. These units were to serve in many theatres of war, including the Western Desert in North Africa, the Arctic Circle, South-East Asia and the Mediterranean. After the success of Lieutenant David Stirling's newly formed SAS, and with the help of the Long Range Desert Group, which worked behind Axis lines in North Africa, the Special Air Service and the Special Boat Service were born. Parallel to this development, the British Special Operations Executive, known as SOE, undertook dangerous operations across Europe, parachuting operatives into Axis-occupied countries to establish communications links, form resistance groups, gather intelligence and undertake sabotage.

In June 1942, the United States formed the Office of Strategic Services (OSS), which undertook similar secret operations using special operatives, before its functions were taken over by the Central Intelligence Agency in 1946. Specialist forces were also formed within the US Marine Corps, one being the Marine Raiders, whose specific task was to secure beachheads prior to major maritime invasions. In Burma, Merrill's Marauders, named after their commander, US Army general Frank Merrill, undertook raiding and intelligence-gathering, much as the British and Indian Chindits did in the same campaign.

The German Army also had specialist units, including the Brandenburgers, who were involved in the invasion of Poland, France and Scandinavia, and undertook commando operations in North Africa, the Balkans and on the Eastern Front. Famous for his paramilitary and secret operations was SS-*Obersturmbannführer* Otto Skorzeny, who came to prominence after leading a daring rescue of Benito Mussolini from imprisonment in the Abruzzi mountains in Italy and flying him to Munich and then a meeting with Hitler. In December 1944, during the German Ardennes Offensive (also known as the Battle of the Bulge), Skorzeny sent English-speaking Germans dressed in American uniforms to spread confusion behind the Allied front line. And in the final months of the war, in an attempt to slow the Allied advance on Berlin, the Werewolf movement was formed and trained in Germany. While it included some SS men, and trained in guerrilla tactics and assassinations, it proved of little worth, with perhaps its greatest success in propaganda and instilling a fear of para-military insurrection behind the Allied line of advance.

Australia was slow to embrace these new ideas; many leaders still saw military operations and infantry deployment much as they did in 1918, and were confused as to how special forces would better the operational proficiency of the Army. However, it was the arrival in Australia of members of Britain's SOE that introduced a new element into the Australian military: an organisation that was to draw from the three services – the Army, Navy and Air Force – and rely on their specialist experience and equipment in covert operations from 1942 to 1945. And from this, and the urging of Britain, the first Australian special-forces units began training in June 1940, with the Australian Army forming commando units, initially known as Independent Companies.

Quite separate to the formation of the Independent Companies, the very secret Special Operations Australia was formed and from this the Services Reconnaissance Department and the Z Special Unit. The success of SOE operations in Europe had not gone unnoticed in Australia. Just as SOE sought to take the war into occupied Europe, so SOA saw their role in a similar way; for here was a chance to take the fight to the Japanese by operating to the north of Australia in enemy-held territory, striking in remote and unexpected places to destroy Japanese manpower and facilities and undermine the enemy's morale. Hence, it was quickly realised that the formation of a 'fourth fighting force' to undertake subversive operations, intelligence gathering and the training of underground native armies was necessary.

After Prime Minister John Curtin approved the establishment of a clandestine SOE type operation in Australia, training began at a secret camp on Wilsons Promontory in Victoria. Later, a special purpose camp was established on Fraser Island off the Queensland coast, and from there over 80 top-secret operations were initiated and planned. While not all went ahead, the operational area was vast, stretching from Timor and Papua New Guinea in the south, through New Britain, Borneo, the Celebes and Molucca Islands, and north to Singapore and Indochina.

During this time, the organisation was able to celebrate successes but also found itself confronted with dismal failures; in particular the Rimau raid on Singapore where 23 men were lost. However, the very nature of these operations – their tactics, weapons, specialist equipment and casualties – meant their operational history was to remain top secret and the files were closed for 30 years, some even longer.

This then is the story of those very secret and special services and the men and women who served in them in the vast Pacific theatre of the Second World War.

ONE

Return to War

As the bells tolled across Australia after Prime Minister Robert Menzies' dispiriting and gloomy announcement of his 'melancholy duty', the country once more found itself at war. It was 9.30 pm Eastern Standard Time on 3 September 1939 as the Prime Minister, in a deliberate and sombre voice, informed the nation of Australia's predicament in again having to come to the support of Mother England. As people huddled around their wirelesses in lounge rooms across the nation, a hushed silence descended as once again a nation must brace itself for austerity, the threat of invasion and the painful loss of its men and women. Unbeknown to anyone at the time, it would be five years before peace could be achieved, the warriors could return and the nation could again prepare for a new and challenging postwar world.

While the war was again far away in continental Europe, if it spread like the last war, which had engulfed Africa, Russia, the Middle East and the Balkans, and even flared up in the Asia-Pacific region, then indeed a world war was upon the nation. For Australians, that last awful tumult had only ended some 20 years before, and with the postwar trauma and suffering of returned men and their families, against the backdrop of an economic

7

depression and increasingly unstable global politics, those 20 years had been harrowing.

In 1919, as the men trickled home and emptied onto the streets of cities and towns across Australia, the country they found on their return was not what they had hoped for. As many returned soldiers were poorly educated, untrained and unskilled, jobs were hard to find, accommodation expensive and the homecoming welcome short-lived and hollow. Raw from their encounters with death, horror and the bewildering slaughter that had been the Western Front, and unable to comprehend how a government could subject its men to such frightful casualties, many would have felt a deep pessimism settle upon their fragile, ravaged bodies. These men knew the scars of war, both physical and mental, would affect them for the rest of their lives.

Yet for some, this lingering hopelessness was replaced with a new optimism and, after the 'war to end all wars', a yearning for a peaceful and prosperous future. The government had not forgotten the returning diggers. Even before they'd left Britain to return home, a wide range of educational courses had been made available to them, including basic literacy and numeracy, technical trades like mechanics, telegraphy and carpentry, farm training including wool-classing, animal husbandry and fruit-growing. There were even art classes and professional training in subjects like law and accounting undertaken by the universities of Sydney and Melbourne.

The government also introduced the Soldier Settler Scheme, which provided grants of land and financial assistance to get the returned men started on their postwar lives. By 1924, over 24 million acres, or 97,000 square kilometres, had been allocated from both Crown and acquired land, providing over 23,000 separate farms. While these farms to a large extent failed over the next ten years, their establishment further developed rural Australia and engendered, as had happened in England, a nostalgia for the countryside and the exaltation of the national character based on the bush ethos and the struggling pioneer.

Yet for all this mixed emotion, already the warning signs of another war were smouldering away in distant Germany, in the country's defeat and the humiliation of the peace negotiations, the reparations and the residual pain that was to see continual political and social unrest and hyperinflation. In Australia, however, this went unnoticed and, anyway, who in their right mind cared? These beginnings would inflame another awful war, one that would take even more than the estimated 15 to 24 million lives of the Great War – nine to 11 million military and six to 13 million civilian deaths – and envelop the entire world. And as with the First World War, the earth would be thrown into further turmoil and bloodshed, with consequences that would reverberate for decades to come.

In spite of the general mood of optimism immediately after the First World War, early consideration had been given to the future of Australian defence requirements. In May 1919, Admiral John Jellicoe, the British naval commander, arrived in Australia, and in October of that year presented the Australian Government with a report titled *Report of Admiral of the Fleet, Viscount Jellicoe of Scapa . . . on Naval Mission to the Commonwealth of Australia.* Apart from outlining the stationing of a fleet in Australia, along with the establishment of naval ports facilities, docks, coastal defences, training requirements and personnel, Admiral Jellicoe identified the Empire of Japan as the most likely threat.

He also emphasised that, given Australia's distance from Britain, 'in the early stages of a war with an Eastern Power, it would fall to the lot of the Fleet stationed in the Pacific . . . to hold the enemy until the British Fleet could reach the area of operations; yet the naval defence of the Commonwealth, as of the whole Pacific, must depend finally on the power of the British Fleet'.[1] When his report was made public in the *Sydney Morning Herald* in October 1919,[2] no mention was made of the potential threat posed by Japan nor its place in strategic thinking. Was this to satisfy the questions being asked by informed Australians about ongoing defence needs, to keep the Japanese purchasing Australian exports, or to keep the population ignorant of the potential of the Japanese threat?

There were some Australian military thinkers who challenged this imperial, British-focused view. One was Major General Sir Granville 'Bull' de Laune Ryrie, ex-commander of the Anzac Mounted Division and federal politician. As assistant minister for defence, Ryrie espoused the view that a world war would return within a generation, and called for a military training programme and the establishment of a cadre of officers and trained men. However, the Washington Naval Conference of 1921–22, the world's first attempt at arms limitation, put ceilings on the size of the navies of Britain, the USA, Japan, Italy and others, including Australia. As a consequence, as the *Official History of Special Operations Australia* recounts:

> nearly half of the ships of the Australian Navy were put out of commission, and it was decided to reduce the permanent staff of the Army to 1600, to maintain the seven military divisions [at] only 25 per cent of their war strength and to reduce training to six days in camp and four days at the local centres a year. Seventy-two regular officers out of a meagre total of some 300 would be retired, and compensated at a cost of £300,000.[3]

It wasn't just Australian military thinkers who were concerned; the Australian Government was also taking careful note of the build-up of the Imperial Japanese Navy and the Japanese expansion southwards. Japan had amazed the world with its victory over Russia in 1904–05 and its subsequent annexation of Korea, thanks to the Treaty of Portsmouth in 1905, which had in turn provided Japan with a new confidence and a new sphere of influence. Then at Versailles, having joined the Allies in the war against Germany, Japan was given control of the former German port of Tsingtao in China as well as German possessions in Micronesia north of the equator.

These occupations provided a centre for Japanese trading and maritime companies, but also for spying and intelligence-gathering operations under the guise of legitimate trading. Strategic raw materials were obtainable: rubber, oil and food, all critical for any future war. It was this vast area that later became Japan's Greater East Asia Co-Prosperity Sphere. These Japanese settlements and the Japanese civilian populations would make their presence felt in the future operations of Australian and Allied operatives throughout this region.

From the early 1920s, therefore, the Australian Government was realising the potential threat of Japan and the subtle British manipulation of their defence needs. The Imperial Japanese Navy went unscathed through the First World War and had slowly grown in comparison to the Royal Navy. Minister for Defence George Pearce asked Lieutenant-General Sir Harry Chauvel, famous for his leadership of the Australian Light Horse in Palestine, to form a consultative committee to review the future military defence of Australia.

Their meeting in January 1920, after the receipt of Jellicoe's report, identified Japan as a threat, in particular at a time when

Britain might be engaged in another European war and unable to rapidly provide military assistance to distant Australia. The senior officers of Chauvel's committee 'recommended that a Citizen Military Force (CMF) of 130,000 men in peace and 270,000 in war should be formed to secure the country against Japanese invasion',[4] but nothing eventuated. Instead, Australia again turned to Britain's Committee of Imperial Defence (CID), ignoring in the process the considered and valuable opinions of its own experienced military advisors.

This subservience was exemplified in imperial defence strategy. Australia's growing concern over Japan, and the evolving naval defensive policy, saw the need for a Pacific–Far East British fleet and a strategically placed base for that fleet. A number of possible sites were considered, including Hong Kong and Sydney, but in 1919, Singapore was chosen, with work beginning in 1923. While Australia, in particular Defence Minister Frederick Shedden, welcomed the British commitment, many considered Singapore vulnerable from air and land attack, meaning it would require support from the Royal Australian Air Force (RAAF) and ground support from the Australian Army.

During the Great War, Shedden had been a lieutenant in the Pay Corps of the AIF, and after undertaking a course at the Imperial Defence College in London, he had prepared a discussion paper on the principles of future imperial defence.[5] In October 1929, he returned to Melbourne and was appointed secretary of the Defence Committee. It was probably the influence of leading military figures in London like Sir Maurice Hankey, Vice-Admiral Sir Herbert Richmond and Dr Hugh Dalton that skewed Shedden's views to support a British rather than Australian perspective on imperial defence, and instilled in him organisational strategies and tactics that would prove useful in the challenging years ahead.

Australians' reluctance to accept their own advice was not new. Many still referred to Britain as 'home' and were anxious about their isolation from 'Mother England' given the proximity of a threatening Asia just to the north. The largest proportion of the population were Australian born, yet they were classified in the census as 'British', along with the large number of British-born residents and new immigrants. Even when the Statute of Westminster was passed in 1931, allowing the dominions of the Commonwealth to legislate on their own behalf and removing the British parliament's right to override dominion legislation if it was in conflict with British legislation, the Australian Government deferred the enabling legislation, 'preferring to remain in a state of formal dependence'.⁶ Such was the state of many Australians' dual allegiance at this time.

Australia raced headlong into the 1920s, taking on the transformation from a colonial outpost based on rural exports to a developing industrialised nation and economic power in the Pacific region. Underpinning this change was Prime Minister Stanley Bruce's three principles necessary for regional and national development, all dependent upon Britain: 'men, money and markets'. Australia needed skilled workers, obtained through a new programme of British migration. The Empire Settlement Scheme began in 1922, and by the early 1930s as many as 212,000 people had come, attracted by a subsidised passage and the provision of land. However, few had farming skills – nor did many of the returned diggers – and soon left the land, living in the cities or returning home.

With the lingering Australian war debt to Great Britain of almost 100 million pounds, added to the cost of repatriation and social services and the expenditure on immigration and the Soldier Settler Scheme, the government found itself in a challenging financial position. To address this, an agreement was reached between Britain and Australia to repay the war debt over 36 years. However, by the end of the 1920s, as the prickly pear infestation took over productive farm land, reducing rural production, with falling wool, wheat and commodity prices, and unfavourable terms of trade, debt repayment only added to the nation's woes.

Then came the crippling Depression, a further drop in exports, increased imports and the failure of many industrial enterprises that had sprung up during the war and now found themselves non-competitive and obsolete. Such was the case of the Sunshine Harvester Company, which, prior to the war, had exported machinery around the world and by the 1920s was the largest implement factory in the Southern Hemisphere. International competition saw the market decline, and in 1930, the company merged with the Canadian company Massey Harris.

The Depression in Australia, as in most of the Western world, devastated the economy. After the stock market crash in New York in October 1929, the USA called up loans it had made to the United Kingdom, which in turn called up loans made to Australia. But Australia could not repay the loans, creating a serious balance-of-payments problem and generating further pressure from creditors. To address this, the new Scullin Government in 1929 reduced government spending to ensure foreign loan repayments were met, and supported Commonwealth initiatives to give preferential treatment to agricultural exports and British-manufactured goods. Even so, it was not until the outbreak of the Second World War in 1939 that Australia really came out of the Depression.

Seriously affected financially by the Depression, like other Commonwealth countries, Australia looked to Britain as a guaranteed market for primary products in return for British-manufactured goods. Again this put Australia in Britain's debt, as Australian produce was more expensive than was available from non-dominion markets. British banks and lending institutions also had large loans owing from Australian governments, both state and federal, as well as banks, public companies and private individuals. The 'Buy British' catch-cry that came from the Ottawa Conference in 1932 not only separated Australian exporters from markets like America and Japan but became yet another factor in Australia's unpreparedness for war after 1939. It seemed that every way Australians looked they were under the political, financial or strategic thumb of Great Britain.

The question of Australia's future defence requirements remained on the minds of governments, military planners and concerned citizens. There was an irresolvable conundrum: the nation still deferred major foreign policy decisions to the Foreign Office in London, and it had to defer defence policy and direction to Britain at a time of need, yet Britain's indifference to Australia's concerns was forcing Australia to think of her own defence requirements and potential threats. In spite of this, many Australians believed Britain owed them a debt for their Great War sacrifice, and as such would provide the protection Australia could neither afford nor determine. So it was that a gullible Australia, with an undeveloped sense of her own nationality and a level of ignorance, blind faith and trust, allowed Britain to completely determine Australia's defence needs.

In September 1931, Japan had invaded Manchuria. To provide a rationale for the invasion, the Japanese staged a provocative sabotage incident by blowing up a section of the Japanese-owned South Manchuria Railway at Mukden (now Shenyang) and then blaming Chinese agitators. But the invasion raised little interest in Australia, with political attention on the upcoming December election and the deepening impact of the Depression. Probably the only material implication for defence movements was realised on the part of Britain, which put a renewed effort into the construction of the Singapore naval base. Even more alarming was that the fledgling League of Nations failed to curb or generate consequences for Japan, as it would likewise fail to do in the years to come with Nazi Germany. Now, no one stood in the way of further Japanese expansionism south, not the League nor the United States, hampered as they were by the conditions of the Washington Naval Conference.

What was being heard in Australia was an alternative case being put by the Army, many of whose militarily informed and veteran members saw flaws in the British naval strategy. For example, Major General Julius Bruche, who had been on the staff of General Sir John Monash in 1916, disagreed with the British notion that the Singapore base was impregnable, and as such would deter the Japanese and prevent war. Others added their voices to the chorus, pressing the Australian Government to consider its own defence needs outside of what was seen as the unlikely assistance from Britain should the Japanese suddenly move south. This further opened the divisions between those supporting the British Committee of Imperial Defence strategy and the Australian mavericks who were pushing for their own defence strategy based on both Army and Air Force units, rather than just the Navy.

Now that broader community demands were being heard, the treasurer, Richard Casey, responded:

> With reference to defence, I can assure you that there has been
> no stinting of money here in Australia. Three years ago we
> were spending five or six million pounds a year; two years ago
> we were spending eight million pounds and this year we are
> spending eleven and a half million pounds . . . Defence is the

only department of the Commonwealth Government that, from
the financial point of view, has been able to 'write its own ticket'.
Any money defence wants it can get, and I can assure you that this
situation will remain.[7]

In fact, the Army had little apart from what had come home
with the troops after the last war. It had no tanks or any type of
armoured car; no artillery, anti-aircraft or anti-tank guns; nor the
necessary stores for engineers, signals, and medical and ancillary
equipment, to say nothing of equipment for an infantry force.
They were simply not available.

What was emerging, though in a piecemeal and haphazard way,
were plans for defence needs, mobilisation and priorities. General
John Lavarack had determined three major needs: the training
of officers and staff, the provision of equipment and the training of
a part-time militia. Against this were the three planned stages
of mobilisation: first, a defence force 'to meet war with a distant
enemy'[8]; second, defence of Australia against incursions, short
of an invasion of the country; and third, the full mobilisation of
200,000 men in five infantry and two cavalry divisions along with
their assorted elements.

In all of this defence planning, the 'enemy' were clearly identified as Japan, who would, as had long been assumed, attack when
Britain was committed elsewhere, and would attack with carrier-
borne aircraft to eliminate Allied airfields and then impose a naval
blockade. By 1935, the aggression and efficiency of the Japanese
Army had been seen in China, and after the Nanjing Massacre
in December 1937, in which mass executions, rape and looting
occurred, the fear of Japanese invasion became much more acute.

Developments in Hitler's Germany and Mussolini's Italy
were also of great concern. In March 1935, Germany introduced

conscription, always a belligerent prelude to war, and later that year Italian forces invaded Ethiopia. The League of Nations again failed to act against these hostile moves, prompting Winston Churchill to state in the House of Commons, 'We are faced not with the prospect of a new war, but with something very like the possibility of a resumption of the war which ended in November 1918.'[9]

Yet there remained confusion as to the appropriate defence policy for Australia, and the appropriate division of spending between the Army, Navy and Air Force. The British continued to claim that the Singapore strategy would contain Japan and prevent the invasion of Australia, and went so far as to suggest that, should war break out with Germany, Australia be ready to send Army elements to Britain. As the *Official History* notes:

> In military terms this meant that divisions ready to serve in the main theatre as soon as war broke out would be worth far more than an offer to raise, train and arm divisions to take part in operations after the expected crisis had passed – a platitude, were it not that the Dominions lacked equipped and trained military formations.[10]

Against this grim and depressing background, however, Australians found time to experience the pleasures of a new age. The electrification of cities saw many advances in technology in the home. This was the time of the first electrical appliances: electric jugs, toasters, washing machines and, most importantly, the wireless. People could now enjoy radio programmes including music, news, drama serials and sport, with the ABC first broadcasting in November 1923. Sport too was an affordable pastime, with cricket, the various football codes, cycling, horse-racing and even billiards all drawing large crowds who flocked to see heroes like Don Bradman, Bill Ponsford, Walter Lindrum, Roy Cazaly, Hubert Opperman and Phar Lap.

The 1920s saw new freedoms for women and a new morality, testing traditional values of social modesty with make-up, smoking and drinking. Also popular were new musical styles in jazz and swing, and new fashions and provocative dances like the Charleston. Music also came to the home with the gramophone, the piano and the pianola. By the early 1920s, American films dominated the theatres. Buster Keaton's *Cops* and Charlie Chaplin's *The Kid*, along with the extravaganzas of Cecil B. DeMille, completely dwarfed local production, which began a long decline and didn't recover until the 1970s. To compound the problem, in 1928, the first sound movie, *The Jazz Singer* starring Al Jolson, established a new expectation in audiences, as did foreign newsreels, so that by the mid-1930s very few Australian feature films were being screened.

Transport was also changing. Henry Ford's Model T quickly changed lifestyle and leisure; holiday options opened up, and picnics in the country or a day at the beach made life more bearable. There were also improvements in the rail networks across the country and the expansion of electric tramlines and metropolitan transport systems. This in turn allowed people to travel further distances to work, offering new possibilities for industry and business.

Even air travel was expanding, with QANTAS beginning regular mail service between Charleville and Cloncurry in 1922. The possibilities for aviation were further expanded by the epic flights of Ross and Keith Smith, Charles Kingsford Smith, Charles Ulm and Bert Hinkler. International services began in 1935 from Darwin to Singapore, but with the coming of the war, services were disrupted.

As the 1930s progressed, there were further worrying incidents around the world. There was renewed fighting in China and continuing Italian penetration in Ethiopia. In July 1936, fighting broke out between the leftist Republicans and the pro-fascist Nationalists in Spain in what became the Spanish Civil War. While Nazi Germany supported the Franco Nationalists, Britain, America and Australia, while also recognising the Nationalist government, followed a non-intervention policy. However, the broad nature of the Civil War, involving on one side communists, anarchists and left-wing republicans, and on the other monarchists, Catholics, conservatives and fascist sympathisers, attracted fighters from around the world. While Australian law prohibited service in foreign armies and wars, Australians enlisted on both sides, with an estimated 65–70 enlisting and about 15 being killed, mostly with the International Brigade military units, comprising foreign volunteers who supported the Spanish Popular Front, pro-communist government. This Australian involvement further focused attention on the unstable nature of the world and on the need to prepare for war.

This ongoing global unrest stimulated defence spending in Australia. While Churchill lucidly pointed out the aggression of Hitler and Mussolini in Europe, former Prime Minister Billy Hughes, now on the backbench, similarly kept up the rhetoric about a threat to Australia, in particular after General Blamey's 1938 recruitment campaign for the Army. Blamey had raised the militia numbers to 43,000 by the end of 1938, but the problem was not a lack of men but of basic equipment: weapons, vehicles, artillery and aircraft. The Army also lacked a cadre of officers and training staff, as the officer corps had been decimated in the late 1920s and early 1930s with mass retrenchments, demotions and little hope of promotion or active service. These were shortfalls that could not be made up overnight, money or no money, and even the appointment of senior British officers to head the three services did little to raise hopes or ease national concerns.

Treasurer Richard Casey giving reassurance of defence spending was one thing, but it was another to determine where to effectively spend these increased budget allocations to bring the nation's defence to a satisfactory state of preparedness. In December 1938, Minister for Defence Geoffrey Street announced an allocation of 43 million pounds for defence with another 20 million over the next three years, a huge increase from the meagre four-million pound budget in 1930–31. However, much of this went unspent, prompting Paul Hasluck, the official historian, to state that it was 'a tiny proportion of the nation's resources when the dangers were so great and so immediate'.[11]

Yet the idea of establishing a regular Army, as opposed to the very part-time militia, was quite novel to government planning. The question remained: should Australia form an expeditionary force ready for service overseas (a second AIF) under British command, or should it look to the defence of Australia given the worrying developments to Australia's north and train men in a part-time militia. However, an expeditionary force would need to be both volunteer and permanent at a cost seen as difficult to justify. Meanwhile, the training of the militia was seen as a virtual waste of time, money and youthful enthusiasm, and in view of the perceived threat, 'it had failed'.[12]

It was certainly seen as not up to taking on the well-trained armies of Europe or the experienced armies of Japan. What existed was basically a defensive force only and little different to that which existed in 1914, totally ill-prepared and ill-equipped to take on Germany or Japan, even to satisfactorily defend the nation.

When Prime Minister Menzies broadcast that fateful announcement on 3 September 1939 about the nation's 'melancholy duty', it was against a backdrop of a dismal defensive capability. The frontline Navy had just six cruisers, only three of which had been built in the 1930s, and of the five destroyers, all had been launched in the First World War. The regular Army consisted of a small pool of officers, and the training cadre were often veterans from the last war. While there were 80,000-plus militiamen, they were barely prepared for war, were ill-equipped and were simply infantry units, as had been so many of their fathers in the Great War. The support services lacked tanks, trucks, artillery and anti-aircraft guns, and the necessary equipment to take on either the Germans in North Africa, Crete and Greece, or the Japanese in their scattered landings to Australia's north.

As concern grew under new Prime Minister John Curtin's Labor Government – which replaced Menzies' United Australia Party–Country Party minority government in October 1941 – defence policy shifted towards preparations for possible invasion, while still adhering to the British policy of the maintenance of a strong Navy and the standardisation and integration of Australian forces with other Commonwealth units. The government also wanted to ensure that Australian industry could provide the equipment required to maintain a defence capability, given that orders placed with British manufacturers years before had been diverted to British defence requirements, particularly for weapons: artillery, anti-aircraft guns, machine guns and rifles, plus the ammunition for them.

Although the Lithgow Small Arms Factory in New South Wales was able to produce the standard-issue Lee-Enfield rifle and Vickers machine guns, and later Bren guns, the facility had suffered from the Depression, and re-tooling and ramping up production from the late 1930s took time. There were also restrictions placed on which weapons of which calibre Australia could manufacture, given the technology and patent rights needed to produce them.

Suddenly the neglect, the political wrangling and the blind faith in Britain and its all-powerful Royal Navy were coming home to roost. The testing of these assumptions would, in turn, test Australia's bonds to Empire, and see the nation over the next five years go from being a colony of Britain to a satellite of the United States. Old relationships based on heritage, culture and trust were to disappear, and a new strategic focus and a new dependence would emerge in the years to come.

Two

'Now Set Europe Ablaze'

For Australia, following the declaration of war, not much happened. Even in Europe, the 'phoney war' saw little action, a situation that was to last ten months until the German invasion of France and the Low Countries. During these early days of the war, while limited skirmishes did continue, and the blockade of Germany was put in place, it became a period of indecision, war preparation and training. Britain, like Australia, was slow to rearm, providing the bulk of military expenditure on the Royal Navy and in re-equipping the Royal Air Force. The British Expeditionary Force began moving to France on 4 September 1939, taking up a defensive line along the France–Belgium border. Here they remained, digging trench works and training and working with their French and Belgian allies.

On 10 May 1940, German forces pushed into France and the Low Countries, forcing the French and Belgian armies and the British Expeditionary Force to begin a rapid retreat to the French coast. The Germans attacked through the heavily forested Ardennes region of Belgium – a lightly held sector that the French believed was unsuitable for a large-scale invasion – bypassing the Maginot Line. This defensive folly was a series of in-depth and well-prepared fortifications and obstacles built between 1929 and 1939 by the French to deter a German invasion and give the French time to plan their defence. The Germans, however, simply went around the end of the line, rendering it useless.

After three German Panzer corps established bridgeheads on the River Meuse, they quickly overcame the defending armies and raced for the French coast, driving the Allied armies before them by the devastating tactic of Blitzkrieg. This tactic of a coordinated and concentrated rapid advance with armour, mechanised units and air forces aimed to smash through defence lines and confuse the Allies. And it worked.

With the situation now desperate, the commander of the British Expeditionary Force, John Vereker, 6th Viscount Gort (he was awarded the VC in September 1918 during the Great War), met the commander of the French First Army, Gaston Billotte, who informed him that the French had committed all their troops at that point and that there were no strategic reserves available to throw against the Germans. This news astonished Gort, as it had Churchill when he had visited Paris two days before.

After attempting to stall the Germans at Arras in northern France, Gort immediately began planning a massive evacuation of the BEF and Allied forces from Dunkirk. The large town, just six miles (10 kilometres) from the Belgium border, was the third largest port in France and opposite the English coastline, just 40 miles (66 kilometres) to the west. Here there were port facilities, defensive areas of marshland, remaining coastal fortifications and the longest sand beach in Europe, where large groups of men could be assembled and organised.

Planning now began in earnest on Operation Dynamo, headed by Vice Admiral Bertram Ramsay in a disused dynamo room beneath Dover Castle. So began the extraordinary gathering of boats for the operation, from naval destroyers down to small sailing boats and pleasure craft. However, while the larger ships could use the port and the remaining wharves, they could not collect men directly from the beaches, hence the need for smaller boats to ferry men out to the waiting ships.

The Germans were prepared too. Hitler issued a directive to Hermann Goering to prevent the evacuation, and massive German aerial attacks saw heavy bombing of the port, the beaches and the assembled shipping. In one day the *Luftwaffe* deployed 300 bombers protected by 550 fighters, but their casualties were heavy, with the RAF flying 3500 sorties and destroying many German aircraft.

On 28 May 1940, Winston Churchill stood before the House of Commons and warned that, over the next week, the nation must expect 'hard and heavy tidings'.[1] At that moment, across the English Channel, the remnants of the British and French armies were forming long lines across the beaches near Dunkirk. The greatest evacuation in British history had begun. At 9.30 am on 4 June, the last boatload of British and Allied troops were evacuated from Dunkirk and returned to England, a total of 338,000, but the cost had been high. The BEF alone lost 68,000 men, of which 3500 were dead and 13,000 wounded. They also lost enormous quantities of guns, vehicles, stores and ammunition, including 20,000 motorbikes, 2500 guns and 450 tanks. At sea the British lost six destroyers and had 19 damaged, as well as sustaining damage to over 200 other vessels, large and small, while the RAF lost 145 aircraft, including 42 Spitfires, in just nine days.

For Germany, this was an enormous propaganda victory. Hitler declared the following day, 'Dunkirk has fallen! 40,000 French and English troops are all that remains of the formerly great armies. Immeasurable quantities of materiel have been captured. The greatest battle in the history of the world has come to an end.'[2] In the House of Commons, Churchill likewise declared the evacuation 'a miracle', though he was quick to remind the British people that, 'we must be very careful not to assign to this deliverance the attributes of a victory. Wars are not won by evacuations.'[3]

On 22 June, France signed an armistice with Germany in the same railway carriage and at the same spot in the Forest of Compiègne where Germany had signed the Armistice in November 1918. The French capitulation focused the mind of the British leadership, in particular Churchill, as to how Britain could help the French and take the war to the Germans. On 30 June, following a meeting at the Foreign Office, the Minister of Economic Warfare, Hugh Dalton, wrote to Edward Wood, 3rd Viscount Halifax and at the time the Foreign Secretary, suggesting the establishment of 'a new organization to coordinate, inspire, control and assist the nationals of the oppressed countries who must themselves be the direct participants'.[4] By the middle of 1940, Poland, France, Denmark, Norway, Belgium and the Netherlands had all been occupied by Nazi Germany.

Isolated, Britain's fate looked grim. On 16 July – just six weeks after the evacuation from Dunkirk – Hitler ordered that planning and preparation begin for Operation Sea Lion, the invasion of Britain. In fact, he was secretly focusing on his invasion of Russia which he saw as a priority, believing the British were already defeated and it was just a matter of time before they would call for an armistice. Even within Britain, Foreign Secretary Lord Halifax and sections of the British public spoke of a negotiated peace settlement with the Germans, having seen the recent success of the German military and believing there was little chance Britain could defeat this rampant military machine.

Prime Minister Churchill's leadership and persuasive rhetoric worked against this lingering defeatism. In his famous speech to the House of Commons on 4 June 1940, he had declared, 'We shall defend our island whatever the cost may be. We shall fight on the beaches, we shall fight on the landing grounds, we shall fight in the fields and in the streets, we shall fight in the hills.

We shall never surrender.'[5] In an earlier speech to the war cabinet, he had stated that 'nations which went down fighting rose again, but those which surrendered tamely were finished'.[6] With the support of cabinet, Churchill refused surrender, and the British people were now to face a difficult, defensive future.

The Germans intensified the threat of invasion, as the *Luftwaffe* began raids on coastal towns and ports, then factories and air-fields. The front line was now the English Channel, and all that stood between invasion and occupation was the Royal Navy, the struggling RAF and the men extracted from Dunkirk.

While the RAF was undertaking raids on German-held indus-trial areas and cities, little else by way of offensive warfare was apparent. Although Britain had the support of the Commonwealth in men, raw materials and food, and the United States, a sym-pathetic ally and provider of war material albeit still isolationist and neutral, it felt very alone. The Germans were increasing their grip on the occupied countries, imposing military government, severe regulations and curfews on the civilian population, while German U-boats operated with virtual impunity in the surround-ing oceans. Faced with the might of Nazi Germany, the island nation needed to fight back.

There was no chance of retaking France or fighting a conven-tional land war at this time, so the idea of an unconventional war seemed not only possible but appropriate. Unfortunately, the British had failed to either establish 'stay behind' networks in Europe or intelligence networks with suitable radio equipment to undertake intelligence-gathering. Realising the shortcomings of Britain's defensive position, in mid-June 1940, just weeks after the Dunkirk evacuation, Churchill initiated discussion on the formation of a secret organisation to take the war to the Nazis and sought the permission of the war cabinet to do so. On 16 July

1940, he appointed Minister of Economic Warfare Hugh Dalton to form a suitable organisation. After Churchill had outlined the possible duties of this new organisation, he told Dalton, 'And now go and set Europe ablaze.'[7]

Dalton knew little about military organisation or tactics for a subversive guerrilla force, so for a model he drew upon the Irish Republican Army (IRA) during their war of independence against Britain in the early 1920s. He realised that absolute secrecy was crucial, and that the personnel for this organisation needed to meet specific requirements in outlook and skill set: they needed to be loyal and politically reliable, have foreign language skills, be dual nationals and have lived in a targeted country, and be open to working with a range of people of varying nationalities. These individuals would be the replacement army in occupied Europe, and it would be these brave, independent souls who would be risking their life and taking the war to the enemy.

Dalton also understood that the civilian populations under Nazi control were likely suffering and would hold a deep hatred for the Germans. He aimed to harness and exploit this hatred, as it provided an opportunity for retaliatory, unconventional action to strike at the heart of the enemy in an unexpected and demoralising way. While not special forces, potential recruits to this new organisation knew their locality, the people and the vulnerabilities of the enemy and could direct their efforts in this way. Dalton also understood that while people under Nazi control could take action against the occupiers, they needed assistance in the form of weapons, communications and tactical support if they were to be effective; to simply annoy the Germans would attract unnecessary reprisals. Coordinating underground subversive activity and providing British support for action by the people in occupied territories would further help to negate feelings of abandonment and neglect in European allies.

Dalton's new organisation was called Special Operations Executive (SOE), and it brought together three existing secret departments that had been formed before the war to undertake specific roles. The first was codenamed EH, formed in March 1938 by the British Foreign Office, and essentially a propaganda organisation that also began monitoring foreign embassy communications. The organisation was initially named after the building Electra House at 84 Moorgate, London, at the time the headquarters of the Cables and Wireless Company.

The second secret department brought in to SOE was Section D, formed by the Secret Intelligence Service (SIS), the forerunner to MI6. Section D's role was to investigate and report on the possible use of sabotage and irregular, unconventional means of warfare to disrupt and weaken an enemy. The third was a section within the War Office known as GS (R), General Staff (Research). They had been tasked to research underground resistance and guerrilla warfare tactics, which was not a well understood or familiar type of warfare at this time.

The hybrid structure of SOE immediately presented problems, not the least being that the activities and interests of each previously distinct organisation overlapped. There was also a degree of professional jealousy between organisations, something that the new SOE would itself soon encounter from similar and competing intelligence organisations within the British secret service. However, as the heads of Section D and GS (R) (renamed MI (R), Military Intelligence (Research)) knew each other, they quickly began sharing intelligence and agreed on defined areas of research and a division of labour. At the outbreak of the war, these small and covert organisations had few personnel and little means or resources to advance their work. For accommodation, they had not even been allocated offices, finding themselves first in St Ermin's Hotel in Westminster and then another hotel, the Metropole near Trafalgar Square.

After its formation, SOE initially produced military books and pamphlets for training, in particular a handbook on subversive activities, sabotage and the organisation of small, irregular underground militia units. The organisation then attempted to put this knowledge into practice, with the formation of independent irregular units in occupied countries to take the fight to the Germans and to prepare for the invasion of Europe sometime in the future.

With this work underway, the next task was to find a suitable director for SOE. At Dalton's request, Brigadier Colin Gubbins DSO MC was appointed in November 1940. He had been an artillery officer in the First World War, first seeing action in the Second Battle of Ypres in May 1915. He was awarded a Military Cross for bringing in wounded men under fire, but was himself wounded in 1916 and later gassed. It was his experiences in Russia and fighting the IRA in Ireland that had triggered his interest in irregular warfare, something he would bring to his directorship of SOE.

Gubbins' brief was broad. SOE was to support and coordinate resistance movements right across Europe and as far as South-East Asia, by every means possible, including sabotage, murder and the assassination of German officers or collaborators. To do this, SOE operatives had to be skilled in deception, disguise, forgery and guerrilla warfare, as well as the ability and tradecraft to survive in a hostile country. Once inserted, agents were to work with local underground organisations, not only in coordinating their operations but also in establishing escape and evasion lines, particularly for downed Allied pilots.

While their brief seemed clear and the need to strike back evident, unsurprisingly SOE quickly gathered detractors. From the outset, the Secret Intelligence Service (SIS) watched the establishment of SOE with concern. SOE was seen as 'amateur, dangerous and bogus'[8] by the head of SIS, Sir Stewart Menzies, who brought internal pressure to bear to have it closed down. Also, SOE needed personnel, equipment, radios and communication equipment, transport, training facilities and aircraft, all of which were seen to be taken from arguably more worthy purposes.

RAF Bomber Command particularly resented SOE. Aircraft were scarce and their allocation to SOE, whether for attacking enemy targets or dropping agents and supplies into occupied Europe, became a sore point. SOE's work was also seen as ungentlemanly by Air Chief Marshal Charles Portal, then commander-in-chief of Bomber Command, who wrote to Gladwyn Jebb, the Chief Executive Officer of SOE:

> I think that the dropping of men dressed in civilian clothes for the purpose of attempting to kill members of the opposing forces is not an operation with which the Royal Air Force should be associated. I think you will agree that there is a vast difference, in ethics, between the time-honoured operation of dropping a spy from the air and this entirely new scheme for dropping what one can only call assassins.[9]

Air Chief Marshal Sir Arthur Harris, the commander-in-chief of Bomber Command after Portal was promoted to the Chief of the Air Staff, was even more against the use of RAF aircraft for anything other than strategic bombing. Harris even saw the invasion of Europe as unnecessary, as he believed that the intensive bombing of German industry and cities by the RAF would force the Germans into surrender. In Harris's view, diverting aircraft to drop supplies and agents, or to support this unnecessary and unconventional war, was a waste of energy and resources, and it was only after Portal ordered Harris to provide these aircraft that they were made available.

While few knew of the existence of SOE – and, in fact, even those recruited for SOE would not have known the full purpose of the organisation nor its formal title – it was not long before this criticism and contempt revealed itself through malicious nicknames and codenames. After SOE moved from their hotel accommodation to offices at 64 Baker Street in late October 1940, its operatives were for a time called 'The Baker Street Irregulars', 'Churchill's Secret Army' and, because of the disdain some felt for its covert work, SOE was called 'The Bureau of Ungentlemanly Warfare'.

Finding suitable individuals to recruit into SOE was another challenge. While SOE had the authority to organise the transfer of serving members of the armed forces, many men did not have the necessary cultural background, experience or language skills. The organisation expanded its search parameters to include civilians – it was said even criminals were included – and also exiled members of the military from now-occupied countries, all of whom needed to be trained in a new range of skills. For this, SOE required the establishment of training facilities, instructors and a specialised syllabus to prepare its new members for their very special tasks ahead.

Initially women were rejected, as it was against military law to expose them to hostile duties, which in turn provided no legal mandate to engage women actively in unconventional warfare. While both men and women caught in civilian clothes could be tried and shot as spies or terrorists, women were not included in either the 1907 Hague Convention on Land Warfare nor the

1929 Geneva Convention as they were not seen as likely combatants, so they were not offered protection under international law.

It was not until April 1942 that the first women were recruited. It was found that women possessed good language skills, and were more able to appear innocent and bluff their way out of situations where a man would have been considered suspicious or even dangerous. It was also felt that women were less conspicuous than men, so they were often employed as spies and couriers to transfer messages and small parcels, and to collect despatches from dead-letter drops. Dead-letter drops allowed the transfer of a document, perhaps a photo or a report, between an operative in the field and their controller via a third person, who collected the message from a secret location and handed it on, so that no-one knew others in the process – therefore maintaining operational security.

Churchill had supported the recruitment of women and their operational deployment to continental Europe, but it was understood that if this became public knowledge, the involvement of women outside of England would have been actively forbidden. To cover the recruitment of women to SOE, they were commissioned into either the First Aid Nursing Yeomanry, known as FANY, or the Women's Auxiliary Air Force, the WAAF.

Women recruits came from all walks of life: some barely out of school; many from the working class; some from stately families and the aristocracy; and others with mixed nationalities, like Noor Inayat Khan, who was executed in Dachau in 1945 and was posthumously awarded the George Cross.

Captain Selwyn Jepson was the senior recruiting officer for SOE:

I was responsible for recruiting women for the work, in the face of a good deal of opposition I may say, from the powers that be. In

my view, women were very much better than men for the work.
Women have a far greater capacity for cool and lonely courage
than men. Men usually want a mate with them. Men don't work
alone, their lives tend to be always in company with other men.
There was opposition from most quarters until it went up to
Churchill, whom I had met before the war. He growled at me,
'What are you doing?' I told him and he said, 'I see you are using
women to do this,' and I said, 'Yes, don't you think it is a very
sensible thing to do?' and he said, 'Yes, good luck to you.' That
was my authority![10]

Although women were in many ways suited to the work of
SOE operations, a number of female agents were captured,
tortured and executed, some in notorious concentration camps
like Dachau and Ravensbrück, some in the last weeks of the war.
Of the 470 agents sent to France, 55 were women, and of them,
13 died in action or in concentration camps.

The selection process was rigorous and tough. Initially, basic
training was undertaken at Wanborough Manor on the Hog's
Back near Guildford, Surrey, or one of six country estates where
recruits would be sent. Here they would confront a Guards
officer, a shrewd judge of character who would put recruits
through a range of tests like getting them drunk and seeing how
they reacted. Another test was the 'honey trap', in which young,
attractive women would be introduced to male recruits and
would ask questions, again testing the recruits surreptitiously. If
they were successful and proved their potential, they would go
on to the next stage: field training in northern Scotland, where
they learnt unarmed combat, killing by stealth, how to live off
the land, map-reading, and had training in explosives, weapons,
radio, tradecraft and deception.

A crucial part of training was wireless telegraphy. Recruits were trained to operate the equipment, which was often bulky and delicate, as well as how to use codes, understand aerial theory and erect aerials of 70 feet in length. The Germans were active in radio interception – mobile vans would plot illegal transmissions by triangulating the radio's location, and it was estimated that a German intercept unit would take about 30 minutes to plot an illegal transmission – so coded signals needed to be short, precise and detailed, sent at irregular times on a range of wavelengths and from various locations. This required secure locations that were ideally remote, but to which agents would need to transport conspicuous radio equipment around the countryside.

Training therefore included instruction in how to write concise, unambiguous, detailed messages. Operators also needed to understand how to make certain mistakes in their transmission, perhaps an incorrect word or a spelling mistake, that would alert SOE they and their codebooks had been captured, and they were being forced by the Germans to send false transmissions. SOE agents were dependent on a high level of security and training with their transmissions, and this security relied on the capabilities of the radio equipment they were issued with, the security of the transmission procedures and the use of codes, ciphers and the placement of these deliberate mistakes, known as 'security checks', should they be captured and forced to transmit.

The first radios issued to SOE for the initial deployment of agents were heavy B2 sets, which required a strong power source and were not always reliable in the field, although this set did have a range of 500 miles (800 kilometres). These were replaced by an SOE-designed and manufactured radio which weighed only nine pounds, including the battery and the necessary accessories like a headset and microphone. It could be packed into a small briefcase or suitcase, easily hidden.

Ciphers were issued from the Secret Intelligence Service. These ciphers, known as 'poem codes', were a cryptographic method whereby a pre-arranged poem was used as the basis of the code. While poem codes were simple to use, as their decoding didn't require codebooks and cipher pads, they were quickly found not to be a secure method and so were replaced by Leo Marks, SOE's chief cryptographer. Marks had joined SOE in January 1942, and while initially regarded a misfit, he quickly proved his worth and his cryptographic skills. He replaced the poem codes with single-use ciphers printed on silk. These were then sown into the agents' clothing and were undetectable in a casual search.

SOE agents were captured on a number of occasions with their radio and codebooks, and the Germans used these operatives and radios to report to SOE in London under their control. But the security checks – those innocuous mistakes agents were taught to insert into their codes to show they had been compromised – were not detected or seen in London. This was an inexcusable and disastrous oversight, as at this time more agents were being sent into France and in particular to Holland, only to be captured when they landed.

The disastrous SOE operation in Holland between late 1941 and late 1943, which the Germans called *Das Englandspiel* or the 'English game', saw 54 agents inserted and immediately captured, and their radios used against SOE. All of them were sent to Mauthausen concentration camp, where 36 were executed in September 1944 with just eight surviving, all due to lax operating procedure in London.

From the earliest days of SOE, questions were asked by the military hierarchy, politicians and the Foreign Office, including

SIS, about its operational raison d'être, in particular inadvertently affecting other operations and drawing German reprisals on civilians in the occupied countries. Hugh Dalton was quick to espouse an aggressive terrorist war against the Nazis across Europe, which immediately drew criticism of both himself and the fledgling organisation.

Dalton was warned about the unexpected consequences of this unconventional, violent war, for example the creation and sustaining of underground armies, but despite his many critics, Dalton had Churchill's support, patronage that kept SOE from being disbanded and dispersed in France and other countries. Others claimed that by supporting acts of sabotage and murder, SOE was also inviting reprisals from the Nazis on the local civilian populations, which would in turn bring further German attention on the formation of underground armies in all occupied countries at the time. That might prove to be disastrous, as these movements of civilian resistance were deemed essential for the eventual invasion of Europe by the Allies.

The SIS, controlled by the Foreign Office, required a different modus operandi in the field, with operational procedures developed over many years. Instead of the instability and social unrest created by SOE, SIS preferred to undertake operations as quietly and unobtrusively as possible, limit the damage and work with legitimate local authorities. They were also concerned about extremist organisations, in particular the communists, something SOE refused to worry about. It is said that at one stage, when SOE attempted to place their agents into occupied France, SIS actively worked against them.

SOE also found critics in the European governments then in exile in Britain. Claims were rightly made that SOE was conducting illegal operations in their countries without their knowledge and permission, and in the process was provoking heavy reprisals by the Nazis on their civilian populations. This was particularly clear where political opponents were fighting the Germans and also fighting among themselves, as was the case with the politically diverse leftist EAM and the ELAS in Greece, or between splintered groups within the Chetniks and the communists in Yugoslavia. The questions for the British became: who should they recognise as legitimate, who should they provide weapons and supplies to, and what was the future of this difficult arrangement.

These underground activities also threatened Britain's relationship with neutral countries and compromised the Foreign Office, which needed to smooth over unanticipated tensions and keep SOE in its box. Neutral Spain, connected to fascist Germany, was a major problem, as were the Scandinavian countries, which, while neutral, were still trading with Germany and supplying raw materials and manufactured goods as they had done in the First World War. Neutral Switzerland, a large part of which was German speaking and even pro-Nazi, also encountered difficulties with SOE operations and the flight of SOE agents across the Swiss border. In spite of all of these criticisms and obstacles both expected and unanticipated, SOE generally lived by the motto 'No bangs without Foreign Office approval', which in most cases pre-empted such difficulties.[11] In reality, however, the Foreign Office went along with SOE operational plans, given the support of both Churchill and Lord Mountbatten, who at the time was Chief of Combined Operations Headquarters, for their work.

Of course, the Germans had a very different opinion of SOE's operations. While the British naturally saw them as legal, the Germans interpreted hostile activities and resistance as an illegal form of warfare. They viewed SOE agents as saboteurs and assassins, outside the law, and the multiple French resistance organisations were lumped into the same category by the German occupying administration as criminals and terrorists.

Looking briefly at a few SOE operations gives an insight into the breadth of offensive missions and territory, and the effects on the enemy. Given the early criticism by SIS and the reluctance of the RAF, in particular Bomber Command, to provide aircraft to support SOE operations, the eventual success of SOE must have been gratifying for Churchill, whose early support gave SOE life and breath, and for the 13,000 people who were recruited, trained and in some cases died for the organisation. After the war, SOE's work was widely praised by Allied generals, who believed its operatives had helped to shorten the conflict.

One of the first SOE operations was Josephine, launched in June 1941, when a group of French SOE agents attacked the Pessac power station, south of Bordeaux, destroying six of the eight transformers. This put the U-boat base at Bordeaux out of action. The operation was SOE's first success and greatly enhanced its reputation, particularly in Whitehall, causing a rethink as to the value of carefully targeted sabotage as opposed to aerial bombing.

Another notable operation was Operation Anthropoid, the assassination of SS General Reinhard Heydrich, the 'Butcher of Prague', considered a major architect of the Holocaust. At the request of the Czech government in exile, SOE was tasked with organising his elimination, which was successfully carried out on 27 May 1942. However, the SS took revenge, destroying two Czech villages and murdering 1300 people, as well as the SOE operatives and their supporters.

SOE operations in Poland, in conjunction with the Polish Home Army, provided the Allies with the first evidence of the Holocaust in June 1942 and valuable intelligence on developments in the Nazis' V-2 rocket programme. In late 1942, SOE attempted to disrupt the rail movement of supplies through Greece to Rommel's Afrika Korps. SOE agents met up with two Greek guerrilla organisations, the pro-communist ELAS and the republican EDES, who provided Greek partisans to assist in the attack. On 25 November, they blew up three spans of the viaduct at Gorgopotamos, cutting the rail link between Thessaloniki and the port of Piraeus.

In Norway in February 1943, SOE agents destroyed Germany's heavy-water plant at Vemork, preventing the Nazis building an atomic bomb. In Denmark, an SOE operation with the Danish resistance movement secured shiploads of roller bearings destined for Germany and developed a burst transmitter for the rapid transmission of pre-recorded Morse-coded messages.

While the Axis countries were difficult to penetrate and establish contacts and a safe working base within, operations began in Italy after the fall of Mussolini in mid-1943, particularly in the north where the resistance harassed the retreating German forces after the landings in Sicily and Anzio. Operations were even planned in Germany, including Operation Foxley to assassinate Hitler at his mountain retreat, the Berghof, near Berchtesgaden. While plans were well advanced and a sniper team made ready, the operation was cancelled. Another operation, codenamed Periwig, sought to deceive the Germans about the existence of a large, secret army within Germany, and to this end several Germans were trained and parachuted into the country.

Some other countries were considered unimportant to the war effort or too difficult to establish a reliable underground connection in. Two groups of agents were dropped into Hungary 'blind' and were never heard from again. In Albania, attempts were made to organise the resistance, but as with Yugoslavia, an ongoing internecine war was being waged by communist and republican forces.

By the end of the war, SOE had a staff of 13,000 people. Of these, 470 agents had been dropped into 14 countries in Europe, and over 100 agents were tortured and killed. However, the detractors and critics still remained, and after Churchill lost the general election on 5 July 1945, the new Labour Prime Minister, Clement Attlee, saw no future in SOE and had it absorbed into MI6. On 15 January 1946, SOE was officially dissolved, the end of an important and highly specialised organisation in the defeat of Nazi Germany.

THREE

A Fourth Fighting Force

Following Prime Minister Menzies' announcement, Australia had declared war on Italy in mid-June 1940. In 1941, Australian forces had fought at Bardia and Tobruk in North Africa, and in Syria, Greece and Crete. Australian airmen were fighting in the Battle of Britain and the bombing of Germany and the Royal Australian Navy was involved in the Mediterranean and in convoy duty in the Atlantic. Of the four Australian divisions of infantry, three were in the Middle East and one had been captured in Singapore. The nation's defences, after years of neglect and diversion, were virtually non-existent and the gate was wide open for invasion and conquest.

Now, just weeks after Pearl Harbor, the Japanese were pouring south, landing in Timor, capturing Rabaul and humiliating the British Empire forces in Malaya with the capture of Singapore and the surrender of 130,000 Allied troops, including 15,000 Australians. On 19 February, Japanese carrier-based planes, the same aircraft that had bombed Pearl Harbor just ten weeks before, made two heavy raids on Port Darwin. Not only was Australia within the range of enemy aircraft but invasion seemed imminent. By this time, Japan controlled half of China, French Indochina, Malaya, Dutch East Indies, the Philippines, Borneo, Timor and half of Papua New Guinea, and were pushing east towards Guadalcanal and Fiji.

This translated to a growing fear within Australia, fanned by a vociferous press. In October 1941, even before the bombs fell on Pearl Harbor, the *Border Morning Mail* in Albury had warned, 'Australia must be ready to meet Japanese attack.' This fear only grew with the fall of Singapore (15 February 1942) and the first air raids on Darwin. On 17 February, the *Sydney Morning Herald* declared with bold headlines, 'NO SURRENDER CALL TO AUSTRALIAN PEOPLE' and 'INVASION THREAT'.[1] Indeed, the Japanese were sweeping south in rapid and ominous steps, driving the Allies before them and showing no mercy.

With Australia's back to the wall, another way needed to be found to take the war to the invincible Japanese. The establishment of a secret fighting force by Special Operations Executive in London, trained to undertake subversive operations, surveillance and the training of underground armies, had not gone unnoticed at General Headquarters (GHQ) in Melbourne. As a result, GHQ 'directed attention to the urgency of initiating special operations behind the expanding Japanese lines' and 'to harass the enemy in every possible way' by 'all forms of fifth-column activity'.[2]

Australian commanders also saw secret operations as an important element in future strategic planning, as 'a fourth fighting service' in addition to the Army, Navy and Air Force which should 'be immediately established'.[3] The idea of taking the fight to the Japanese, of striking unexpectedly in remote and unforeseen places, seemed a good option for Australian military planners. The defiant words of Churchill – 'we shall fight on the beaches' – found resonance with the beleaguered Allies in the Pacific, as did the idea of silent, aggressive patrolling against the Japanese, who had already shown their brutality and contempt for Allied prisoners.

Given the challenges that SOE faced from its establishment in late 1940, not only with Nazi Germany but also with the prejudice and jealousy from within British intelligence, it had little time to think of offensive operations outside mainland Europe, certainly not in South-East Asia and the Pacific areas. This area was in fact not under British military control but American, and became the South West Pacific Area (SWPA), established by General Douglas MacArthur in January 1942. In July 1941, before the Japanese entry into the war, the British Army had established a training camp near Singapore with plans for a number of stay-behind parties, but this idea was abandoned for fear of frightening the public by dispelling the myth of invincible Singapore, safe behind an impenetrable jungle and the massive guns that protected the harbour.

After the Japanese landings in northern Malaya in late 1941 and their rapid advance south through early 1942, General Thomas Blamey, commander-in-chief of the Australian Military Forces, proposed the formation of an Australian version of SOE. At the time there were a number of secret intelligence-gathering units active in the region, including the RAN's Coast Watch Organisation (also known as the Coastwatchers), established in 1919; the Australian–British Special Operations group, the propaganda intelligence organisation; the Far Eastern Liaison Office (FELO); the Dutch intelligence organisation NEFIS; and the American Philippine Regional Section (PRS). All were working on similar and parallel operations, and while they had been under-resourced and marginalised within their respective military apparatuses, they were now brought together under one intelligence organisation, the Allied Intelligence Bureau, or AIB, in early July 1942.

In March, Prime Minister Curtin had approved the establishment of an SOE-type organisation within Australia to undertake subversive operations under the direct control of the commander-in-chief and GHQ. The organisation was to be completely independent, top secret and funded by an undisclosed and separately funded financial vote. Special Operations Australia (SOA) would be outside the budget of the Australian military and be jointly funded by the Americans, Dutch and Australia. It needed to have a separate, undisclosed budget to retain secrecy and the allocation of funds.

To head up the new organisation, SOE London first ordered Captain Ambrose Trappes-Lomax, then commanding a section of SOE in Singapore, to fly to Australian GHQ in Melbourne. He arrived on 11 March and was followed soon after by Major Edgerton Mott, ex-head SOE Java, on 17 March. As he was senior to Trappes-Lomax, Mott became the principal advisor on special operations to Colonel Ronald Hopkins, the Director of Military Operations.

Mott and Trappes-Lomax were provided a small office within Victoria Barracks in Melbourne and began work with both Colonel Hopkins and the Director of Naval Intelligence, Commander Rupert Long. While Hopkins was not familiar with secret operations, Long 'proved to be exceptionally well informed'[4] and worked closely with Mott to establish an SOE-equivalent organisation. Taking into account the experience of SOE London and recent operations against the Japanese in Malaya, it was accepted that, 'in theatres of war, SOE operated under the direct control of the C-in-C [commander-in-chief]. Therefore, it was recommended that if an SO organisation be set up in Australia, it should function directly under the C-in-C, maintaining at the same time very close liaison with all the services.'[5]

In early April, just weeks after his arrival in Melbourne, Major Mott met with General Blamey and Lieutenant General Vernon Sturdee to discuss the formation of a special operations organisation as part of SOA, which would come to be called the Inter-Allied Services Department (ISD). Mott was instructed to prepare an operational outline of the new organisation, along with a budget for 12 months, to be submitted to both the prime minister and General MacArthur.

At the meeting, Blamey had stressed that the new organisation should be under the operational control of the SWPA's commander-in-chief: 'as foreign policy was no longer of concern in any of the territories where SO (Secret Operations) Australia would operate, he considered that civil cover was unnecessary and undesirable and that the organisation should be controlled and run by the High Command.'[6] Ten days later, MacArthur approved the plan, though with some disagreement about the provision of funds. Blamey ordered Mott to establish the HQ of the organisation in Melbourne, and immediately promoted Mott to Lieutenant Colonel to undertake the role.

To rein in this enthusiasm of ISD, in particular contain their proposed area of operations, General Headquarters SWPA formed the overarching organisation, the Allied Intelligence Bureau (AIB), in June 1942. In addition to their reservations about the organisation's lack of accountability, the Americans also suspected that the British and the Dutch were more interested in defeating the Japanese to reclaim their colonial possessions to the north of Australia – Malaya, Singapore, British North Borneo and the islands of the Dutch East Indies – than in following General MacArthur's plan to defeat the Japanese.

While the AIB was placed under the overall command of Colonel C. G. Roberts, an Australian officer, his deputy and second-in-command was an American, Lieutenant Colonel Allison W. Ind, who also acted as the organisation's financial controller. By this means, should ISD step out of line or propose operational plans unacceptable to the Americans, they could simply refuse financial support to starve the project of funds and a future.

Mott had set to work but there was much to do. While he had no budget initially, London had approved the expenditure of monies brought with him from Java. After some time, an agreed allocation of funds from the USA, the Netherlands and Australia would be made available. In the interim, Mott needed to recruit and appoint military and civilian personnel, purchase the necessary stores and equipment, develop a training programme, secure transport and find suitable training facilities and camps.

On 17 May 1942, Mott moved from Victoria Barracks to 'Airlie' at 260 Domain Road, South Yarra, along with a small staff of six officers and three secretaries. Within weeks, Mott had selected a number of men to begin training as operatives at a special facility in Foster, 90 miles (150 kilometres) east of Melbourne. This camp was found unsuitable as it was cold and lacked the necessary security, so Blamey agreed to the establishment of a suitable tropical training camp in Cairns – with conditions closer to those of the Japanese-occupied territories – with the cover name Z Experimental Station (ZES).

The site, which contained a large house named 'Fairview' in the hills above the town, was chosen by Commander Roy Kendall because it had good radio reception. The home belonged to Richard Kingsford, the grandfather of Sir Charles Kingsford Smith and at one time the mayor of Cairns. It came to be known as 'the House on the Hill' and, after being established in July 1942 as a wireless relay centre, it was to become the operational base for the early ISD operations.

With the establishment of ZES, in June the Chief of General Staff had created within ISD a separate raiding unit designated 'Z Special Unit', formed with a core of British SOE-trained officers who had escaped the fall of Singapore. With them were a number of British and 'alien refugees from the east . . . all with intimate knowledge of the territories overrun by the Japanese [who] could prove invaluable to SO and military intelligence'.[7]

As the *Official History* states, the Z Special Unit 'had no war establishment and no equipment table. It had a *carte blanche* authority to draw ordnance, and, as it was controlled, run and paid by ISD, held a unique position in the Australian Army. Its formation increased security and was of great assistance in stabilising ISD's stores arrangements with the maximum of security.'[8] But, for the fledgling ISD, issues of control and coordination quickly arose, mainly due to the role of the Allied Intelligence Bureau.

To separate responsibilities, AIB had been broken into four sections. The ISD would become Section A, the British Secret Intelligence Service would become Section B, the Combined Field Intelligence Section became Section C and the Military Propaganda Section became Section D. Even so, it was soon found that there were still overlapping responsibilities, and no clear lines to separate where the duties of one section ended and those of another began.

It also became apparent that the new structure was problematic and unwieldy. While AIB's role was 'the allotment of priority of objectives, the provision of transport . . . and to keep SO in the picture regarding general strategy, so that SO planning could proceed with regard to the C-in-C's plan', the *Official History* notes that 'this conception proved to be erroneous'.[9] There were problems with defining the role of Section A (special operations) as distinct from that of Section C (intelligence).

To address this, Lieutenant Colonel Mott wrote, explaining, that while GHQ saw ISD as 'a subsidiary Intelligence Organisation'[10] and tried to 'run it on orthodox Intelligence lines', he believed this approach was not practical or sustainable. He suggested that ISD come under General Stephen Chamberlain, the Assistant Chief of Staff in MacArthur's HQ, in charge of Operations and responsible for the planning and execution of MacArthur's SWPA campaigns.[11]

Being still the early days of ISD, Mott also highlighted the problems of overlapping roles, confusion and loss of security, expenditure issues and the compromising of operatives by the Dutch section. It came down to differing opinions as to how AIB and ISD should work; should it be for intelligence gathering on one hand, or special operations including sabotage on the other.

To further compound the issues, the Americans thought one thing, the Australians another. For Mott's part, he told GHQ the organisation could not do both, and if this was required, another reorganisation was necessary – which caused further friction between ISD and AIB. When Mott reported his concerns to Blamey, his job as director of ISD-Section A became untenable. As a result, in February 1943, ISD ceased to exist and Mott was relieved of his role and returned to London. The future of special operations in Australia looked grim.

Meanwhile, training continued at ZES Cairns. To complement this, a secret base, the Lugger Maintenance Section (LMS), was established at East Arm, ten miles (16 kilometres) from Darwin, to support operations in Timor and Papua New Guinea. While Section A had no difficulties securing the necessary stores, rations and fuel, they did have a major problem securing suitable transport. As there were long distances involved in dropping operatives into enemy territory, the only suitable alternatives were specially prepared aircraft and submarines, both of which were in short supply, and those available had already been tasked for offensive operations.

Following the return of Mott to London, he was replaced by Lieutenant Colonel P. J. E. Chapman-Walker, formerly a London solicitor. Chapman-Walker saw the importance of special operations to the north of Australia and recommended the establishment of a new organisation, Special Operations Australia (SOA). Most importantly, SOA would report and fall under the control of the Commander-in-Chief of Allied Land Forces, rather than SWPA. This way, it could operate more independently, both within SWPA, but also outside of the designated SWPA. While still under the overall control of MacArthur, SOA could operate in a much larger operational area and also potentially work in cooperation with SOE Far East, while at the same time not being under SOE control.

To push his idea forward, Chapman-Walker submitted a memorandum to AIB on 6 April 1943 outlining the adjustments to be made to the administration of the former ISD. His suggestions included the establishment of a new training camp, approval for SOA operations 'in adjacent theatres of war',[12] the approval process of operations by both GHQ and other necessary headquarters like the Dutch, the approval of appropriate personnel, that any intelligence obtained from SOA operations be provided to London after GHQ approval, and that the channels of communication between SOA and GHQ be clarified. He also asked to be placed on the staff of the controller of AIB, to advise on secret operations in both SWPA and areas outside of SWPA's control. Chapman-Walker was denied direct access to the SWPA Commander-in-Chief General MacArthur, although Brigadier General Charles Willoughby, who served as MacArthur's Chief of Intelligence, 'later assured [Chapman-Walker] that he could in practice have direct access to him'.[13]

In May 1943, yet another name change occurred, this time from SOA to Services Reconnaissance Department (SRD). Initially, the Z Special Unit was to be retained by AIB, but it was subsequently transferred to SRD, while a similar unit, known as M Special Unit, was established and maintained by AIB. At this time, Chapman-Walker opened a forward office in Brisbane, but retained his headquarters in Melbourne, as he considered it important to be close to the Chief of General Staff and more importantly General Blamey.

Within the new SRD organisation, Chapman-Walker created subsections to cover operational areas including the Netherlands East-Indies, Malaya, Borneo and Sarawak, Timor, and a special Raiding and Partisan section. Next, as he realised the need for training, he suggested that dedicated specialist schools and camps be established to teach communications, language skills and how to live off the land, as well as weapons and explosive training. Most important was training in 'insertion'; the operational placement of a patrol of operatives into enemy territory on a mission and their later 'extraction'.

The fledgling SRD had much to do. Three training camps had already been established. The first, known as Camp Z, had been set up in September 1942 at Refuge Bay in Ku-ring-gai Chase National Park, north of Sydney, another on Wilsons Promontory and a third in Cairns. While ZES in Cairns continued as a holding and training camp, it was found to be increasing unsuitable for the role as initially envisaged. Cairns had become a major troop assembly area, which compromised security, and there was a shortage of training staff. There were also transport problems out of Cairns and delays caused by the lack of aircraft. The search was on for a more suitable and remote training location.

The answer was the virtually uninhabited Fraser Island, off the Queensland coast, 150 miles (240 kilometres) north of Brisbane. Apart from a small forestry camp and an RAAF radar station, there were no permanent inhabitants. The island also had areas for jungle training and freshwater lakes for kayaking and parachute drops. The Fraser Commando School was opened in October 1943, for which buildings were erected along with a power plant and pumping station, and barge transport was provided by the Australian Army's 52 Port Craft Company. Specialist instructions came from the Army, the Jungle Warfare School at Canungra in the Gold Coast hinterland in Queensland's south, established in November 1942 to train troops for jungle combat. Here operatives were trained in signals, jungle craft, weapons, navigation and map-reading, unarmed combat, the use of folboats (folding kayaks), parachuting and physical training, and some had even learnt basic Malay and Japanese. From the Fraser Commando School, training raids were also undertaken on the aerodrome, port and railway infrastructure in Maryborough, nearby on the mainland.

In time, specialist training was also provided at a number of other locations, including the School of Eastern Interpreters in Melbourne, the Special Boat School at the Careening Bay Camp near Fremantle, Camps 6 and 8 at Mount Martha near Melbourne, and at Advanced Training Camps at Darwin and Morotai Island in Indonesia. Use was also made of the Parachute Training Unit at Richmond, New South Wales; the School of Military Engineering at Liverpool; and the Signals Training School at Bonegilla on the New South Wales–Victorian border.

While some men trained hard on Fraser Island, others were attending lectures at the School of Eastern Interpreters. Here they were given instruction in Japanese counterespionage, planning and organisation; the Malay language; how to build cover stories and use fake identity cards; interrogation systems; how to recruit agents in the field; internal communication methods such as secret ink, disguises and cyphers; and how to pick locks and enter and search buildings.

At the Careening Bay Camp, on Garden Island about 15 miles (24 kilometres) south-west of Fremantle, training was undertaken on the secret Motorised Submersible Canoes (MSCs). These were steel canoes with electric motors powered by batteries and controlled by a hydroplane and rudder, which gave them great manoeuvrability as offensive weapons. They could carry nine limpet mines (a six-pound charge), which were sufficient to sink two 10,000-ton ships if correctly placed.

Initially, when ISD had been established, there were three sections: a Papua New Guinea section, a Timor section and an NEI (Netherlands East-Indies) section. As operational work increased, it became necessary to form a planning section to select possible targets, collect intelligence, prepare plans and submit these for approval to GHQ. This joint Planning/Technical Section was commanded by Major C. V. Holland, with the assistance of Captain Sam Carey and Sergeant G. Mackenzie. Over time this section was enlarged, and with increased operational pressure, further separate sections were formed: Planning, Intelligence, Technical and Country, as in the country in which the operation was to be undertaken.

The process of approving an operational plan passed through a number of stages. First, a brief outline of the proposed operation was submitted by the originator to the Director of Operations. Here it was discussed and considered, and if approved for further development was then passed to the Directorate of Plans. Now the real work began, in consultation with the Country Section. Once this was completed, the plan then went back to Director of

Operations, who, with the assistance from the Country Section, submitted the plan to the DGS (Directorate of General Staff). If it was approved, it was then passed to Plans, where further work was done, including consultation with various other directorates. This resulted in a formal plan for submission to the Director SRD.

Finally, if approval was granted at this stage, it went on for final approval at GHQ. Once GHQ approval was secured, it became necessary for the relevant Country Section head to liaise with the leader of the operation, and in this conference details were finalised. From here, an operation order was prepared by the Director of Operations and circulated to those who needed to contribute in some way to the plan.

This Australian clandestine organisation, like its British counterpart SOE, soon drew critics and sceptics among the military bureaucracy. In particular, the Americans were concerned that unconventional, even maverick British officers would begin independent operations – what the Americans saw as harebrained schemes – outside the strategic master plan for the defeat of the Japanese. Even though General MacArthur had sanctioned the formation of the organisation now known as SRD, he was concerned about what he saw as secret and uncontrolled Allied initiatives in what was his sphere of influence, the American South West Pacific theatre of war.

To assist SRD operations, a number of support units were consumed while others established. These included FELO, the Far Eastern Liaison Office, which had been around since 1942, RAAF 200 Flight, the Royal Australian Navy's 'small boats', and the specialist instructors and linguists who all contributed to the successful preparation of SRD personnel, as well as their insertion, resupply and extraction. These men and women were drawn from the three services of the Army, Navy and Air Force, in particular

volunteers from the Second AIF, but many were specialist individuals recruited from civilian employment, specifically signals
and technical experts, linguists and expats from the occupied
territories like Borneo, Sarawak and Papua New Guinea.

Beginning with just five personnel, by the end of the war,
FELO would grow to an establishment of 475, including five
Japanese POWs.[14] Its objectives included all combat propaganda
directed against both the enemy and civilian populations under
enemy control. This remit embraced the lowering of 'the morale
of the enemy forces and so impair their fighting efficiency, to
mislead the enemy regarding our military intentions and to influence subject populations in enemy-occupied territories to impair
the enemy's war effort and to assist Allied forces'.[15]

FELO dropped propaganda leaflets, operated frontline broadcasting stations, ran mobile propaganda units that worked with
SRD operatives and assisted with the insertion and running of
agents, often under an Australian officer, in Japanese-occupied
territory. Apart from enlisting the support of people in occupied
territories with intelligence-gathering, FELO also attempted to
deprive the enemy of native labour and food, and information on
Allied movements and intentions. As well, FELO was involved
in rescue work, in particular with air crews, by providing and
hiding rescue kits, and briefing and preparing air crews on surviving in the jungle. This included the teaching of 'languages of the
areas over which they would be flying and production of special
leaflets to obtain native co-operation'.[16]

An important part of the work of FELO was the production
of leaflets aimed at both the enemy and people under Japanese
occupation. From a main production centre in Brisbane, leaflets
were first drafted in English and then translated. Special attention
was given to ensuring the authenticity of both the design and

content of the leaflet, with the issuing authority being the government of whichever country had administered the area before the Japanese occupation. To add authenticity, experts were consulted about adding totem signs, symbols and cultural representations and talismans to strike at the traditional heart of the people, also ensuring that the leaflet contained nothing offensive, in order to maximise the leaflet's psychological effectiveness. Extensive use of photographs and artwork showed 'proof' of the Allied success and strength: images of sinking Japanese ships next to lines of Allied tanks, aircraft or landing ships.

Within FELO, a separate unit known as Frontline Broadcasting Units was established to broadcast propaganda, in particular news, talks and Japanese music, in an effort to further break down enemy morale. Equipped with lightweight, portable public-address systems, including turntables and generators, and operating within 1000 yards of the enemy, these units were able to also broadcast sound effects of gunfire and explosions, all with the purpose of demoralising the enemy and keeping them awake. While these units had limited operational value, they assisted after the close of hostilities in contacting Japanese parties in the jungle to notify them of the surrender.

To further assist morale-building for the locals, Mobile Projection Units operated in areas recently vacated by the Japanese to show these people suitable propaganda to advance the Allied cause. This 'show' began at dusk with the broadcast of popular music and recorded 'sing-sings', and when enough people had congregated films and slideshows were presented. Propaganda included news of Allied victories, footage of Japanese ships sinking, the destruction of Japanese facilities, Japanese atrocities, and instructions to locals to assist Allied airmen and to avoid Japanese contact. Also included was local information and news appropriate to particular populations, including health issues and messages from friends.

In July 1944, GHQ requested the establishment of what became the Psychological Warfare Bureau, which was required for service with the US forces in the Philippines and in the push towards Japan. After training with FELO, the nucleus of the bureau was formed by 17 officers and 20 men from the US Army. Attached to this unit were experienced FELO officers, in particular two AIF warrant officers; one made eight operational landings with American forces and the other became the only Australian to serve with US forces on Okinawa.

As a curious example of how FELO and other Australian units became involved in propaganda, in a memo dated 21 June 1944 and headed 'SUBJECT: DROPPING OF ASHES OF ENEMY DEAD', the story is told of the discovery in Hollandia – now known as Jayapura, the capital of the Indonesian province of Papua – of the urns of Japanese dead and a proposal to drop these from an aircraft and return them to the enemy. As it happened, the aircraft with the ashes crashed,[17] but what is of interest is the reasoning behind going to this trouble and losing planes in the process. The memo goes on to state:

> At the time, it was hoped that the fact of returning ashes to the
> enemy would have the following effect: (i) It would impress upon
> the Japanese soldier that he is fighting 'gentlemen', and therefore
> offset the Japanese propaganda which has been to the effect that
> Europeans have no sense of tradition and are rather brute beasts.
> At the stage when Japanese morale is beginning to crack, this
> may be an important contributory factor. (ii) It would cause
> considerable embarrassment to the local Commanding Officers.
> If the leaflets were properly designed they would inform the

troops of our action and the Commanding Officer would not dare to ignore the return of the ashes.[18]

In the file that contains this memo, there are numerous references to how to use dead Japanese soldiers for propaganda purposes: photographs of their graves and of their cremation, and even when and how this might be released to the press for the biggest propaganda impact.

Given the ongoing problem of transport by sea or air for SRD-Z Special operations to the north of Australia, a range of support options were considered and used over the course of the war. These included US and British submarines operating out of Perth, Exmouth and Darwin, US and RAAF Catalina flying boats and, later in the war, a dedicated RAAF unit with specially equipped aircraft for the insertion, resupply and extraction of SRD operatives. Prior to 1945, SRD had used aircraft from the USAF 380th Bombardment Group, along with modified B-24 Liberators from No. 24 Squadron RAAF.

As SRD operations increased, specially trained crew in specially modified aircraft became necessary, and it was agreed in June 1944 to form a secret and separate unit, known as No. 200 Flight. While it was not until early 1945 that this unit was established at Leyburn, near Toowoomba in southern Queensland, it began training not only air crew, many of whom had been transferred from No. 99 Squadron RAAF, but also engaged in the parachute training of operatives. By the time No. 200 Flight became fully operational in March 1945, they flew six B-24 modified Liberators, nine 11-man air crews and 450 ground crew to support the flight.

Aircraft were also modified, with the removal of the mid-upper and ball turrets and all armour so that the craft could carry the weight of operatives and their weapons and equipment. As well, a special slide at the rear of the aircraft was installed to drop operatives and supplies.

On 15 March 1945, two B-24s left Leyburn, bound for McGuire Field on Mindoro in the Philippines, which had been liberated by American forces in mid-December. From here, No. 200 Flight undertook their first aerial reconnaissance over Borneo as part of the Semet I operation on 18 March, and two days later made two unsuccessful attempts to insert an SRD party of eight operatives. On 23 March, the insertion by parachute was successful 'in the mountainous and largely unexplored hinterland of Borneo'.[19] Unfortunately, the aircraft, flown by Squadron Leader Harold Graham Pockley, the commanding officer of No. 200 Flight, failed to return, and, in the days after, searches of the area were unable to find any survivors or evidence of the missing aircraft.

No. 200 Flight were to lose two more Liberators and 46 men – two crews of 11 men plus SRD operatives – after one aircraft was believed shot down over Timor on 17 May and the second off the coast of Borneo four days later. The last operational flights were to drop leaflets in September 1945, after which the flight was demobilised on 15 December 1945.

The Royal Australian Navy also provided specialist boats and crews. With the expansion of its operations, SRD required purpose-built vessels and turned to the RAN for help. In January 1944, a naval section had been established within SRD with two vessels, but more were needed. Four trawler-type vessels then under construction for the Army at Williamstown in Melbourne were transferred to SRD. These became known as the 'snake boats'; by the end of the war, seven were in service.

To assist in the stealth required for the SRD's dangerous missions, it was proposed to modify the vessels to look like junks that were common in the operational waters to the north, especially around Borneo, the Moluccas, the Philippines and Singapore. They were armed for defensive purposes only, with two Oerlikon 20 mm cannons along with Browning machine guns and Brens.

In all, there were seven snake boats: HMAS *Black Snake*, HMAS *Coral Snake*, HMAS *Diamond Snake*, HMAS *Grass Snake*, HMAS *River Snake*, HMAS *Sea Snake* and HMAS *Tiger Snake*, along with HMAS *Krait*, named after another deadly snake found on the Indian subcontinent. Along with these were a range of smaller ex-Army vessels like *Alatna*, *Karina*, *Nyanie* and *Misima*, which had a range of 3000 miles (nearly 5000 kilometres) and a top speed of 20 knots, ideal for the insertion and resupply of SRD operatives. There were also three 'mother ships': *Anaconda*, *Mother Snake* and *Taipan*, a converted junk which provided depot facilities to the smaller snake boats. At war's end, most of the snake boats were handed over to the British Borneo Civil Administration, including *Krait*, which was rediscovered in 1964 in Borneo before being purchased and returned to Australia. The *Krait* is now part of the collection at the National Maritime Museum in Sydney.

While initially SRD was a small, secret and poorly equipped unit, the importance of its work was to see not only parallel support from all three services, but virtually an open chequebook for the requisition of both personnel and supplies. By war's end, this cooperation and sacrifice saw a range of extraordinary operations undertaken: SRD was to initiate 81 covert operations across a wide area, from New Guinea through the islands around Timor, the Lesser Sunda Straits and Java, through British North Borneo and Sarawak, the Celebes and Moluccas, the Malayan Peninsula, the South China Sea and even in Indochina. By July 1945, the month before the Japanese surrender, SRD personnel comprised

205 officers and 996 men, plus additional Dutch, naval, Air Force and local personnel.

Many of these operations were implemented at great human cost. The British and Australian service casualties were high, with a total of 74 men dead or missing. Some were killed in firefights, some were executed by the Japanese or died as POWs, some drowned and many were listed as missing. The *Official History* tells us that during the course of operations, the Japanese had a total of 2095 casualties, with 1846 killed and a further 249 captured.[20]

The story of SRD and the men of the Z Special Unit remained a secret until the release of Ronald McKie's book *The Heroes*, first published in 1961, some 15 years after the war. Many of the files were not released until the late 1980s and files were still being cleared into the 1990s.

FOUR

'We're Going to Singapore'

Just days before the surrender of the Singapore garrison by General Arthur Percival, a 60-year-old Australian master mariner, Bill Reynolds from Williamstown, took matters into his own hands. Reynolds had been a member of the Royal Naval Reserve in the Great War, had captained merchant vessels around South-East Asia, possibly even worked for MI6. As the Japanese advanced down the Malayan Peninsula he had been tasked to destroy any facilities in Singapore that may be of use to the enemy. It was while he was at the docks that he found himself staring at a dilapidated Japanese fishing boat, the *Kohfuku Maru*, abandoned and unattended. While not the ideal means of escape, it did offer an interesting cover, a chameleon of a boat that, if spotted by the Japanese, would be considered one of theirs. And it had other potential uses, disconnected ideas that would soon form into an audacious plan.

During the chaos of the fall of Singapore, Reynolds met Major Ivan Lyon of the Gordon Highlanders, who worked for MI6 and SOE Far East. While Lyon's position was unknown to Reynolds, they discussed the idea of using this unassuming boat on a return mission to Singapore, which they codenamed Operation Jock. This was later renamed Jaywick by Lyon, after a seaside village on the Essex coast 'where fishing boats similar in looks to *Kohfuku Maru* were commonplace'.[1]

The Japanese had pushed into Indochina in September 1940 and then landed in northern Malaya at Kota Bharu on 8 December 1941, one hour before the Pearl Harbor attack, which was 7 December Hawaii time. The Japanese Army advanced quickly down the Malay Peninsula, bulldozing British, Indian and Australian forces before them. The British Army organised stay-behind groups of Malays under a British officer to continue the war after the anticipated fall of Singapore. Lyon, along with Freddy Spencer Chapman[2] and others, worked to establish these irregular units while assisting the civilian evacuation of Singapore. Through all of this, Lyon believed he had a good understanding of the Malay situation, as he knew Singapore Harbour and the waters and islands nearby, and realised the potential strategic importance of Singapore to the Japanese.

With the Japanese closing in on Singapore, Reynolds departed on 12 February 1942, steering the *Kohfuku Maru* east through the Rhio Strait to Bintan Island, where, evading capture, he was able to rescue as many as 1500 people from islands off Singapore, including women, children and nursing staff, many from ships sunk trying to escape south. Others he fed or moved to safer locations, all the time under direct threat of Japanese aircraft and difficult conditions. He was later decorated for this rescue. Reynolds then sailed from Sumatra, via the Strait of Malacca, to Ceylon. Meanwhile, Lyon and his batman, Corporal 'Taffy' Morris, sailed separately to Ceylon, where they met up with Reynolds and talked of a return raid on Singapore.

In Ceylon, Lyon organised a meeting with General Archibald Wavell, the commander-in-chief of British forces in India and the Far East. Wavell, Lyon found, was very supportive of unconventional warfare and took little convincing to consider a raid on Singapore, though he suggested an attack from the east rather than the west. While Lyon was meeting with Wavell, Reynolds was planning to sail his fishing boat *Krait*, newly renamed after the deadly Indian snake, to Australia, but there were problems with the diesel engine so the vessel was shipped to Sydney as deck cargo. It had been hoped that the boat would be ready to begin immediate operations, but even after repairs in Bombay, *Krait* was still plagued with engine problems, an issue that would continue for some time.

Lyon also sailed for Australia, arriving in July 1942 with the intention of recruiting personnel locally. Upon his arrival in Sydney, he learnt of the capture of his wife, Gabrielle, and their young son Clive when their ship, the SS *Nankin*, had been captured by the German raider *Thor* en route from Fremantle to India, whereupon they were handed over to the Japanese and interned. At war's end, Mrs Lyon and her son were repatriated back to Australia.

It was at this time that Lyon also met up with another mate from Singapore, Lieutenant Donald Davidson, who he invited to become his second-in-command. Although Davidson was British, he was an ex-jackaroo and timber worker who had been working in Borneo and had escaped from the Japanese at Sandakan, so he was familiar with Singapore and the surrounding waters.

Lyon and Davidson were soon discussing their plans with the director of AIB, Colonel Caleb Roberts, and the head of ISD, Lieutenant Colonel Egerton Mott. Both were in support. However, after discussions with Colonel Merle Smith and Brigadier Charles Willoughby of US Army Intelligence, Lyon found the Americans had no plans for an attack on Singapore and were more interested in using trained operatives in Timor. Lyon then sought a meeting with the then governor-general of Australia, Lord Gowrie VC, with the help of 'Lyon's family friend'[3] (this was the governor of

Victoria, Sir Winston Duggan, who Lyon was staying with at the time),[4] and, along with support from the Naval Board, the plan was finally approved by the Australian commander-in-chief, General Sir Thomas Blamey. This cleared the way for Davidson and Lyon to begin the selection process for men to be involved in the operation and, after arrangements were made with the naval authorities, personnel were selected from Flinders Naval Depot, south of Melbourne.

Initially, 40 men volunteered, and from these, 17 were selected for six weeks' training at the Frankston Army Physical and Recreational Training School on Port Phillip Bay. There, it was said, 'Davidson put them through their paces, watching closely for any weakness or character flaws as they boxed, wrestled, climbed, ran and learned unarmed combat.'[5]

At the end of the training period, six men were returned to their unit, leaving just 11 to continue. These operatives were then transferred in early September 1942, first by train to Sydney and then by a nine-mile (15-kilometre) boat trip from Cottage Point, into the maze of waterways in the Hawkesbury River, then to their secret training base at Refuge Bay.

Training now took on a new urgency and focus. This camp, while not a long way from Sydney, was in very rugged sandstone country surrounded by cliffs and thick scrub, with the waterway the only means of access, making it an ideal location for the training ahead. The training notes state that the purpose of this camp was for the men 'to reach a state of perfect physical condition, capable of being maintained for six months', so they would 'be able to cover long distances over land and water: 50 miles a day on foot over roads . . . 40 over rough trackless country; 30 by kayak on rivers, estuaries and open sea and 30 by land and water combined'.[6]

After establishing a tent camp, the men began a tough training schedule under the watchful eye of Davidson, beginning at 7 am and working through until 10 pm. It was here that the men were introduced to kayak training and boat-handling skills, which soon became the focus of preparation. This involved long periods of paddling, sometimes for 200 miles (320 kilometres) over four days, not only in the calm waters near the camp but in the open sea and between lakes, meaning the kayaks required porterage. The men would also practise attacks on RAN ships and on the 4.7 inch guns of the West Head Battery. At all times, the watchful eyes of Lyon and Davidson were on the men, as they carefully made their final selection of the fittest and most reliable of the operatives.

Davidson trained the men in the swiftest and most effect means of killing. In his diary notes he states, 'Temple – good hard blow will kill. Eyes – gouge out in fighting, jab with two fingers in sudden contact and finish him off at leisure. Ears – pull off, bite off. Hands – tear fingers apart and split hand – bend fingers back and break.'[7] The men were trained to use a range of weapons, including the Sten, Owen, Bren and Lewis guns and explosives, and were trained in unarmed combat, movement by stealth and operating as a team.

Davidson's training notes make interesting reading, as do his personal assessments of the men, as he does not hold back. He writes of one man that 'he has the gentle outlook of a girl', and of another, 'inclined to be a buffoon . . . could not be trusted to think or act quickly in an emergency'. One man is described as 'Rather lazy, gutless, no stability . . . weak face, receding chin, would not dare rely on him even in small things; mentally childish'. Another is called 'Lazy and surly. One cannot like the man however hard we try.' Another: 'He remains a bumptious little gutter snipe and will always be a serious irritant to all around him.' And finally: 'A cheeky, flash, larrikin type. On one occasion . . . he was seen . . . with his arm around some harlot that had just strolled up . . . A bad type and difficult to knock down.'[8]

In spite of these harsh assessments, Davidson was well respected with the men, who had a high opinion of his experience and leadership. As one of them, Horace 'Horrie' Young, later said, 'he was a very, very decent guy; very capable, competent fellow.'[9]

After the tough training and selection process, 14 men were finally chosen to undertake the mission to Singapore. Alongside Lyon and Davidson was the captain of *Krait*, Lieutenant Hubert Edward Carse (RANVR), ex-British Navy and merchant marine with master mariner qualifications, while Lieutenant Bob Page of the AIF was the other officer. The other ranks were Corporals Andrew Crilly (cook) and 'Taffy' Morris (medic), Leading Telephonist Horrie Young (radio operator), the Irishman Leading Stoker James 'Paddy' McDowell (mechanical engineer), and three Leading Seamen canoeists, Walter Falls, Arthur Jones and Andrew 'Happy' Huston. There were also two reserve canoeists, Mostyn Berryman and Fred Marsh, while Leading Seaman Kevin 'Cobber' Cain was the coxswain.

The crew were less than impressed with the *Krait*. Horrie Young first saw the *Krait* when he joined the rest of the crew in Cairns. He said:

> I thought it was the most dreadful thing I'd seen in my life, the state of it, untidy, ropes scattered everywhere and filthy, dirty looking, I thought, 'My God.' She was dirty, untidy, and full of cockroaches the like of which I've never seen in my life. They were monster big cockroaches. You could almost hear them walking around they were that noisy. It looked so crook. It was terrible.[10]

On 17 January 1943, the *Krait* left Refuge Bay near Sydney for Cairns, the very first leg of their extraordinary journey. Quite soon the voyage became a nightmare, with the *Krait's* engine failing and the narrow beamed boat rolling and pitching, to the distress of the crew. They were forced to stop for engine repairs in Brisbane, where they were joined by Paddy McDowell, and Kevin Cain. Setting out, they again became beset with engine problems; *Krait* finally broke down and needed to be towed to Townsville. This was a major setback for Captain Lyon, particularly in view of a secret message to him which stated in part, 'in view of the complete break-down of the engine . . . it appears that the Expedition . . . must now be abandoned'.[11]

Krait was finally towed to Cairns in mid-March, where a new Gardiner diesel engine was fitted, but this delayed their departure. Given the difficulty recruiting specialists and the time taken to undertake this, their availability and the wasted time sailing from Sydney, it was not until Cairns that the final four members of the operational team joined them: Captain Lyon, Lieutenant Page, Ted Carse and Horrie Young. They came together at the 'House on the Hill', Z Experimental Station above the town, which was at that time an important operational centre for the Z Special Unit.

Page was a young lieutenant, a second-year medical student at the University of Sydney. His father, Major Harold Page, was a First World War member of the 26th Battalion AIF who was awarded both a Distinguished Service Order at Gallipoli and a Military Cross for actions in 1918. He had been wounded three times and returned to Australia in March 1919. Sadly, Major Page was lost on 1 July 1942, along with a thousand other POWs and civilians, in the sinking of the Japanese passenger vessel *Montevideo Maru* off the Philippines, something unknown to Page at the time.

On 9 August 1943, *Krait* left Cairns on the first leg of her journey to Exmouth Gulf in Western Australia. She carried supplies for a four-month operation: weapons, folboats, a huge amount of explosives and a quantity of cyanide tablets should the need for quick death arise. In the event of capture, an operative would have the choice to take their own life rather than be tortured and, in the process, reveal information about their operation and their mates.

There were also medical supplies, trade goods like cigarettes and Dutch guilders, a range of spare parts including a propeller, and distilled water in two-gallon tins. They carried intelligence information including diagrams of Japanese ships and aircraft, and detailed instructions for the collection of a wide range of intelligence information. But as Arthur Jones later stated, 'It was very cramped, terribly cramped, and meals were only two a day – two meals a day, breakfast and an evening meal.'[12]

Their journey north from Cairns was uneventful, with *Krait* humming along, powered by the new Gardiner engine. At one point, the boat grounded briefly on a coral reef, but skipper Carse was able to back off without damaging the hull timbers. On Friday 13 August, *Krait* arrived at Thursday Island before setting out again the following day. While close to the Australian mainland they were still within range of enemy aircraft, so the RAAF provided aerial cover as they headed westwards. After they turned south and were travelling past the Monte Bello Islands, not far from Exmouth Gulf, the seas became rough and the decision was made to jettison the heavy tar – bulletproof material that Lyon had instructed be applied in Cairns. The weight was slowing the boat, so Carse told Lyon it had to be stripped off and thrown overboard.

After 18 days at sea, *Krait* reached Exmouth Gulf on 27 August. Here the party took delivery of four specially designed kayaks.

However, on inspecting them, Lieutenant Davidson noted that he was 'never so disappointed in my life as I was in them . . . the workmanship put into them is shoddy . . . is not to my design at all. I do honestly think we have been done an awful bad turn by someone.'[13] But Captain Lyon stated they were better than their training kayaks, and was 'quite content to take on the world in them'.[14]

At 1400 hours on 2 September, *Krait* slipped quietly out of Exmouth Gulf on its secret mission. Over the following days, it ploughed north at just over six knots in clear, calm weather. On 8 September, 950 miles (1500 kilometres) north of Exmouth, they sighted land dead ahead and slowed down to time their arrival in the Lombok Strait after dark. They had been informed that at this time of the year they would be provided the benefit of a sea haze, but as their log notes, they still had 'perfect visibility'.[15]

The men, of course, still knew nothing of the mission nor the destination, such was the level of secrecy imposed. Lyon, after first raising the Japanese flag, called the men together. Horrie Young recorded the following of his speech to them:

> Lyon called them 'Clear the lower deck' and got all the troops up
> forward. Then he started to issue his, 'We're going to Singapore.'
> Nobody said anything. Taffy later told me that he nearly fell over
> the side. He'd only just got out of Singapore in the surrender
> circumstances. Going back he thought Lyon must have lost
> his lid. Nobody else seemed to be greatly concerned. He said,
> 'We'll be flying under the Japanese flag and you've all gotta
> stain yourselves black and wear sarongs like Malay fishermen.
> Nothing, but nothing, is to go over the side. No tins, no paper,
> no nothing that would betray the presence of Europeans to any
> sub that may happen to be charging his batteries on the surface
> and something floats past. These are the rules.[16]

Approaching the Lombok Strait, they felt their first real pang of fear. As Arthur Jones later recalled, 'a search light came up on our port side and started to swing towards us and it lit the water up around us but the main beam didn't get as far as us, it was too far away'.[17] It was 'very tense' as the crew knew there was a Japanese airfield and Army garrison nearby, as well as naval units and patrol craft. Carse spoke up to relieve the pressure, stating, 'That searchlight is 20 miles away and you will be well down on the horizon. They wouldn't be seeing you. Not yet anyway.'[18] The men 'breathed a sigh of relief'[19] and felt grateful for the captain's experience and maritime capability.

Upon entering the strait, the sea conditions became difficult and 'confused'. They found they were pushing against a tidal current which was at times over seven knots and actually pushed them back. At one point, the log notes, 'Since entry into the Straits, until four hours later, distance made good was under five miles at full speed.'[20] The report goes on, 'Dawn broke to find *Krait* not clear of the Straits as she should have been, but well and truly in them, approaching the northern exit to the Java Sea. At this moment, the promised haze in the Pilot book developed, and under cover of this, she slipped out at full speed into the open sea beyond.'[21]

They pushed on through the narrows, the sight of land tracking with them on each side. To the observer they were a Japanese fishing boat, complete with a Japanese merchant ensign, the crew now made up to appear as Malayans or Indonesians, with their skin darkened, thanks to a special skin dye provided by the cosmetic company Helena Rubinstein in Sydney. Around them, the waterway was busy with small prahus – multi-hull sailing boats that were common in the region – and other sailing craft, and Japanese reconnaissance aircraft were flying back and forth above them. The *Krait* pushed on, the sea at one point 'an olive green colour' with a comforting haze and little wind, while at another point it was 'very discoloured in patches'.[22] For the operatives there was little to do, so they sat around whispering quietly, careful not to let out any noise that would carry across the water and give them away. Into the Java Sea, they chugged north at six and a half knots still shrouded by sea haze; the voyage at this point was noted to be 'dull and uneventful'.[23]

By dawn on 14 September, they reached the Karimata Islands, off the south-west coast of Dutch Borneo. Carse then set a course to the Temiang Straits and the entrance to the Lingga Archipelago, immediately south of Singapore, and on to Pompong Island, which had been previously selected as a transhipment area. Here the operatives and their folboats could be dropped off and they had a direct line of approach to Singapore.

However, Pompong Island was found unsuitable so the decision was made to investigate instead the islands of the Rhio Archipelago, which lie between Pompong and Singapore. In the *Krait* log it is noted that, 'During that evening much enemy activity, in the form of searchlights, floatplanes and transport aircraft, made it evident that this was not a healthy spot for the *Krait*.'[24] The log goes on, 'While sailing north to the Rhio Archipelago *Krait* passed right under the nose of the Japanese observation post located on Galang Bahru at the southern end of the island group. She apparently aroused no suspicion so the course was maintained until darkness.'[25]

As the men needed to find a base, they decided to return to a small island, Panjang Island, which had been observed on the way north and turned out to be suitable. *Krait* arrived on 17 September and by 0500 the following morning, all operatives and their kayaks, operational gear and rations for one month were landed without problems. When asked to describe the mood of the crew at the moment the six operatives left the *Krait*, Horrie Young said, 'Very sad in a way, because I think by that time we had a feeling that what they were gonna try and do was almost mission impossible. We didn't think we'd ever see them again. It was pretty sad.'[26]

Having completed the drop-off, *Krait* weighed anchor and set sail for safer waters near Borneo, with instructions to return to Pompong Island on the night of 1–2 October.[27] As Young related:

> As soon as we dropped them we went off back towards the coast of Borneo. We ran *Krait* up and down in the shallows off the edge of the coast there. We kept her there in the shallows so no vessel larger than her could get in there. They'd have to be the same size almost. So that was Carse's idea to keep her in the shallow water. Anyone that wanted to have a look at her they had some chance of defending themselves. If they were out in the open sea they could have been gone, finished.[28]

Following the departure of the *Krait*, the six operatives – there were in fact four canoe teams, but the reserve team of Berryman and Marsh did not go – completed the concealing of their stores and equipment, and an observation post was set up to observe their approach to Singapore Harbour. As *Krait* chugged away from the beach on Panjang Island before dawn, the six operatives realised they were now alone, deep in Japanese-held territory, with no chance of rescue or escape. Return to Australia relied on communication with that ugly wooden boat disappearing over the horizon, the ominous Japanese rising-sun flag limp on the rear mast. As the six men turned away and walked silently inland, their minds were on the task ahead: the dangerous paddle into

Singapore, the mission and the long, exhausting paddle and rendezvous with the *Krait*.

After dawn broke, the operatives on Panjang Island surveyed their island home. Thick jungle grew to the rear of a small arcing beach, which they named Otter Bay after a family of otters they saw playing there. They moved their stores, folboats and weapons inland and established a camp by a waterhole, hiding their stores in a cave in the nearby cliff. When they returned to the beach, they were pleased to see that an army of soldier crabs had totally obliterated their tracks across the sand. Searching further, they discovered a village on the other side of the island, about a quarter of a mile away, but no tracks were found leading to the beach or to near their camp.

With their stores safely hidden, and now ahead of schedule, the men had time to rest. During the day of 20 September, they carefully assembled their folding kayaks and packed them with 'food and water for a week, operational stores and men, a total cargo of approximately 700 lbs [300kgs], were very low in the water and sluggish'.[29] Just as they were about to leave, a large Japanese patrol launch appeared about a mile off the beach, but, having observed this vessel on its patrol on the two previous nights, they were unconcerned by its presence.

When the noise had receded, they pushed out into deeper water. Arthur Jones related that the men 'wore blue japara silk suits that covered the whole of your body and they didn't breathe except where your arms went and your neck, you know. They were buttoned up and of course in that climate you sweated like the devil.'[30]

With two men in each of the folboats, they settled into the hard wooden seats as the three boats took up an arrowhead formation, Lieutenant Davidson acting as navigator and taking the lead. They continued to head out and were consumed in the darkness.

After paddling ten miles (16 kilometres), the three kayak teams arrived at Kaloh Island, at the entrance to the Bulan Strait, where they found a suitable camp spot on Bulan Island, 'a small uninhabited knoll with a sandy beach'[31] two miles to the north. Here they rested for the day, observing the passing shipping and venturing out for a swim off the small beach. Meanwhile, the *Krait* was steaming south-east towards Borneo to lose itself in the many islands and archipelagos before returning for the rendezvous in the first days of October.

Just after dusk, the three kayak teams set off again towards Singapore. The narrative of the operation states that, 'owing to the constant alarms at unfounded dangers, we made poor progress'.[32] In fact they travelled 12 miles (19 kilometres), but, as they feared being caught paddling in daylight, they found a campsite on what was described as 'a sand-fly infested swamp'[33] opposite a village across a narrow stretch of water just 300 yards away. Arthur Jones related that 'Davidson could speak Malay and they heard them talking about three canoes so we were on our toes from there on'[34]. Their late arrival was a valuable lesson: they must allow time to find a safe and protected campsite, and not risk discovery due to poor planning or preparation.

With the arrival of darkness, the men quickly gathered and moved out into the channel. They made good time and reached the end of the strait, from where they could see the lights of the old Dutch oil terminal on Sambu Island. They paddled on to their predetermined final observation post on Dongas Island, a mere hump of land with a swamp on the south side and only one landing place, a sand spit that went back into the jungle which provided 'every facility for concealment with some comfort'.[35]

The following morning, the men carefully explored the island and found that from a sheltered spot at the top, they had an excellent view of the Roads and the entrance to Singapore Harbour. The Roads was an area along the Singapore Harbour frontage, where originally a breakwater, known as the Detached Mole, ran parallel with the shore. Within this was an area known as the Inner Roads, while on the seaward side was the Outer Roads where larger vessels would be anchored.

After finding water in a disused well, they rested for the day and prepared for the final paddle and attack. During that time, Lyon observed shipping transiting the harbour into various anchorages and discussed the options and the line of attack with the rest of the party. While Lyon was the leader, he relied heavily on Davidson for his maritime knowledge and because he spoke Malay, so Lyon said to the men, 'We'll follow Davidson from now on, whatever he says goes.'[36] They then rested, exhausted after their long paddle.

During the daylight hours of 24 September, the operatives carefully observed the harbour area, the shoreline and the movement of shipping, in particular patrol craft. Heavily laden ships were observed coming from the east and quickly docking; then, when emptied of their cargo, returning to sea via the Strait of Malacca. Also noted was the unfavourable tides, which would be heading out towards sea as they approached Singapore, but as Lyon later wrote, 'the nature of the target was such that an attempt seemed imperative'.[37] This perhaps was typical of Lyon and his determination to destroy anything Japanese: it was simply too tempting not to attack it. The men were ready and keen to go. As Arthur Jones said, 'I think we were all confident, I was confident we could do the job, but I was a bit doubtful about getting away.'[38]

At 2000 hours on 26 September, the three folboat teams set out and paddled towards the target area. Their passage was uneventful until midnight, when they were about halfway across the strait, and for half a minute a searchlight swept the area. Jones retells the story:

> . . . a search light opened up on our port side and it flamed down on the water and it came towards us and we headed the canoes into the light to cut down the silhouette and I slid underneath, down as low as I could get down in the canoe, and Bob Page sat up on the back of the canoe and sort of just paddled with one paddle. We had single paddles, just paddled with one paddle like the fishermen do and hopefully they wouldn't take any notice of us. But anyway, it got almost to us, the light, the water was light around us, and then suddenly it flipped up in the air, went across over our heads and then out. Of course we said a prayer.[39]

They were not detected, but ten minutes later, the searchlight swept the water again:

> [the light] started coming towards us and of course we thought, 'Oh, they've woken up, there's somebody out there or something out there and they're a bit suspicious,' you know. So we went through the same routine again and they did it again too, they got almost to us and then went up in the air and over the top and out.[40]

However, as anticipated, the tide was flowing directly against them, and at 0100 Lyon abandoned the attack and all three kayaks turned back towards Dongas. While Davidson and Page were able to make Dongas before dawn, Lyon and his mate Huston could not keep up. Arthur Jones, the paddler with Lieutenant Page, noted, 'Lyon did very little training with us actually. He lived in Sydney and would just come out on weekends every now and then up to where we were at Broken Bay. So he didn't get a lot of training and he was a pretty fragile-looking fellow – tall and thin.'[41]

As a result, Lyon and Huston were forced instead to find shelter among boulders on the shoreline, where they spent an uncomfortable day exposed and lashed by rain. At nightfall, they left their hideout at 1900 hours and rejoined the other two teams to find that a hot meal was awaiting them.

During the day, Davidson had rethought the line of attack on the harbour, given the problem of the tides, and made plans for an alternative hiding place ready for an attack on the night of 26–27 September. And so, after dark on the 25th, the operatives moved off to the bracken-covered island of Subar, some nine miles (14.5 kilometres) away, arriving just before dawn. Here they could observe shipping in the Examination Anchorage and harbour, an estimated 100,000 tons, but the exhausted men needed sleep, so during the course of the day observation was limited.

Late in the afternoon, the final determination was made on targets and the areas within the harbour each team would attack. The men readied their folboats, agreed on the return route and the escape south, and then checked their limpet mines – each team having eight limpets, plus plastic explosive, detonators and three magnetic holdfasts. These holdfasts were simply a stick to allow them to attach the limpets about five foot (1.5 metres) below the water line at a spot on the ship's hull to do the most damage; for example, by the engine room or near the rudder and propeller. Each team also carried emergency rations, water, their operational clothing (a blue-black tracksuit of japara outfit with black socks and sandshoes), plus a .38 revolver with 50 rounds and a knife.

Now ready, they took one more look across the water. Singapore had no blackout and was lit up, the war seeming far away, with cars visible coming and going along Beach Road.

Lyon noted that, 'No harbour or navigation lights were burning and all shipping was stationary.'[42]

At 2000 hours, the raiders set out, their clothing and faces black and their paddles matt to reduce reflection. Lyon and Huston, in Canoe No. 1, initially remained with Page and Jones, in Canoe No. 3, while Davidson and Falls in Canoe No. 2 headed for the Empire Dock area. Silently they slid across the water, paddling 'at an easy pace, making good progress on the cross tide'.[43] With their profile low, they were virtually invisible, even when at midnight a searchlight, believed to be on the Cathay Building, briefly swung in an arc across the harbour. It did not pick them up, but an anxious minute passed as they stopped paddling and remained motionless. The operatives were also fortunate that no patrol boats were out. At 2130, Lyon and Page, in Canoe No. 1 and 3, reached the vicinity of Jong Island, where they split up and headed for their designated target areas.

Page and Jones paddled parallel to Bukom Wharf (which was about five miles (eight kilometres) in a direct line south-west of Keppel Harbour, the main harbour right by the city) and found it well lit up with arc lights and busy with workers and welding crews. As Arthur Jones later said, 'there's probably no way possible that you could get in there, probably paddle your canoe in there, without being seen because there's so much light.'[44]

Seeing a larger target, a freighter, the operatives paddled in and, getting right alongside it, attached their limpets with a loud and frightening *clang*. Jones continued, 'We watched a sentry walking up and down on the wharf and about from there to the road they were working on another ship all lit up and doing some repair work.'[45]

Having completed their attack on this ship, Jones looked out into the harbour: 'And when you look out [you think], "Oh God," and you see all that water and light and you think no way can you get out again. That was the tensest moment, I think, going out and not knowing what's behind you and whether they're going to discover you or not.'[46]

Page and Jones paddled to their next target, a ship hugging the darkness away from the wharf. 'We went under the starboard side bow and we were just about to get ready to start putting the first limpet on and we looked up and there's cigarettes with blokes hanging on to them hanging over the side, and so we had to back paddle then and go under the bow and around the other side and just hoped to God there was nobody there.'[47]

Passing on to the next ship, heavily loaded and low down in the water, they needed to scrape away rust and barnacles to attach the limpet and make it grip. As it was by now getting towards 0200, they headed back to the beach at Dongas, where they met up with the other two teams.

Lyon and Huston arrived in their target area between Bukom Island and Keppel Harbour at 2230 to 'find that all shipping, except tankers, were blacked out and completely invisible against the background of the hills'.[48] Of more interest were the two tankers at anchor, identified by their lights. Approaching the stern of the first tanker, they placed two limpet mines against the engine room and a further limpet on the propeller shaft. However, Huston drew Lyon's attention to a man watching them intently out of a porthole, just ten feet above them. As Lyon later wrote, 'He continued to gaze until just before we left the ship, when he withdrew his head and lighted his bedside lamp. He took no apparent action and we set off for Dongas 12 miles away.'[49]

Like the other two teams, Davidson and Falls left Subar Island and headed out for their designated target area: Keppel Harbour. They too pushed against a starboard tide which made progress slow and difficult, but as with the others, they encountered no patrols or potential threats apart from the odd searchlight. They were nearly run down by a large steam ferry which apparently did not see them so they paddled on until they came to the pylons of the Keppel Harbour boom, a net to prevent submarines entering this inner harbour area.

With the boom gate open, they entered the protected area, where two ships were tied up against the east wharf. Davidson and Falls considered the ships not worth attacking, so they paddled on in search of a suitable target. A little further, they came upon the Empire Docks, but they were not worth the risk given they were brilliantly lit.

Back across the boom, they headed for the Roads, where Davidson later reported, 'Here were many excellent targets and we selected three of the largest cargo vessels.'[50] The first target was a heavily laden cargo ship of 5000 to 6000 tons. The second was of similar weight, also heavily laden, and a modern vessel. This Davidson identified as the *Taisyo Maru*, which they had seen entering the Roads a few days before. The third ship, again of similar weight, was an engines-aft cargo vessel riding high in the water; it was un-laden and could not be identified.

Fearing being seen by the lights of Singapore, Davidson and Falls attacked each ship on the dark port side, confirming their time by the chiming clock on what they believed to be Victoria Hall. By 0115, after they had attached their limpets with a seven-hour delay to the three ships, they cleared the Roads area and headed east for the Rhio Straits, 40 miles (64 kilometres) ahead.

At 0515, Lyon and Huston arrived at Subar as the first explosion lit up the dawn sky. A few minutes later, Page and Jones arrived and both teams raced for the protection of the mangroves, from where they could observe the reaction of the Japanese and of any villagers nearby and across the water. Arthur Jones later related:

> all you could see was a lot of smoke going over the harbour so one of the oil tanker's holds must have been caught alight and all you could see was black smoke everywhere. We couldn't see what was happening to the others, but we heard seven separate explosions and so we knew then that Davidson got his three and we got three and Lyon got the one tanker. So we knew that obviously they'd done their job and were on their way hopefully. Yes, everybody shook hands all around, a good job well done.[51]

The Japanese had no idea how this sabotage had come about, and certainly would not have expected operatives to have travelled all the way from Australia to undertake such an audacious mission. Arthur Jones further recalled, of that morning after the mission:

> Aeroplanes were buzzing around and we didn't know whether they were looking for submarines or what they were doing. And there were what looked like patrol boats, big launches, moving around, and so we stayed there until dark on this island and waited and then away we went.[52]

At 1100, in broad daylight, the four men made a quick crossing of the narrow passage, returning to their old campsite on Dongas. There they remained in hiding all day, resting and preparing for the first stage of their return trip south. Davidson and Falls had decided to take a longer route, by way of the Rhio Straits and along the east coast of Batam Island on to Panjang and then Pompong Island. Lyon and Page had planned their route to the west of Batam, which, while shorter, was more dangerous and exposed. Meanwhile, Davidson did not know the fate of the other two crews, but given there were no sirens or gunfire, it was hoped they too had made their escape and were paddling for the agreed rendezvous with the *Krait*, which had been keeping a low profile.

At dusk on 27 September, the two canoe teams of Lyon–Huston and Page–Jones set out. They had anticipated problems in passing the island of Sambu from patrols and searchlights, but nothing eventuated as they paddled south into the narrow Bulan Strait. At one point, the two canoes found their progress blocked by an anchored patrol boat, the one that had been observed over the previous nights. As Arthur Jones noted, 'There was nobody on deck keeping a look-out that we could see, but we couldn't do anything about it so we just took our paddles out of the water and let ourselves drift with the current until we got past. I could have reached out and touched the anchor rope that it had out at the stern.'[53] Exhaustion overtook them, and they located a well-concealed hiding place in what they found the next day to be an old Chinese cemetery. After hiding their canoes, they fell asleep.

After remaining undiscovered all day, they again set off on the night of the 28th, paddling first to Bulat, where they again rested, before paddling through a violent storm to their old camp at Otter Bay on Panjang Island. They remained there throughout 30 September, expecting to continue their paddle south that night, but heavy clouds and the threat of ominous weather prevented their departure.

To keep to schedule and make their rendezvous with *Krait*, they were forced to take the dangerous option of a daylight paddle. As Lyon later noted, 'To risk a day passage of 28 miles was a serious decision, but it was amply justified by the violence that later developed.'[54] As Arthur Jones added, 'We sort of were against it, the rest of us, but he decided, he'd made up his mind that he was going to take the risk.'[55]

On the other side of Batam Island, Davidson and Falls were encountering the same dangerous weather conditions. They had landed early on the 29th at Otter Bay, where they retrieved some of the cached stores and left a note for Lyon, just before a storm swept across the island and forced them to remain there all day. They rested and set out at 1900 for the final leg to Pompong, but again faced a violent storm 'with a deluge of rain, thunder and lightning, lashing the sea into a fury'.[56] They finally arrived at 0100 on 1 October and the following morning the *Krait* arrived just after midnight to await the returning paddlers.

Horrie Young recalled of the rendezvous with Davidson and Falls:

> Well we weren't too sure what the hell we were going into, we had to sneak past this blasted Japanese observation post and fortunately there was no moon, so we were pretty right. Carse went in and dropped the anchor and everybody's waiting there with their fingers on the Owen gun triggers and the Brens and things like that, cos we weren't too sure what the hell was gonna happen. Then it was Davidson, playboy as he is, tried to sneak on board undetected. He was a bit lucky he didn't get a burst from a Bren gun. The blokes were pretty trigger happy. Davo slipped over the stern and closely followed by Falls. Naturally we were more than delighted to see them. But boy, they were really beat cos they'd paddled 60 miles from Sambu down to Pompong. It was pretty stressy stuff. They were pretty beat. Pretty knocked about. Particularly with hands blistered, blisters on the seat and all that sort of thing.[57]

On the morning of 1 October, the other two folboat teams left Otter Bay, heading south into a difficult headwind, with an interval of an hour between their departures. During the day, enemy aircraft passed overhead, but failed to see them. They also passed the Japanese observation post at Gual Island, where, Lyon said, 'We must have been clearly visible to the OP [Observation Post].'[58] They paddled on, arriving at Torte Island, where they rested for a few hours before setting out on the remaining 16 miles (26 kilometres) to their rendezvous point at Pompong.

After making a circumnavigation of Pompong in search of *Krait*, the exhausted men slept on the beach after hiding their folboats in the jungle. Fearing the *Krait* had already left for the return trip to Australia, they began planning for a long stay, starting work on a hut and bartering food from local Malay villagers. Lyon had even contemplated capturing a junk and sailing it to Ceylon, a similar trip to the one he had made after the fall of Singapore.

The *Krait*, which had also been circling the island, returned at 2200 the following night and took both parties and their folboats aboard before immediately putting to sea. As Arthur Jones noted, 'we went aboard and of course celebrations everywhere and we got noisy and Crilly, our cook, had a nice big feed waiting for us. I think he might have put a few tins of bully beef in and some tinned vegetables and made a bit of a feast out of the dehydrated mutton. Everybody was happy.'[59]

Horrie Young added, 'They were all elated that everyone had been picked up and the operation had been a success. We suffered no casualties, the morale was really very high.'[60]

Setting a southerly course for Exmouth Gulf, Carse, Lyon and the men felt the rising exhilaration of success. The Japanese, while no doubt searching for them, had no idea who had carried out the attack or where to look for them. Their vengeance was unfortunately taken out on the local population, in what became known as the 'double tenth massacre'. The Japanese secret police, the Kempeitai, took over the investigation about the explosions on 10 October, some two weeks after the attack, and rounded up local Malays, Chinese and Europeans who were subsequently tortured, at least 15 of whom were executed.

The *Krait*'s passage across the Java Sea was uneventful. Although at one point a large, four-engine Kawasaki flying boat flew over them on the way to Singapore, it didn't alter course or seem to pay any attention to them far below. Ahead, they still faced the treacherous Lombok Strait, the Japanese Surabaya airfields, the naval patrols and the tides. To add to the danger, along with a full moon, the weather was clear and visibility perfect. As darkness fell and a fresh southerly wind sprang up, though, the sea became choppy and waves broke across the boat, drenching the men yet providing them some temporary cover.

After entering the Lombok Strait at dusk on 11 September, they picked up the south-flowing tide, and with engines full steam headed into the gathering darkness. On watch were Wally Falls and Arthur Jones, sitting on the top of the wheelhouse staring into the blackness. At midnight, Jones turned to Falls and said, 'Look there's something white over on Lombok side, just in the lee of the island, and it seems to be moving with us. Wally Falls jumped down and he said, "It's a warship, it looks like a small destroyer or a corvette." At this point, Lyon he told Davidson to go into the wheelhouse and get the tin of cyanide tablets in case anyone preferred to take them in the case of emergency.'[61]

Suddenly, the men were awakened by an approaching vessel, its white bow wave clearly discernible against the dark horizon. Carse immediately turned for the Bali shore as a huge warship approached, and the men went into action stations. Should the warship force them to stop, they could manoeuvre alongside and, in an act of suicidal desperation, fire the huge box of plastic explosives mounted on the deck. While there was enough to destroy the enemy ship, the men of *Krait* would be atomised, a thought that no doubt ran through the men's minds as the threatening ship approached.

As the Japanese ship came closer, the men broke out a Bren gun and Captain Lyon offered each of the men a cyanide pill, stating, 'I'll leave it to yourselves individually,' knowing the men had their own personal views about taking the pill. The warship then drew parallel and alongside, in what one crewman said was 20 minutes but Carse actually timed as five. The Japanese neither challenged the *Krait* nor shone a light upon her. It then dropped back astern. Jones recalled that the Japanese ship:

> . . . followed us for a while and then all of a sudden it came up in the same position again and of course we thought that's it, they're suspicious and we could be going to cop it. It stayed there for a while, another few minutes I suppose, it seemed a long time, and then suddenly it just turned to port and wheeled away and went back across to Lombok and we never sighted it again.[62]

After a frightening time, the ship steamed off northwards, the men following it until it disappeared over the horizon.

Early on the morning of 12 October, the *Krait* cleared the Lombok Strait and headed south for Exmouth and home. As darkness overtook them, they hauled down the Japanese flag, now confident they were clear of Japanese naval and air patrols. The following day, they broke radio silence and sent a coded signal to the US naval station at Fremantle. They were still afraid of an unexpected attack by an American vessel or submarine, so they ran up the naval ensign for safety. As Horrie Young remembered, 'we were more nervous of American submarines than we were of perhaps even Japanese ships. The Yanks have got a habit of being a bit trigger-happy.'[63]

As they closed on the Australian coast, the men were able to get news from Australia and the course of the war. At 1400 on 19 October, the *Krait* arrived at Exmouth Gulf, 47 days after they departed, a journey of over 4400 miles (more than 7000 kilometres) over hostile seas. The raiders were credited with the sinking of seven ships weighing about 40,000 tons total and the shattering of the Japanese myth of invincibility in the port of Singapore.

During this extraordinary voyage, Arthur Jones states, 'there was never an argument or a bad word, I never heard it on the whole trip. So that sort of goes to show that not only brain and brawn, but the temperament. And I never heard anyone whinge or argue, they were all pretty good.'[64]

Horrie Young echoed these sentiments when he said, 'I can't remember hearing any brawls, arguments or things that I would have regarded as not being in the best interest of the ship's company. They all got on very well together. I'll say that Lyon and Davidson picked the crew very carefully.'[65]

Upon their return to Exmouth, the men underwent interrogation and a comprehensive file of intelligence information, photographs and drawings was handed over. The details of Operation Jaywick remained top secret for decades, with the files only released in the early 1980s. While this was classed as an SOE Far East operation and not strictly an SRD task, Jaywick set an example and a model for future SRD operations right through to the end of the war and after. The news of its success, while not made public, spread among operatives in other secret

Allied organisations, in particular with SOE in London, and no doubt stimulated offensive planning and operational ideas. In turn, the story of Jaywick encouraged other operatives to emulate these very brave men.

FIVE

The Early Days –
Operations in Timor

The island of Timor had rarely been visited by Australians. After the infamous mutiny on the HMS *Bounty* and his epic open-boat journey from Tonga, Captain Bligh had finally come ashore there, but there were few encounters between the Timorese and the British or Australians in the centuries afterwards. This all changed with the Japanese declaration of war against the United States and United Kingdom on 8 December 1941. At the time Timor was divided in half, with Portuguese and Dutch sections. The Portuguese quickly declared their neutrality, but the Dutch sought the Australian Government's help to protect their remote colonies of Timor and Ambon, an island to the north of Timor, from the impending advance of the Japanese.

Prior to the war, an arrangement between the British and Portuguese governments had been signed, agreeing to the provision of Australian troops should a threat materialise from Japan. In response to the Japanese declaration, the Australian Army formed 'Sparrow Force', with men from the 2/40th Battalion (Tasmanian) and other units, including the 2/2nd Independent Company, for deployment to Timor. A second unit, 'Gull Force', was deployed to Ambon, and a third contingent to Rabaul and Kavieng in Papua New Guinea, known as 'Lark Force'. Sparrow

Force left Darwin on 10 December 1941 and Gull Force a week later. Little did these men realise what they were sailing into: the terrible fighting ahead, and for many inhumane treatment by the Japanese as prisoners of war.

The Portuguese found themselves in a quandary. They had a small contingent of 700 troops on the way to Timor, but would they arrive in time? If not, and if they accepted the Australian troops, they were going against their neutrality agreement. If they ejected the Australian troops, they could be seen as cooperating with the Japanese. And if the Portuguese troops did arrive before the Japanese invaded and they resisted, this would mean war with Japan. In the end, it was decided that, since the Australians were already at sea, the Portuguese had no choice but to accept their presence, though the Portuguese Government bitterly objected at first. The Portuguese ship *MV Jano Bele* was recalled and its troops steamed home.

On the night of 19–20 February 1942, a force of more than 1500 Japanese began landing at Dili, the capital of the Portuguese section of Timor to the island's north, and soon other large Japanese forces – some 4000 men and light tanks – came ashore on the undefended south-western side of the island. As the Australians retreated inland and towards the north-east, they were cut off by Japanese paratroopers and ambushed; some prisoners were tortured, while others were tied to trees and killed. However, a decisive counterattack killed all but 85 of the 850 paratroopers who had landed.

As the Australians continued their retreat and as more Japanese forces disembarked, the radio link to Australia was lost. The men were exhausted, short of ammunition, water and food, and hopelessly outnumbered, so they surrendered to the Japanese on 23 February. Eighty-four Australians had been killed and a further 132 wounded in the two weeks of fighting, and the men of Sparrow Force would suffer greatly as prisoners of war in the years ahead.

Into the fray came a new fighting force, the elite troops of the AIF's independent companies. The establishment of these units came at the suggestion of the British Army, who subsequently sent specialist instructors to Australia and assisted in the selection process, the training schedule and the building up of an Australian cadre to carry on this specialist work. In time they were to be renamed commandos but not before 12 independent companies were raised and saw service in the early part of the war.

One of these was the men of the 2/2nd Independent Company who continued their own private war in Timor after the capture of Sparrow Force. They comprised one of initially four independent companies formed – each of about 300 troops and made up in large part by men from Western Australia. Under the command of Major A. L. Spence, the men were well trained, tough and resourceful, and prepared for the fighting ahead.

In Australia it was believed they had been captured along with the rest of Sparrow Force, so the men were listed as missing for three months. In fact, after they'd been unable to hold the Dili airfield, the 2/2 had retreated into the mountains, and on the night of 19–20 April the men were able to make contact with Darwin on a makeshift radio cobbled together from parts recovered from several inoperable radio transmitters. Known as 'Winnie the War Winner', it was built using a range of salvaged material, including a 60-foot aerial and a crude generator to charge the battery. (Today, this small radio is on display in the Australian War Memorial, Canberra.) Initially the military authorities in Australia believed this was a Japanese ruse, and it took some time for them to be convinced that the unit was still operating.

With communications established, the unit was now able to call in resupplies and provide crucial intelligence, and their survival provided hope and good news in a time of low morale in Australia, with Darwin and other northern towns under Japanese aerial attack. The radio contact increased the potential for unit operations, ambushes and contacts with the Japanese, who quickly realised they were dealing with a very different enemy than the Allied forces they had overrun and captured in the first days after their landing.

Within a few days, the 2/2 had killed an estimated 200 Japanese with few losses, but a party of 16 Australians were ambushed and captured, and a number were tied up, pushed into a roadside ditch and shot. One man, Private K. M. Hayes, somehow escaped, crawling into a rice field where he was found and rescued by local people. After tending to his wounds, they took him to a nearby Australian post, where he told his mates the story of the massacre. From this time on, the 2/2 men vowed there would be no Japanese prisoners. They would be killed outright.

By now, news of the 2/2 Independent Company and their successes had been passed from General Blamey to General MacArthur. Blamey suggested an expeditionary force be sent from Australia to retake Timor, but the Japanese build-up over the preceding three months would preclude this. MacArthur, realising the nuisance value of the 2/2 and the fact that its men were keeping a large number of Japanese troops from being redeployed to the Papua New Guinea and Guadalcanal campaigns, responded to Blamey in very direct terms on 11 June. 'The retention of these forces in Timor will greatly facilitate offensive action when the necessary means are at hand. They should not be withdrawn under any circumstances. They should remain and execute their present missions of harassment and sabotage.'[1]

The Japanese commander, Colonel Sadashichi Doi, sent the Australian honorary consul in Dili, David Ross, a message asking him to track down the unit and demand they surrender. Doi likened the Australian resistance to that of the Boers in the Second Boer War, stating they were fighting a good fight, but making the point that with further Japanese reinforcements the Australians would be finally driven from the hills and captured. To this request Ross agreed and had, on this occasion, promised Colonel Doi he would pass on the message and return, which he did. Doi sent Ross on a second mission, but again the Australians ignored his request. Ross, having not given his word he would return as he had done on the first occasion, was evacuated to Australia.

The Japanese were tiring of the unit's incessant attacks, and in August 1942 began a series of aggressive operations against their Timorese sympathisers to cut off support for the Australian commandos. The Japanese 48th Division of 15,000 men, commanded by Lieutenant General Yuichi Tsuchihashi, was sent from the Philippines. Outnumbering the Australians 100:1, the Japanese launched a massive offensive with the aim of pushing the Australians into a small area along the south coast from where they could be eliminated as a threat. Pushing out from Dili, four large and heavily armed Japanese units advanced towards the centre of the island and captured the town of Maubisse, but still they failed to destroy the mobile and well-trained Australians.

In September, the 2/2 were reinforced by the 450 men of 2/4th Independent Company, known as 'Lancer Force', to continue to put pressure on the Japanese. However, during the landing of the 2/4th, the Australian destroyer HMAS *Voyager* ran aground near the port of Betano on the south coast and could not be removed from the beach. It was attacked by two Japanese aircraft, one of which, a bomber, was shot down, but the second reported the ship's position and the *Voyager* was again attacked. A column of 700 Japanese troops were sent from Maubisse, but they were constantly ambushed and harassed along the way by the men of the 2/2. With few options, the crew of the *Voyager* were safely extracted by HMAS *Warrnambool* and HMAS *Kalgoorlie*, and the *Voyager* was destroyed by demolition charges. The men of the 2/4, however, were safely ashore and able to join with the 2/2 in their fight against the Japanese.

It was soon realised that the increasing Japanese pressure on the units, the toll on Timorese civilians, the exhaustion and ill health of the men and the problems of resupply were not worth the effort. Ten months after the Japanese had invaded Timor, there were 28,000 enemy troops on the island, with more arriving, along with naval units and aircraft. There seemed little point in further resistance. Needing to evacuate Timor without the Japanese knowing, small parties gradually trickled out, the first group leaving on the night of 11 December, and by 15 December the last of the 2/2 men were evacuated. Between December 1942 and January 1943, the two independent companies were withdrawn, along with Dutch troops and loyal Timorese civilians, and the next phase of the Timor campaign began in earnest.

While the fighting units returned to Australia, a small group of 20 volunteers under Lieutenant Harry Flood of the 2/4 Independent Company remained. Known as 'S Force', the men were led inland by Flood to an area he felt was relatively safe, yet from where he could strike at Dili only 30 miles (50 kilometres) away. Along the trek north through the centre of the island, his small group was joined by other Australian stragglers who had been lost or missed the evacuation opportunities to Australia.

S Force found that the enemy were quickly on their trail. The Timorese, after threats and reprisals by the Japanese, were no longer prepared to support the Australians with either crucial intelligence or food. As Japanese pressure increased and the Australians' food and ammunition caches were discovered, the men were forced on the run, exhausted and weak and with nowhere to hide. After jettisoning their heavy radios, they were in an even more desperate situation, cut off from possible resupply and evacuation.

Lieutenant Flood remembered having been told of the existence of an SRD unit some 30 miles (50 kilometres) to the south-west of Dili, an area he was now in. While there were native people always ready to assist the Australians, this help had diminished as a result of Japanese brutality and a system of native spies and informers. Initially it was believed to be mere rumour, but with local help, Flood was able to meet the unit, made up of Captain I. S. Wylie, Captain Douglas Broadhurst and two privates who also had radio comms with Darwin. Flood was able to get a message notifying HQ that S Force had joined with Wylie's unit and requesting evacuation as soon as practicable. His men were weak, exhausted and sick, and, after hiding in a swamp near the coast for two days, were evacuated by the US submarine *Gudgeon* on the night of 10 February 1943.

While this ended the Australian resistance on Timor, it should be remembered that over the 12 months since the Japanese invasion, the commandos killed an estimated 1500 enemy troops for the loss of 40 Australians, and importantly had drawn about 30,000 Japanese troops onto Timor at a crucial time, preventing their deployment to other far more strategically crucial fronts like Guadalcanal and the north coast of Papua New Guinea.

While Timor was tactically important to the defence of Australia, both MacArthur and Blamey realised now that there was no hope of invading the island and taking it back. It was estimated that the Allies would need three divisions – some

50,000 men – for such an offensive, plus strong naval and Air Force elements. Timor was also 400 miles from Darwin, which made close support and resupply from the sea or air difficult. This would have been crucial for the large Allied force necessary to retain an offensive momentum against the Japanese and who could not 'live off the land' as some military planners in Australia had suggested. At this time in early 1943, the Australian Army was tied up in fighting in northern Papua New Guinea, in particular at Buna, Gona and Sanananda, and given there were few available resources and men, Timor would have to wait.

Other means of continuing the fight, retaining the support of the Timorese people and preparing for the ultimate invasion to repel the Japanese, needed to be considered. It was decided to expand the secret operations of ISD as it was at the time, which had begun on the island in July 1942 and were to continue until the end of hostilities in August 1945. Although Timor itself was of little strategic value and there were few targets of importance on the island, the belief was that as the war progressed it would be retaken by the Allies, so pro-Allied partisan forces under European leadership needed to be in place and ready.

Initially in the first phase of operations, a series of un-coordinated and at times poorly planned operations had been embarked upon by Dutch, Australian and Indonesian personnel in the broad region of the Aru Islands, Ceram Island, the Celebes and Java. This was a time when SRD and its operational potential needed to be tested, its *modus operandi* honed and the detractors proven wrong. It was still in its earliest stages of development as an offensive organisation, without proper training, intelligence sources, specialist equipment and communications. And this was borne out in the initial operations as noted in the *Official History*: 'Of 13 parties inserted or planned, four were successful, seven were captured, one was unsuccessful and one did not leave Australia.'[2]

The second phase of SRD operations, known as the Partisan Phase, saw the landing of a four-man party in mid-July 1942, codenamed Lizard I and followed by other Lizard operations. This evolved into a series of insertions and extraction missions, the main one being the disastrous Lagarto, inserted and continued until the capture of the Lagarto party and the total compromising of all Allied missions in Timor.

A third phase began in early 1944, with operations conducted under the codenames Mugger-Sounder, in which a series of resupply bases were established on the sea route to Timor to facilitate the insertion of operational parties. After January 1945, a fourth phase extended this line of bases to within striking distance of Japanese territory and potential operational areas once the Japanese were forced to retreat. And finally there was a fifth phase, comprising five operations, to ensure that postwar information was gathered, POWs released and secret caches of weapons and store recovered.

Let us begin by going back to the second phase, Operation Lizard I. This was launched at the crucial time in the Timorese campaign when the Australians were embattled but realising the strategic value of the island to the Japanese and its potential in the years ahead. The four-man party comprised Captain I. S. Wylie and Captain D. K. Broadhurst, with an ex-Timor resident, Lieutenant G. H. Greaves, and a signaller, Sergeant J. R. P. Cashman. The men (minus Greaves who was in hospital and subsequently joined Lizard II) landed at Suai, in Sao Domingos province in Timor's south, on 17 July 1942.

Their immediate task was to observe the strategically important north–south road between Baucau near the north coast and

Beaco in the south, and to keep the Timorese locals working with the Allies. The party were also tasked with establishing observation posts to watch enemy ship movements and the construction of any new airfields, to support the Portuguese administration, to counter enemy propaganda among the Timorese and to support the local currency against the introduction of Japanese money.

The party joined up with the 2/2 Independent Company of Sparrow Force at Mape, 21 miles (35 kilometres) north-east of Suai, and spent time familiarising themselves with the district and meeting various administrators and people of influence. On 8 August, a Japanese warship and two troop-carrying tenders (rowing boats) were observed off the coast, and it was believed they planned to encircle the commandos and drive them from their mountain hideout. The commandos and the Lizard party moved out and, by a circular route, headed to Same, a further 20 miles (32 kilometres) north-east of Mape. But the main radio was lost to hostile Timorese locals, and the Lizard radio was handed over. The Lizard party decided to withdraw, along with a number of wounded commandos, and were extracted by Catalina flying boat and returned to Darwin on 18 August 1942.

After the party had time to rest and debrief, they were tasked with Operation Lizard II, and were reinserted on 2 September by motor launch at Beaco. The operatives quickly moved inland, burying stores in caches along the way and making contact with Sparrow Force, local commanders and officials from the Portuguese administration. Due to Timorese hostility towards the Japanese after atrocities inflicted on them, the Australians were able to raise and arm a small guerrilla army and establish the basics of an intelligence network. This was followed by the provision of 100 rifles along with ammunition, which was put ashore at Aliambata Beach in mid-October. With local help, the Australians were also able to utilise the telephone system to send and receive intelligence reports, especially from agents in Dili.

A new problem arose for the Australians: a series of revolts against Portuguese authority by the Timorese locals, which forced the Portuguese governor to seek protection from the Japanese for Portuguese residents. This resulted in many Portuguese demanding evacuation to Australia, which in turn saw many natives supporting the Australians in the hope of also being flown to Darwin. But the Japanese retained their pressure by occupying the central road and important landing points on the south coast at Aliambata and Beaco.

On 1 October, 27 Portuguese administrative officials, non-commissioned officers and troops were massacred by Dutch Timorese natives under Japanese control at Aileu, 25 miles (40 kilometres) south of Dili. This was part of a broad strategy of terror to concentrate the Portuguese at two small towns, Liquica and Maubara to the west of Dili, and to eliminate any vestige of Portuguese control and administration across this part of Timor. Parallel to this, Japanese air, land and naval activity greatly increased as they began occupying inland towns and coastal anchorages.

As a result, the Portuguese administration began breaking down everywhere except in the province of Sao Domingos, where the anti-Japanese Lieutenant Manuel de Jesus Pires, a Portuguese Army pilot and the administrator of Sao Domingos province, maintained control and the support of the local population. On the suggestion of SRD, Pires wrote to General MacArthur requesting arms and support, and this initial letter was followed by others, each more pleading and desperate. Pires asked for an Allied invasion, but he and other local leaders were informed, 'in the bluntest terms',[3] that a major invasion operation was not possible. This news put Captain Wylie, the Lizard leader, in a difficult position, as the group's security and operational future would be compromised. As a minimum, Pires requested an intense bombing campaign against Dili, and for several days in early November 1942, Dili and surrounding targets were heavily bombed.

On 17 November, after further requests by Lizard for arms and support and the evacuation of Wylie with malaria, three more operatives arrived, Lieutenants F. Holland, J. E. Grimson and W. T. Thomas, along with a signaller, A. K. Smith. Accompanying them were two officers, Captain R. C. Neave and Lieutenant L. W. Ross, who were tasked with sourcing and exporting rubber. However, while Neave and Ross were successful in evacuating a few tons of rubber,[4] because of the extent of Japanese activity around Dili a further 150 tons could not be secured. The reinforcements also brought with them 100 rifles, making 300 in all now supplied, along with a few Bren guns, allowing the operatives to begin training and arming the remaining loyal Timorese.

The Japanese concentrated their offensive operations on the eastern end of Timor, an area that had until late 1942 remained relatively safe for the Australians. By now, the commandos of the 2/4th Independent Company could do little more than hold territory and tie down Japanese forces. The decision was made to begin the evacuation of the unit, along with loyal Timorese and their families, and men of the Royal Netherlands East Indies Army. During this attempted evacuation, HMAS *Armidale*, a new corvette, was sunk by enemy aircraft off Betano Bay on 1 December with the loss of 100 men, including a raft with about 20 men who survived the sinking but could not be recovered. The other members of Sparrow Force were successfully evacuated, leaving Lancer Force still confined to the mountains and limited in what they could achieve offensively.

Just before Christmas 1942, Lizard's headquarters were hit by Japanese mortar fire and ten Timorese soldiers were killed. This began a series of well-directed attacks after the defection of a once-friendly chief named Joachim, who informed the Japanese of the Australians' positions, especially observation posts that were transmitting valuable target information to Darwin. Before dawn on 28 December, Lizard's number-one camp was attacked by a large force of Japanese troops, and while the Australians were able to escape, they were again attacked at another hideout by Japanese infantry and aircraft. As the Japanese closed in on all sides, Lizard radioed for evacuation, not knowing that the men of the 2/4th Independent Company, Lancer Force, had by this point been withdrawn, on the night of 9 January.

The Japanese advance, along with the increasing number of Portuguese looking to be evacuated, seriously compromised security, and as the decision had already been made to evacuate the 2/4th, the Lizard team now found themselves continually on the run, along with a number of important Portuguese administrators and local chiefs. They began to review their purpose and value in Timor.

By early 1943, the civilian situation was becoming grave. Not only would there be dire consequences for Timorese locals should they assist the Australians or provide any opposition to the invasion, but the Japanese were very successful in turning many Timorese against the Portuguese administration and against their own population. Without help from Australia in the form of more commandos, the supply of weapons or more intense bombing of Japanese strongholds, many Timorese would look to the Japanese for protection; even the Japanese-led atrocities and raids on villages were not enough to confirm loyalty to Australia. Support for the Japanese among the Timorese would further alienate any pro-ally locals, and it was understood that if the remaining Australian commandos attacked pro-Japanese locals, they would not only draw more fire on themselves but also on the people they were trying to protect.

The concern at GHQ was that the departure of all Australian operatives would have a devastating effect on the morale of the remaining Portuguese and loyal Timorese who continued the fight. The first challenge was to return Captain Wylie and another signaller back into Timor to retain communications with Darwin, but this became impossible in the rapidly changing circumstances.

By now, the situation was critical for both the Lizard party and a number of commandos who had volunteered to remain behind. On 19 January 1943, Lizard informed Darwin that a party of 100 'valuable men' were awaiting evacuation, but were told to remain in hiding and keep radio silence, 'there being no immediate possibility of evacuation'.[5]

The Lizard party continued to be hunted down and harassed by the Japanese, and a number of Timorese supporters were caught and executed. Reluctantly, on 21 January, the loyal Timorese moving with Lizard were forced to disband and return to their villages. The reduced Lizard party continued to move westwards, into an area less frequented by Japanese, but found they were being tracked by 200 Japanese with local guides. At times the Japanese fired mortars and machine guns, and aerial reconnaissance increased.

Fortunately, Allied search aircraft located the party and were able to drop supplies and radio sets and, the following day, 3 February, food and batteries. With the Japanese hard on their heels, the party arrived at the mouth of the Dilor River. Here they were able to contact the US submarine *Gudgeon* and, as we have heard above, be extracted and returned to Australia.

The departing Australians left behind a confused and unstable situation. The Japanese continued to exploit the growing tension between the Portuguese administration and the Timorese people, particularly in places where a Portuguese administrator fled his post or the administration relinquished control to the Japanese. A pro-Japanese attitude extended through most of the six provinces, and it was only within Sao Domingos to the south that any semblance of pro-Allied support remained, where consideration might be given to establishing a small subversive force to sabotage Japanese installation and where the provision of weapons and supplies might not be wasted.

While the future looked grim for the Allies in Timor, High Command saw a glimmer of hope in a few remaining loyal and effective local leaders. In a report headed PROJECT 24 and received in Melbourne on 2 January 1943, written by an unknown person with the code name 152, the various dispositions of pro-Allied Timorese units were reported. In one area there were 150 local armed soldiers, divided into nine sections, with one Bren gun between them. In another there were 50 rifles and one Bren, and in another 40 soldiers armed with ex-Portuguese army weapons 'and a few relics'.[6]

The report emphasised the resilience and loyalty of these leaders. One, simply referred to as ABC, was 'more staunchly pro-ally than ourselves (if that is possible). He has been steadily at work spreading anti-Japanese propaganda and instilling in the native mind the ultimate certainty of Allied victory in the face of overwhelming Japanese superiority in the past, and at present and in the immediate future.'[7]

The report was scathing about the Portuguese: 'we see the "flower of the Portuguese" having no thought but escape to Australia. This goes for a good 90%. Worthless rats! The lords and masters of Portuguese Timor deserting and leaving erstwhile serfs to stand in defence of their country.'[8] The report goes on:

> We only ask you to evacuate them [the Portuguese] because they are so worthless that they do more harm than good. For selfish skin-saving they win the prize. The patriotic and loyal natives 'in the know' despise them and grudge them the safety and ease of a life in Australia. The rats take it as a right that they be evacuated and blab to the world that they are to be taken out although no promises have been given. They are a frightful danger to our boats coming in.[9]

The writer of this report, Captain Neave, having clearly stated his opinion of certain Portuguese officials, also makes an interesting observation: 'We are more concerned now with the evacuation of families of our leading natives. It is fair to them and of the greatest value to us as *hostages* [emphasis mine] of good faith.'[10]

The operatives on the ground were most concerned to assist those who had helped the local people and their families, but among them were those who just wanted to flee. The operatives also provided an incentive to those still in Timor, that if they assisted the Australians, this might be a ticket to leave Timor in the future.

The return of the Lizard party to Australia on 18 February 1943 marked the end of the first SRD operation in the South West Pacific Area. While the party did not have concise objectives and strategic outcomes, it was able to establish an intelligence network that reported back to Australia. The official report on the operation noted: 'It is most disheartening and so much unnecessary labour giving bombing targets and nothing happens . . . Nothing gives our natives more thrill than to see our planes.'[11]

The party were also able to foster 'a subversive movement among the natives which was capable of holding down large Japanese forces in this area at comparatively small cost'.[12] These successes, and the fact that a radio link was left behind along with valuable experience for future operations in this area, were seen as an effective start for Australian special operations.

The radio link became crucial for the next stage of operations in Timor after the Australians left. This was not a carefully planned operation, but an informally arranged group of mixed-race Timorese, Cantonese and Portuguese sympathisers, numbering about 60 men, who agreed to keep a communication line open with Darwin and to facilitate future operations on the island. In return, they would be supplied with weapons, money, food and radios, and would await the hoped-for future invasion. The group came to be known as Portolizard.

The leader of the sympathisers, Sergeant Martines, was an audacious and determined fighter who had evaded the massacre at Aileu and escaped from a Japanese prison in Dili, bringing with him important intelligence which had led to successful Allied air raids on the town. He was well equipped, having taken over the stores and weapons left by the Lizard party. He also had two radio sets, operated by locals who were trained by Lizard men and also some former telephonists from the Portuguese government who had joined the Lizard party in November 1942. In fact, the Portolizard signallers were so efficient that their first signals came just two days after the departure of the last of the Australians. Throughout February, a stream of messages came from Portolizard, at times four a day; most sought arms and stores drops due to the increased pressure upon the group by the encircling Japanese.

The first drop to Portolizard came on 7 March. Three days later the party split, with one section going to Barique in the centre of Timor, while the radio section went to Melolo, from where 'useful intelligence emerged from the party's signals'.[13] While active Japanese patrols remained a problem, food became a serious issue, as the prices for rice and maize rose steeply due to shortages, a drop in the value of currency, and because the local chief wanted to force the party from his area.

Other issues created complications and diversions. The Japanese had been inflicting atrocities on the locals and taking local women for forced prostitution since their invasion of Timor. Then, with food scarce throughout the island due to crops not being planted and the Japanese requisition of grains, the locals now rose in revolt. Meanwhile in Melbourne, the recently evacuated Pires was putting pressure on the Australian Government to seek diplomatic ways, via the Portuguese Government, to extract both Portuguese and Timorese residents from the island. However, the Portuguese Government were either not across the problem or indifferent to the plight of their nationals, and no action was taken.

As a result, further demands were put upon the Australian military. SRD proposed the insertion of an evacuation party, led by Pires, which was named Lagarto. It landed on the night of 1–2 July 1943 at the mouth of the Luca River, and a week later its men made contact with Darwin. But the operation that Lagarto became would haunt the history of the SRD and Z Special forever.

Six

The Great Tragedy
of Lagarto

With the despatch and landing of the Lagarto party in early July 1943, a sad and painful chapter began in the history of SRD operations. While initial success saw the evacuation of both Portuguese and local civilians from Timor, Lagarto, and the series of Tiger and support operations that followed, were in most cases a disaster, and the information provided by operatives to the Japanese under interrogation and torture seriously damaged future SRD operations.

The original plan for Lagarto was to insert two parties into Timor: one into the eastern and one into the western districts. It was hoped that a spirit of competition might develop between the two to enhance and extend their operational success. The eastern party went in under the codename Lagarto – 'lagarto' is the Portuguese word for lizard or 'a cunning fellow' – under Lieutenant Pires. With him was a Portuguese civilian and six locals. However, before the second party could be inserted into western Timor, the only pro-Allied leader in the area, chief Dom Alexio, and his family were massacred by the Japanese. As such, this part of the operation was cancelled.

Prior to landing, Pires was briefed on the objectives and tasks to be undertaken by the Lagarto party. These are detailed in the

Official History: 'To create and operate a secret network covering the eastern part of the colony for the purpose of reporting on all enemy activities, to maintain the morale of the Portuguese and Timorese, to arrange the evacuation of the refugees assembled with Portolizard, and to establish OPs (observation posts) to cover enemy movements.'[1]

With these instructions, Pires set out with two other men, leaving Perth by US submarine on 18 June 1943 and landing at the mouth of the Luca River on the night of 1–2 July. During the landing they were assisted by members of Portolizard, but due to heavy conditions at sea they lost three radio sets in the surf. They proceeded ashore, met six natives who joined their party, and the following day made radio contact with Australia.

The men were familiar with the area around the Luca and Dilor rivers, and there they remained in hiding, but on 9 July were attacked by a large force of 200 Japanese troops using mortars and machine guns. The men of Portolizard escaped, and in so doing left behind much of their equipment, but managed to retain one radio. They were attacked again two days later and, as they continued to be hindered in their flight by numerous locals, radioed Australia for evacuation.

Back in Australia, SRD had no intention of extracting the Pires party, even though Pires declared they were weak and sick. Then a planned evacuation of civilians set for 22 July by two RAN motor launches was cancelled by Pires due to the encroaching Japanese and rescheduled for the night of 3 August. At this time, SRD inserted an Australian signaller, Sergeant A. J. Ellwood from Victoria, who had been a member of the 2/4th Independent Company and had stayed behind after their evacuation with the Lizard party. They also embarked a number of civilian refugees and returned them to Darwin.

The decision to insert Ellwood into the all-Portuguese party was to ensure the operational work of the Lagarto party was undertaken as required, but also so that Ellwood could report on what was happening separately to SRD, on his own radio and with his own codes. Pires was considered a hothead and seen to have a poor grasp of English, and in SRD's view he could not be trusted to understand their orders or provide clear and precise reports back to them in return. The arrival of Ellwood quickly created a tension between the two men, with Pires denying Ellwood access to intelligence information. He also refused, as he had been directed by SRD, to allow Ellwood to check the text and content of messages before they were sent.

The day after Ellwood's arrival, a party had been sent to recover a cache of buried stores, but were ambushed and forced to flee, losing the small arms, ammunition and rations they were sent to recover. Then within days, the Japanese were again hard on the heels of the party. Having been pre-warned of the Japanese advance towards their headquarters, they travelled north towards the coast, but were continually harassed, forcing the party to keep on the move. Ellwood reported that the movement of the party was very slow, due to what he referred to as the 'circus' of natives and camp followers; at one time there were 34 of them, including Pires' and another man's mistress, one of whom was pregnant. Within weeks of the landing of Ellwood, not only were relations with Pires continuing to deteriorate, but the Japanese were closing in.

Now, keeping this lumbering party fed was also a problem, and they were forced to eat wild potatoes, yams and certain leaves. Food and assistance to the party was further compromised by the Japanese torturing and killing village chiefs who fed or in any way assisted the Lagarto party. As a result, many local people looked to avoid contact or providing help – whether offering safe passage, hiding the party, or giving necessary information that would aid their survival – for fear of retribution.

To secure intelligence from the Dili area, where a large concentration of Japanese were now confirmed, a party of six men were despatched in early August. By the end of the month, they had established an observation post above the town between Laclo and Remexio, a distance of about ten miles (16 kilometres) from Dili. While they were able to supply some intelligence, this was sent to Lagarto by runner as the radio operator was incompetent, and quite soon contact with this OP was lost. It was later found that the men had been discovered and captured in an ambush by the Japanese, and imprisoned in Dili.

With two separate lines of communication back to SRD headquarters in Melbourne, one via Pires and the other via Ellwood, there was some confusion in Australia as to what was going on. Pires reported 'the party's existence would be impossible after the end of August', adding 'as I have always told you'.[2] Ellwood was reporting that the Lagarto party could not succeed 'due to the numbers, the lack of discipline and secrecy, slowness of the march and the extensive food requirements', and went on to state, 'the party is a bloody farce'.[3] In response, Melbourne ordered Pires to split his party. Pires replied that this was not possible under the circumstances, due to the pressure of the Japanese and pro-Japanese local troops.

Ellwood was also keen to split the party, in part to get clear of Pires and his ever-increasing mood swings and deteriorating mental state. With the Portuguese civilian radio operator, Patricio Luz, and a Timorese local, Jose Tinocco, they separated, hoping to get assistance from friendly locals. But the Japanese were still increasing their pressure on the chiefs, who now avoided the Lagarto party. Realising the futility of continuing, Ellwood requested the extraction of Pires 'and his circus',[4] but SRD responded that seaplanes were not available for the task at that time.

On 18 September, the now-reduced Lagarto party were surprised by a patrol of pro-Japanese local troops with dogs as they attempted to cross a road, but were able to make their escape. Soon after, Pires sent a request for stores, but Ellwood considered the list to contain 'a lot of bloody unessential rubbish'[5] and argued that only the bare essentials be sent.

Unbeknown to the party, one of the Portuguese troops had been followed as he returned to the party. The Japanese were closing in, and on 25 September Sergeant Ellwood reported to Melbourne that the deteriorating situation made it very difficult to operate and stay on in Timor, that the once supportive natives were now too afraid to assist and an imminent Japanese search operation would further close them in. With now nowhere to go, he requested extraction from the Laleisa River mouth on 26 September or else face 'a sticky end'.[6]

SRD Melbourne sent a blunt reply: 'Impossible to arrange evacuation suggested. Party too large. Must divide into smaller groups. GHQ will not provide urgent air transport for women or so large a party. Can you reach Baucau caves or any other area where we can supply you by dropping . . .'[7] To this, Ellwood replied:

We repeat, it is impossible for the party to carry on. It is equally impossible to send any of the natives away or divide the party into smaller groups. Whenever we have left natives behind Japs have captured and tortured them into telling everything. We cannot receive stores from air. Jap drive now is not same as February drive. It is a grimly earnest business of torture and killing. In the last fortnight big chiefs have been killed . . . All natives very afraid.

Say they will give us enough food . . . but no one will offer to guide us. As a last resort we could jettison our natives making number for evacuation ten.[8]

Pires was, at the same time, also pleading for help, signalling, 'All people when see us hide for frightened to be killed by the Japs and at all moments we wait to be betrayed by the natives. Send quickly tomorrow 28th some flying boat for to save us . . .'[9] Again the message came back: 'Regret RAAF state flying boat out of question. Only alternative is extraction from south coast. We will lay on any bombing required.'[10] With the broad support of the party, Ellwood then urged Pires to march south-west, but the Portuguese lieutenant refused due to a sprained ankle.

The Japanese and Timorese troops continued to close in. On the morning of 29 September 1943, a party of pro-Japanese natives were seen, and the Lagarto party attempted to move away. After travelling a short distance, they were fired on by a strong Japanese patrol with machine guns, and a number of the Timorese in the group were killed. By midday, with the party still closely pursued by the Japanese, Ellwood dug a pit and buried his diary, ciphers, signal plans and all his private papers. But the party were caught between two enemy patrols while still attempting to evade capture, and soon after, Pires along with Ellwood and three locals in their group, surrendered.

Stripped of their weapons and equipment, the party were marched to a nearby road, blindfolded and bound, then placed on a truck. They travelled eastwards to an unknown village, where they were further secured and retained in a small cell. Though exhausted, they were forced to stay awake, the guards kicking and beating them with rifle butts to prevent even a moment of sleep or a chance to speak.

The following day, still blindfolded and heavily bound, the group were loaded onto a truck and driven to the military police barracks in Dili. Here Pires and the locals were interrogated and gave the Japanese the details of Ellwood, including his name, rank and nationality. After another night, bound and without sleep, they were taken to another building, where their blindfolds were removed. Facing them were a number of Japanese officers, including a major general and his staff. They were told through a translator that they were to be charged with espionage and, if found guilty, would be executed. If they were found to be lying or failed to answer their interrogator's questions, they would also be executed. The options looked grim.

At this point Ellwood told the Japanese that he was a prisoner of war, a serving soldier in uniform, and as such could not be charged with espionage. He was immediately struck and silenced. After completing this initial interrogation, physically and mentally suffering, the prisoners were marched off and placed in separate cells. Ellwood did not see the members of his party again, but stated later that he did on occasion hear their screams and voices during their continued, brutal interrogation.

Handcuffed and heavily bound around his wrists and elbows, Ellwood found himself in a frightful, filthy condition in a small cell beneath the verandah of the interrogation house. Without bedding or a toilet, his clothes in tatters and rotting from his body, his skin was further exposed to mosquito and insect bites. His feet were puffy and swollen as they were confined in his boots and he soon developed malaria, beri-beri and dysentery.

Ellwood's health further deteriorated as he was not allowed to wash for the first month in captivity and was provided only two small bowls of salted rice and filthy, salty water for sustenance each day, which had a severe weakening effect, and his thirst became more unbearable than the floggings to which he was subjected during interrogations. His condition was made worse by his not being allowed to sleep, his guards beating him into wakefulness every little while. Under these circumstances he was in no condition to think connectedly or put up any prolonged resistance to his interrogators.[11]

During daylight hours the savage interrogation continued, along with that of the other members of the party, and the Japanese were able to compare the answers given by each man. As the questioning continued, with sword belts and whips, the Japanese captured details of documents, lists of names and unit codes, ciphers and messages, and were able to piece together an extensive dossier of SRD strategy and operational procedures.

Pires was breaking under torture. He stated his aim was simply to secure the governorship of Timor, and that he hated the Australians and just wanted to use them to this end. He accused Ellwood of being anti-Timorese, and sought safety in offering himself to work for the Japanese. Ellwood himself continued to endure prolonged torture.

However, having recovered Ellwood's diary, codebook and ciphers, the Japanese were able to ascertain his signal plan and operational details of great intelligence value. Totally exhausted, his body bloodied and wracked by disease, Ellwood finally told the Japanese enough to allow them to open a radio communications link to Melbourne with the codes, ciphers and his wireless.

After testing the system with a false message from Pires' radio, the Japanese forced Ellwood to operate his set and sent a further signal to SRD in Melbourne. As each Morse operator had a distinctive way of tapping out his message, the Japanese guided Ellwood's fingers on the Morse key, sending a message which read, 'Our position very serious. Are hiding near Obaqui. Have not eaten for three days.'[12] SRD Melbourne replied, offering a food drop of tin rations and requesting information about the condition of the party and if in fact they had split up. The following day, Ellwood was again forced to contact SRD, and provide the location of the Japanese drop zone for the resupply. This took place soon afterwards, and the airdrops continued right through until the end of the war, the whole time SRD believing the Lagarto party were operational. At times Ellwood was taken to the drop zone and forced to signal the aircraft dropping supplies, while close by the Japanese were covering him with rifles.

After about one month, Ellwood was provided better food and some medicine, and had his wounds and sores dressed. He also received letters and the odd magazine in the resupply drops, and was given two changes of clothes. In his weakened condition, his arms and legs debilitated, he found he could slip his hands out of the handcuffs, while at other times lenient guards allowed him to remove them.

SRD in Melbourne remained blind to the odd signals and the inconsistency of information and travel directions. With the information relayed to what they presumed to be the Lagarto party, HQ continued to forewarn the Japanese of the insertion of other Allied parties, the location of airdrops and other intelligence of great use to the enemy.

Late in December 1943, SRD radioed that another party, Cobra, was to be inserted. This was led by Lieutenant John Cashman with a signaller, Sergeant Eric Liversidge, two local chiefs and a guide. The plan was for a three-week mission to locate a suitable point to land a long-term SRD party to establish an intelligence network among the locals and to transmit intelligence gained back to Darwin. The party landed on the south coast on 29 January 1944, where they were met by and identified locals to act as guides. After the stores were dropped on the beach and the RAN launch had pulled away, the party moved silently inland.

As the Cobra party moved off the beach in single file, they had no idea that the Lagarto party had been captured and compromised, and their 'friendly natives' were in fact pro-Japanese. After trekking in darkness for an hour, the party came to a road where the leading local, intimating he was lost, requested a torch. This was provided. Immediately after the light clicked on, the party were attacked and overcome, the Australians knocked unconscious and tied up. Two of the locals with the Australians fled into the bush, but were soon captured.

Lieutenant Cashman, Sergeant Liversidge and one of the local chiefs, Cosmo Soares, soon found themselves in much the same situation as Ellwood. Stripped of their weapons, equipment and radios, they were tightly bound and taken by truck to a nearby military post, where they were charged with being spies. They were then moved to Dili and placed in solitary confinement. The *Official History* states, about their treatment:

> Here began a period of systematic starvation, degradation
> and torture which lasted until May 1944. The prisoners were
> handcuffed and bound about the arms and feet constantly for
> many weeks. They were kept in solitary confinement; they were
> prevented from sleeping; their wounds were not dressed. For two
> months they were unwashed, and in the bound state, wearing
> one-piece overalls, even the most elementary sanitary arrangements
> were denied. Torture of various kinds was used upon them,
> comprising beating about the face, body, hands and joints with
> cane whips, and a process of kneeling on the log with another
> behind the calves, and being rocked backwards. These tortures
> were concurrent with interrogations.[13]

SRD Melbourne had no idea that this party, like the Lagarto party before them, were captured along with their radios, ciphers and, most importantly, a notebook of Sergeant Liversidge, which contained the secret number of the party's cipher and authentication word. This particular authentication word, if not inserted in a message, meant the party's radio had been compromised and was now operating under duress and the control of the Japanese.

Although this procedure had been followed by Ellwood in trying to warn SRD, his message of duress was not noticed. Once ignored, this resulted in the two-way flow of information and (false) intelligence and the insertion of the Cobra and other parties and their subsequent capture. This was an inexcusable and astonishing breakdown in communications between operatives and HQ. It's worth noting that a similar failure to note a warning through the prearranged use of the authentication code words had led to the total collapse and failure of the SOE operation in Holland, where, between 1941 and 1944, all but a few of the 52 SOE operatives sent in were captured, tortured and killed.

The interrogation of Lieutenant Cashman began on 4 February, five days after they landed. He was told that, because the Japanese had not signed the Geneva Conventions for the treatment of prisoners of war, he could be tried not as a combatant but as a spy, and if found guilty, executed. The Japanese interrogator was quick to make use of the cipher and Liversidge's notebook, questioning Cashman on the authentication code. While there was some confusion in understanding this system by the interrogator, the Japanese were eventually able to open a second radio link with SRD and begin transmissions.

Back in Melbourne, the message was received, but no questions were asked nor suspicions raised as to why the first transmission was five days late. In late February, SRD were able to decode a

Japanese signal which stated that Cashman had been captured. SRD challenged Cobra about this, and in Cobra's response the all-important authenticated code was excluded. This should have worried SRD, but again the simple, clever warning went unseen or unrecognised.

SRD Melbourne again signalled Cobra, adding further questions, but again failing to detect the hidden message indicating the Cobra party were not following procedure and therefore transmitting under duress. The Japanese realised an authentication word was missing, and although the men of Cobra were initially able to pass this off, further challenges from SRD left the Japanese suspicious. When the second message arrived from SRD containing the authenticator, the Japanese realised the importance of the code and subjected Cashman to eight hours of extreme torture, then refused him food and water for two days. After further torture, he revealed the authenticated code, which again allowed the Japanese to open a radio link with SRD.

To further compound Cashman's situation, SRD signalled they were ready to deliver funds in gold and radioed Cobra to suggest a safe delivery method. The unusual request prompted further questions from his suspicious interrogators – although Cashman was also unsure of the meaning behind it – which saw him further tortured. Two days later, the Japanese again sent a message via Cobra's radio, stating they did not understand what was required. Further messages passed back and forth, and even included reference to Lagarto and the inclusion of their authenticator word, 'compact'.

The Japanese, feeling they had extracted what information they could from the Australians, slowly improved their conditions and diet, and allowed them one bath each week and the chance to wash their clothes. During one of these occasions, Cashman saw his signaller, Sergeant Liversidge, emaciated and 'almost a skeleton' from the ravages of malaria. He also heard from a Lagarto survivor, Matos de Silva, that Ellwood was still alive, but Cashman never saw these men again, and was only to meet Ellwood after the end of the war, when they were repatriated to Australia together.

Still imagining both Lagarto and Cobra were active operations, SRD began a bimonthly supply drop. On one occasion, Cashman was forced to accompany a large Japanese party to the drop zone, just as Ellwood had been earlier, where, under the muzzles of rifles and machine guns, he was compelled to signal Allied aircraft with a signal torch operated by a Japanese signaller while another Japanese soldier, dressed as an Australian, held a smoke candle. Even though very large quantities of supplies were dropped, requiring many locals to transport them from the drop zones to the bases, again SRD did not ask how so many bearers were able to be assembled despite the hostility and pro-Japanese sympathies of many of the locals.

SRD were now considering the insertion of a third group, and requested Cobra's help by despatching a welcoming party. Cobra was able to subtly warn SRD that the proposed entry point had few loyal locals in the vicinity, so the idea of a reception party to meet the incoming team was dropped. The news did not deter SRD, who moved ahead with the plan to insert a party for one month into the Lautem Plateau area at the very eastern tip of Portuguese Timor. This party was to obtain intelligence, mainly on Japanese road and aerodrome construction and aircraft movements, and on the extent of Timorese cooperation with the Japanese. The party, known as Adder, comprised Captain John Grimson and Sergeant Jack Shand, both AIF, and three Portuguese men.

Each of the three attempts to insert the Adder party failed. On the first attempt, the landing craft running the stores to the beach was swamped in the surf and the stores lost, some later believed to have been recovered by the Japanese. The second attempt was made in mid-June 1944, but the motor launch inserting the party was spotted by Japanese aircraft and the party returned to Darwin. On the third attempt, while the party were stopped off on Melville Island en route to Timor, Sergeant Shand injured his hand and again the mission was cancelled. To replace Shand, Sergeant Ernest Gregg was flown from Melbourne to Darwin, and it was not until the night of 21 August that Grimson and Gregg were able to depart Darwin for Timor. After arriving, and while the stores were being transferred to the shore, Grimson carried out a recce in the area, feeling reasonably certain he had landed at the correct location. The motor launch then returned to Darwin and the Adder party moved quietly inland. They were never seen alive again. Having received no radio transmission from Adder, RAAF aircraft swept the area for three days between 5 and 7 September, but found no sign of the operatives.

SRD sought Cobra's assistance to search the location, but a message came back on the compromised Cobra radio stating that the presence of Japanese patrols prevented further investigation of the area. The RAN were tasked to patrol the section of coast where the party had been inserted, but their only sighting were some fires, later considered to be a Japanese barge staging point. It was later learned that the Adder party had been intercepted within hours of landing, and that in the subsequent firefight both Grimson and Gregg had been wounded. When the Japanese questioned Lieutenant Cashman about the personal details of these men, he was unable to help his interrogators, but was told soon after that both men had been ambushed and killed. After the war, he learned that Grimson and Gregg had died of their wounds and starvation in early 1945.

During 1944, messages flowed back and forth between the captured operatives under Japanese control and SRD in Melbourne, about the possibility of extracting Cobra. The planning for this operation went on over many months, first under the name of Pidgeon. SRD undertook aerial reconnaissance to find a suitable place for the insertion of a parachute party, and Timorese operatives were requested to undertake ground reconnaissance trips. By September 1944, plans were suspended due to the unavailability of suitable aircraft. It remained in abeyance until early 1945, when the rescue operation was renamed Starfish and then Suncob.

As part of the scheduled resupply drop, both Cobra and Lagarto had been requested to report certain intelligence information, but SRD discovered that this request was included in intercepted Japanese transmissions. Each party had been questioned if they still had their copies of their operational instructions, their designated tasks and the type of intelligence required. It was the responses which came back to SRD from the field that triggered the first concern that both parties had been compromised and were now in Japanese captivity. This must have raised serious concerns at SRD headquarters, as the operators there well knew the length of time the operations had run, the men and stores inserted since the possible time of the operatives' capture, and the likely damage in intelligence and security breaches.

However, standing by were the long-planned relief party; aircraft had been tasked for the rescue, and the men trained. What to do? First, the idea of informing Cobra of the date and location of the party's arrival was to be dropped, along with the idea of a reception committee. Instead, plans were made for a blind insertion, to place operatives in the field before seeking to notify either Lagarto or Cobra.

On 2 July 1945, the two-man Suncob team, made up of Captain P. Wynne and Corporal J. B. Lawrence, were inserted by parachute from a Liberator of No. 200 Flight (RAAF), the RAAF unit that had been formed to serve SRD. But a heavy wind separated the two operatives, and instead of landing in an open paddy field, Lawrence became caught in a tree. Able to free himself, he went in search of Wynne, but was captured by a Japanese patrol in the days after. Wynne also set out for the pre-arranged rendezvous point, but failed to meet up with Lawrence. Wynne tried to signal Allied search aircraft, but his ground signal was not seen. After two weeks on the run, he too was captured and taken to Baucau, where he was interrogated and tortured for 16 days. From there he was taken to Dili, and remained in solitary confinement until he was released on 1 September.

Yet another operation was hatched, called Cobrexit. The plan was to extract the Cobra party by dropping stores and a rubber boat to them, after which they would be extracted by Catalina on 2 August. The stores and rubber boat were duly dropped, but straight into the hands of the waiting Japanese. SRD waited for an acknowledgement from Cobra, but it never came. Instead, on 12 August, just three days before the Japanese surrender, Cobra sent to SRD Melbourne its last transmission: 'For ACB [14] from Nippon. Thanks for your information this long while.' The last Lagarto transmission stated, 'Nippon for LMS [Lugger Maintenance Section Darwin]. Thanks your assistance this long while. Hope see you again. Until then wish your good health. Nippon Army.'[15]

At war's end, the story of the Lagarto and Cobra parties was able to be pieced together and the men debriefed. For Cashman and Gregg of Cobra, their captivity slightly improved after they had provided what information they could, although they remained on a very poor diet in solitary confinement, with little chance of exercise or healthy conditions. During this time, three men of their party died through torture, starvation, malnutrition and disease. The surviving operatives were finally released on 21 August, six days after the Japanese surrender. While they remained in prison, the survivors were able to meet and discuss their horrendous experience, the first time they had spoken since they had left Australia. On 1 September, they were taken to Bali, and the following day to Singapore.

In hindsight, it could be asked if the radio traffic between Cobra, Lagarto and SRD, and the details provided as to the date, time and place of this insertion, led to the capture and death of the rescue parties. It was also subsequently found that the operational planning for the mission was poor: no recognition signals had been agreed upon, and no contingency plans carried out should radio communications fail. As a result of this experience, a plan was drawn up which became standard operating procedure for the insertion of all rescue parties in future wars.

After the landing of the first Australian units in Timor in December 1941, Sparrow Force and the 2/2 Independent Company, SRD had also realised that to resupply operational units, a series of small supply bases needed to be established between Australia and Japanese-occupied Timor. This would allow small ships and motor launches of limited range and capacity to collect and transport arms and supplies, saving the need for long, dangerous sea voyages and making the insertion, resupply and recovery of field operatives safer and more efficient. From mid-1944, Hornet Base at Cape Voltaire on the Kimberley coast and a series of bases including Montalivet, Browns and Sandy Inlet, and Cartier and Ashmore Reefs, were established for store dumps. Supplies could then be transferred by sea and concealed in hidden caches on the Australian mainland, ready for distribution to active units.

From the beginning, problems arose, not the least being the repairs needed to both HMAS *Krait* and HMAS *Alatna*, before they could help with resupply efforts. By late 1944, a revised plan to undertake this work, called Mugger–Sounder, was submitted to the Australian Intelligence Bureau (AIB) for approval, but due to the relocation of priorities and the necessary aircraft it required, the plan was abandoned.

The establishment of various caches on the mainland, on the islands and ultimately on Timor and the Lesser Sunda Islands, was covered by a number of SRD operations, including Apache, Wasp, Gnat, Flea and Louse. During this time, the locations of these caches were made available to RAAF aircrew by what was known as the Rogers Points system for downed airmen, which became an important contributing factor in raising morale for aircrew operating from bases in the Northern Territory and Western Australia to Japanese Timor.

Also underlying the broad Mugger–Sounder plan was the possibility of further Allied operations in the area to provide intelligence on all Japanese military dispositions in Timor, the location and reliability of any remaining pro-Allied units, details of landing points, the insertion of pre-landing operatives and the establishment of intelligence-gathering and radio transmission networks. A revised plan was submitted in November 1944, which included the insertion of seven air sorties and nine maintenance sorties, but this was again refused by GHQ. The plan was later revised on a smaller scale under the operational name of Sunfish.

Following the return of the Lagarto and Cobra parties after the war, a report written on the operations was scathing:

> It is the story of hardship, death, torture, humiliation and degradation meted out by a ruthless enemy. It is a story of

colossal waste since all subsequent operations in the area for a period of two years depended on the assumption of Lagarto's freedom. It produced nothing whatever of value and neither did the subsequent operations. To this failure can be ascribed the wretched deaths of nine Australians, some Portuguese and scores of loyal natives. Even the Japanese must have despised the gross inefficiency and criminal negligence with which it was conducted.[16]

When asked to comment about SRD operations in Timor, Captain Keith Stringfellow of SRD said:

Our casualty list was very high. It was caused mainly by somebody in the Darwin office who didn't read the signal properly and didn't pick up that they were in enemy hands. He queried it which he never should have done and the Japs knew exactly . . . and we kept sending in people on requests for people and ammunition and food and they never queried it. Very poor staff work and mainly from our Darwin office. It should never have happened.[17]

This really said it all, but for SRD and the men of Z Special, these hardships were only the beginning.

SEVEN

The Insect and Fish Operations – Papua New Guinea

While the Japanese were pushing the British and Australian forces back down the Malay Peninsula with the final fall of Singapore on 15 February 1942, they were also sending naval and army forces against strategic Allied bases further south. Even before the start of the Pacific War, in fact going back to the 1920s, the threat of Japanese aggression loomed large and Australian military planners had realised the potential of strategic Japanese airfields within range of northern Australia. Although the three small infantry forces of 'Lark Force', 'Gull Force' and 'Sparrow Force' were despatched between April 1941 and January 1942, as part of what was called at the time the Malay Barrier, they would in time be overrun and their men captured, brutalised and interned at the hands of the Japanese.

At 1 am on 23 January 1942, 5000 Japanese troops landed at Rabaul in New Britain and Kavieng in New Ireland. Rabaul was a defendable harbour with good port facilities and within reach of the upcoming objectives, including PNG and the Solomons, but also mainland Australia. Upon landing, the Japanese were confronted by about 1400 Australians of Lark Force who they quickly overran and dispersed. A group of 180 were cornered and massacred at the Tol Plantation, while many of those captured were lost in the sinking of the Japanese freighter *Montevideo Maru* off the Philippines on 1 July 1942.

A week later, the Japanese landed at Ambon, a large Dutch military base and now part of the Maluku Islands of Indonesia. In December 1941, it was reinforced by 1100 Australians of the 2/21st Battalion known as Gull Force. It was Gull Force and about 2800 Dutch colonial troops of the Royal Netherlands East Indies Army who faced the first Japanese landing on 30 January. As with the Rabaul and Kavieng landings, these Allied units were quickly overrun, and while the casualties from the fighting were relatively light, the Japanese were to carry out systematic torture, massacre and ill treatment of the survivors, with three quarters of Gull Force losing their lives before the end of the war. To the west, the Japanese had by this time invaded and taken Timor, where the men of Sparrow Force fought on, in particular the commandos of the 2/2 and 2/4 Independent Companies.

The Japanese now turned their attention to the north coast of Papua New Guinea as part of their broader operational plan for the south-west Pacific. The Japanese strategy was to drive east, capturing all of Papua New Guinea and the large islands to the north, then the Solomon Islands, and from there, eastward across the Pacific to the New Hebrides, New Caledonia and finally Fiji. This would interdict the sea route and strangle Australia of military personnel and supplies. To begin this, Rabaul had become a major supply base and the Japanese needed to secure it, but also needed to build ports and airfields to support this advance.

While MacArthur had hoped to deny the Japanese further land bases and staging points along the Papua New Guinea coast and to the north of Australia, his forces were unable to undertake a counterattack and the Japanese landed virtually unopposed at Lae and Salamaua on the island's north-east shoreline on 8 March 1942. The small Australian detachment of the New Guinea Volunteer Rifles and some members of the 2/22 Battalion withdrew from the area after blowing up a bridge and, after a brief encounter with the Japanese, retreated into the hills towards Mubo.

On the morning of 10 March, two days after the landing, a major bombing raid was launched on Japanese shipping and stores dumps at Lae by American aircraft from the carriers *Lexington* and *Yorktown*, stationed in the Gulf of Papua, and bombers from Garbutt Field in Townsville. They sank a number of troopships and damaged other vessels, which was a major psychological blow to the Japanese, who to date had found little resistance in their advance south. The raid also alerted the Japanese Navy to the presence of American aircraft carriers and the threat they posed to their supply lines and forward bases.

The Japanese had also decided that Port Moresby was a key strategic target and a possible launching pad for any future invasion of the Australian mainland. While the Australian population held great fears about an imminent Japanese invasion, we now know this was never seriously considered by the Japanese. An invasion was simply beyond their capacity in shipping and ground forces, and in fact no military planning was undertaken.

The capture of Port Moresby, which would become part of the Japanese Operation MO, would therefore deny the Allies a forward base. The operation involved a number of services, including the establishment of two seaplane bases, one at Tulagi in the Solomons and another in the Louisiade Archipelago off the south-east coast of Papua New Guinea. It also involved the landing of troops near Port Moresby, covered by a light cruiser and the despatch of two carriers to eliminate the Allied units who were expected to respond. The deployment of these vessels resulted in the Battle of the Coral Sea between 4 and 8 May 1942, which, although a turning point in the Japanese advance and a strategic victory for the Allies, saw the loss of three American ships, including the carrier USS *Lexington*, the destroyer USS *Sims* and the oiler USS *Neosho*.

As the Japanese had failed to take Port Moresby by a coastal landing, their planners looked to capture the city with a two-pronged attack: overland, from bases on the northern coast, and from a base to be established at the very eastern end of Papua New Guinea at Milne Bay. The Japanese drive over the Owen Stanley Range, which runs down the centre of Papua New Guinea, was stopped just 30 miles (48 kilometres) north of Port Moresby. The Australians also defeated the Japanese landing force at Milne Bay with American support, a battle that ran from 25 August until the Japanese were forced to evacuate on 7 September. The defeat of the Japanese at Milne Bay was both a strategic victory in preventing the Japanese establishing an operational base closer to Port Moresby, and a huge morale boost to the Australian population threatened by invasion. This is believed to be the first time the Japanese were defeated on land during the war and clearly showed they were not invincible.

In spite of these Allied successes, the Japanese now held a line of strategic bases along the northern coast of Papua New Guinea, and there was no established intelligence organisation apart from the scattered and threated men of the Coastwatchers to provide intelligence. After the First World War, a coast-watching organisation had been established in 1922. While initially for Australian coastal defence, it was extended in 1939 to Papua New Guinea and the Solomons, deploying about 400 Coastwatchers and, later in the war, became part of SRD and was known as M Special.

In April 1942, ISD, yet to be renamed SRD, was tasked to provide a plan for the insertion of specialist operatives for intelligence-gathering and sabotage. Their initial recommendation was to insert eight parties, each of four men, to undertake a range of operational duties including the recruiting of local men to act as guides, interpreters and porters; the provision of propaganda; the establishment of intelligence networks among local tribes under Australian control; and the continuation of a programme of sabotage and subversive work. Due to the difficulties that the island's extensive coastline and mountainous topography posed to resupply efforts, it was proposed to limit the operations to areas of strategic importance to the Japanese, in particular in the Gulf of Huon around Lae and Salamaua, to the west towards Madang, on New Britain around Rabaul and on New Ireland at Kavieng.

Even aside from the threat of the Japanese, the jungle was a frightening and unhealthy place to fight a war. The rain fell constantly and men's clothes were continually wet, quickly rotting and falling apart in the 100 per cent humidity and stifling temperatures. Insects, in particular mosquitos, were aggressive, finding their way into netted stretchers and feasting on the soldiers' exposed bodies. This, along with the scratches and abrasions from prickly plants and sharp branches, meant that men's skin was often blistered and covered with boils and infections.

Shelter was limited and basic. Often tents were not available, and if they were, rotted quickly in the humid conditions. Crude shelters were constructed using bamboo and kunai grass, but these were not water- or insect-proof. Food too was difficult to obtain, and was of generally poor quality. Rations consisted of tinned beef, hard biscuits and rice, but few vegetables or fruit unless these were able to be obtained from locals' gardens. This poor diet led to dysentery and other diseases, with malaria a constant concern. It was found after the war that the Japanese suffered far more casualties through tropical diseases, in particular malaria, than they did battle casualties.

The jungle and coastal swamps also held animal dangers. Giant bird-eating spiders built vast webs that were difficult to push through and stuck to clothes, face and weapons, and huge pythons, some up to 25 feet (7.5 metres) long, consumed whole animals. The coastal rivers, swamplands and the open ocean were infested with sharks and crocodiles, which imposed serious dangers for beach landing, river crossings and the navigation of flooded areas. Rivers too were dangerous as they were often fast flowing, wide and turbulent, and broad rivers like the Markham and the Sepik made crossing difficult, slow and exposed.

Initially it was difficult to recruit civilians with any experience in Papua New Guinea, although many Australian expats had worked in various government jobs, in particular as patrol leaders, while some had worked for the major trading companies like Burns Philp and with geological and mining companies. To secure enlisted men for the operation, arrangements were made for their transfer and redeployment with ISD or similar organisations. Thirty-two men were required for the eight parties: 24 operatives and eight radio technicians, who were trained and sourced from other AIF units.

The training of operatives began in late May 1942 at the No. 7 Infantry Training Centre (Guerrilla Training School) at Foster, Victoria, a remote and rugged location on Wilsons Promontory. Originally established to provide training for commandos of the Independent Companies, the centre also trained ISD operatives until their training moved to Fraser Island, Canungra and the 'House on the Hill' above Cairns.

The radio operators and technicians began their training at the Radio School at ISD Headquarters in Melbourne. In preparation for the first insertion, special lightweight radios were developed by Captain Jensen of the Netherlands Section, as well as the design and manufacture of special food packs and weapons, webbing, backpacks and footwear. But this all took time.

As preparations continued, the eight parties were provided operational codenames: Cockroach, Beetle, Ladybird, Spider, Wasp, Tick, Bug and Locust. As it was believed that Port Moresby would imminently fall to the Japanese, who were gaining ground over the Owen Stanleys, Captain Sam Carey was despatched to New Guinea Force Headquarters as the ISD Liaison Officer and appointed to the General Staff. Carey provided the necessary connection between ISD in Melbourne and the operational needs of the Army in the front line, establishing a base for various secret operations in northern Papua New Guinea. As part of a broad reorganisation, ISD operations were transferred to C Section AIB, the section responsible for Papua New Guinea, New Britain and the Solomons. A radio link remained between operational ISD parties in the field, the Port Moresby headquarters and the Z Experimental Station (ZES) in Cairns.

The first operational party to be deployed was Cockroach. It contained four men: Lieutenants I. F. G. Downs, H. L. Williams and L. K. Searle, the first two ex-patrol officers, and a signaller, Sergeant J. O. Milne. Initially the Cockroach party were to work with native tribes in central Papua New Guinea, in particular the Chimbu, Hagen and Bena Bena people, and from there work north into the lower Markham Valley, where sabotage operations could be undertaken against Japanese installations at Lae.

In late August 1942, the party flew to Cairns and were taken to the ZES for further training and to await departure. After a delay of 25 days due to the unavailability of aircraft, the party then flew to Port Moresby, where plans were already underway for the evacuation of the town. Given the prospect of an indefinite delay, Lieutenant Downs secured a boat and proceeded west along the Papua New Guinean coast, landing near Terapo, where they obtained carriers.

The party set out northwards with 4000 pounds of stores on an arduous south–north crossing of PNG, travelling 225 miles (362 kilometres) to Tungu in the lower Markham Valley, where they established a base about 80 miles (125 kilometres) south-west of Lae. The Japanese were at this time landing at Buna and Gona with 7000 troops, and at Milne Bay further to the east. By the time the Cockroach party reached the end of their trek, the fighting on the Kokoda Trail was at its most intense, with the 2/39th Battalion briefly retaking Kokoda village just two days before.

The Cockroach party established a base camp in early October, and were initially tasked to blow up a Japanese radio locator station at Hopoi, to the east of Lae, as this formed part of a series of locator stations that allowed the Japanese to detect and locate Coastwatcher transmissions. But GOC, New Guinea Force, postponed the plan and changed the operation's role from one of sabotage to solely intelligence-gathering, before control of the party passed from ISD to Section C of AIB in early December.

As GHQ in Australia had no source of intelligence on the Lae area, where it was known the Japanese were strengthening their bases at both Lae and Finschhafen, Cockroach were ordered to proceed to the Huon Peninsula to the north of Lae. After their insertion, they travelled to their operational area by a circuitous route over three stages, using jungle tracks and the rivers, and established a base to conduct intelligence operations and report by radio to Australia. But the AIB had just taken over control from ISD, and the new command wanted to start afresh with operations and so ordered Cockroach to withdraw. With the departure of Cockroach, it is noted in an operational report that 'the only opportunity the Allied forces had of maintaining a base for the transmission of enemy reports from the Lae area was lost'.[1]

On the same day the Cockroach party assembled at ZES Cairns, 21 August 1942, a second group of operatives, codenamed Beetle, were also assembling and preparing for a Papua New Guinea operation. This party was led by Lieutenant K. W. T. Bridge (AIF), an ex-patrol officer from the Morobe District inland from Lae; Lieutenant C. J. Miller (AIF), also a former patrol officer; Warrant Officer E. J. Robson (RAAF), previously a member of the New Guinea Public Health Department; and an AIF radio operator, Sergeant R. K. Henderson. They too were to establish an intelligence-gathering base, west of Salamaua.

Like Cockroach, Beetle was provided 4000 pounds of stores for four months, but were also to face a considerable delay in Cairns as they waited for suitable aircraft to fly them to Port Moresby. It was 43 days before they could be flown into their forward base at Garaina, 80 miles (127 kilometres) directly south of Lae. Here the party made contact with locals from New Britain who had escaped from the Japanese in Lae and were able to provide valuable intelligence on the conditions in Rabaul, troop numbers and supply dumps.

A report written by Lieutenant L. F. Howlett makes an interesting comment about the interaction between the Australians and the locals: 'All the interrogations seem to have been made with the sole idea of getting information and little attempt made to discover how they were treated, what their feelings were or how the natives of Rabaul had reacted to Japanese control.'[2]

A week after the first two parties arrived at ZES Cairns, they had been joined by the four members of the third party, Ladybird, made up of Lieutenant G. Greathead (AIF), a former patrol officer in the Madang District; Lieutenant R. Cambridge, a plantation manager; Lieutenant D. G. H. Chambers (AIF), who had also been a patrol officer; and a signaller, Sergeant T. Mitchell.

In a report written by Lieutenant Greathead, he reported that 'before the war occasional luggers manned by Japanese fishermen landed on Long island [north of Lae and east of Madang]. The crews killed pigs, stole food and raped women, and the natives ran away to the bush and hid.'[3] Given Greathead's knowledge of and experience in the Madang area, it was proposed to fly the Ladybird party into Bena Bena, about 65 miles (108 kilometres) south of Madang, and from there begin intelligence operations in the Madang District, where there were no Australians operating at the time. But the Ladybird party were also delayed, spending 61 days in Cairns before eventually flying to Port Moresby and from there to a staging point at Mount Hagen in the centre of the island. At this point control passed to AIB, and, as with Cockroach, the operatives of Ladybird were returned to Cairns.

The problem of transport was to plague other Papua New Guinea operations at this time. In late August 1942, a four-man party led by an ex-trader and planter from Kavieng, Lieutenant H. J. Murray (AIF), along with Lieutenant R. H. C. Cardew (AIF), an island employee, Lieutenant G. Stevenson (AIF), also a former patrol officer, and Sergeant J. W. Marsh as their signaller, had their operation abandoned after waiting 62 days, as there was no available flying boat or submarine transport. Similarly, the Wasp party, led by an ex-trader and planter from Rabaul, found they too could not get suitable transport to undertake their operation in the Rabaul area. After waiting 61 days, this operation was cancelled and the men were transferred to the Lizard III party in Timor.

After the Japanese had landed at Buna and Gona on 21 July 1942 and began their rapid advance overland to Port Moresby, GOC New Guinea Force asked ISD for urgent and immediate assistance to prepare a party, codenamed Tick, to provide intelligence in the Buna area on the northern coast of Papua New Guinea. In response, a party of four, comprising Lieutenant L. E. Ashton as leader and Lieutenants G. R. Archer and A. M. Hamilton (AIF) and a signaller, Sergeant Marsh, left Melbourne for Port Moresby on 17 September with 3000 pounds of equipment, including weapons, radios, food and supplies.

By September 1942, the Japanese were well entrenched along the Buna–Sanananda–Gona coastline. From here they had been sending supplies south for the fighting on the Kokoda Trail, but after they were repelled by the Allies just to the north of Port Moresby, the survivors of the campaign were returning to this fortified beachhead. The Japanese plan was to resume the overland attack on Port Moresby after they had secured the island of Guadalcanal in the Solomons, but the Australian and American commanders, in particular General Douglas MacArthur, forced the pace on eliminating this strategic beachhead in Papua New Guinea's north. But to increase the Allies' problems, as pointed out in a letter from Army HQ in Port Moresby to FELO in Melbourne, the Orokaiva tribe in that area were considered 'extremely treacherous, a large proportion actively assisting the enemy'. In one intelligence report it stated, 'Information re our intended ops was on one occasion passed very quickly to the enemy.'[4]

Given the importance of their mission, the Tick party were provided the necessary transport, arriving in an advanced base at Adjora just 13 air miles from Buna. At this time, due to the reverses the Japanese were sustaining on Guadalcanal and the concern within the Imperial Japanese Army that Allied forces might land along the northern coast in their rear, the Japanese were beginning their retreat back over the Owen Stanley Range to their bases on the northern coast. This was seen as a strategic withdrawal until a time when the Japanese could re-establish their positions on Guadalcanal and could return to their offensive on Port Moresby. Their initial retreat only took them back to Templeton's Crossing, still well south of Kokoda but the attack by Australian forces drove them to Oivi-Gorari, north of Kokoda, where they were forced to fall back even further.

Meanwhile, the Tick party were moving towards a forward operational base near Buna. While their mission was intelligence-gathering and reporting on Japanese movements and unit strengths, GOC now asked them to undertake demolition work, a strange request given they were carrying no demolition stores. The orders were rescinded and Tick reverted to their original intelligence-gathering task. They were also able to assist American forces who were operating against the Japanese in the Buna area by providing intelligence and guides, as well as leading US patrols into the Japanese defensive areas along the coast. But, as with the other Papua New Guinea operations, command was transferred from ISD to the new AIB, where their structure and role was changed.

The next four-man party to be inserted into Papua New Guinea was Bug. The leader was Lieutenant L. C. Noaks, an experienced geologist in the territory administration, and the remainder of the party comprised Lieutenant C. E. Searle, an ex-rubber planter; Lieutenant W. Ferguson (AIF), an ex-territory oil company employee; and a signaller, Sergeant L. T. W. Carlson. Initially they were tasked with special operations work including sabotage, but as had happened to other parties, this was redefined to intelligence-gathering and reconnaissance.

The Bug party arrived at ZES Cairns in late September 1942, and after a delay of a month awaiting suitable transport flew via Port Moresby to the small, remote airstrip at Garaina. The men briefly established a base then trekked to Ioma, about 125 miles (200 kilometres) south-east of Lae and inland from any Japanese operational area at the time. From here, they were able to operate in the coastal area, about 20 miles (32 kilometres) to the north, and report on Japanese shipping movements, until the control of the party transferred to AIB.

As with many ISD–AIB operations, the Papua New Guinea parties needed to be quickly planned, organised and inserted into the field, but in many cases the operational and strategic situation also quickly changed, so that by the time the men were prepared and ready, the reason for the operation had altered or was considered less important. This was the case with the Locust party.

Concerned with the possibility of the Japanese's imminent arrival in Port Moresby, GOC NG Force thought it necessary to prepare stay-behind parties who would be inserted into Papua New Guinea. These parties would be available to continue sending intelligence and work with the locals to undertake raids and subversion on the Japanese. Locust was hurriedly tasked to undertake this mission, but while the men were still training and preparing at ZES Cairns, the threat on Port Moresby was averted and the original operational plan abandoned. ISD's alternative plan for Locust was equally dangerous and ambitious.

While many of these operations were cancelled or failed to achieve very much, the story of Whiting was very different. As the operational area was over the border in Dutch New Guinea, this operation was controlled and planned by the Netherlands

East Indies (NEI) Section of ISD in late 1942. As in the areas of the northern coast occupied by the Japanese, there was virtually no intelligence-gathering capability apart from some remaining Coastwatchers, the odd ANGAU (Australian New Guinea Administrative Unit) and the few expats still at large.

The plan was to insert a combined Dutch and Australian intelligence party across the border into Papua New Guinea and into the hinterland behind Hollandia (now Jayapura), the capital in the island's north. The group was to be equipped for an extended stay. The mission would be led by Lieutenant Fryer of the Locust operation, who was to guide Whiting to the border and then return, leaving the group to continue to its operational area while Locust established a similar operational area behind Aitape to the east.

The Whiting party was under the control of an NEI sergeant, a Dutchman, H. N. Staverman, and included an NEI Brigadier, D. J. Topman; Acting-Sergeant Leonard Siffleet, an AIF signaller of Australian-Dutch descent; and two Indonesian NEI privates, H. Pattiwael and N. Raharing. Len Siffleet was born in January 1916 in the NSW town of Gunnedah and in September 1941 he joined the AIF where he was posted to the 1st Signals Division before volunteering for special duties with ISD.

Given the remoteness of the Hollandia operational area deep inside enemy territory and the difficulty in inserting a party, it was decided to send the group overland on an extended trek as Japanese control was only along the coast.

The plan was for the two parties, Whiting and Locust, under the combined control of Lieutenant H. A. J. Fryer (AIF), to be flown to the farthest possible airfield from Port Moresby at Bena Bena, some 260 miles (420 kilometres), and for them to then walk hundreds of miles to the Dutch border, where the Locust party would leave them to continue on their mission. As with the leaders of other ISD units, Fryer was a former prospector for oil in Papua New Guinea, so was familiar with the area and the tribes. Also in the Locust party were two other former PNG employees: Lieutenant H. A. Aitkin (AIF), who had worked in geological survey and was equally familiar with the country; and Lieutenant G. Black (AIF), who had for a time been employed by the PNG administration. With them was a radio operator, Sergeant L. J. Baillee.

The combined Locust and Whiting party left ZES Cairns, passed through Port Moresby, with an extensive load of supplies, and were airlifted into Bena Bena on 21 January 1943. Here they unloaded and checked their stores, before distributing them among 400 carriers who had been organised from the local people. In the amazing six-month overland journey that followed, the party travelled an estimated 514 miles (822 kilometres) on tracks through the jungle, and a further 225 miles (360 kilometres) along rivers and across lakes and waterways, arriving at Lumi on 10 June. At this point, Lieutenant Fryer departed with his party, returning to Port Moresby, while the Whiting party headed for Hollandia on 7 July.

Now in their operational area, Whiting began receiving airdrops from Darwin, and after they established a base camp, Sergeant Staverman began intelligence patrols towards Hollandia. Three months after the two parties separated, he and one private, Pattiwael, were ambushed by pro-Japanese natives. Staverman was killed, but the Indonesian escaped into the jungle and brought news of the ambush to the base camp, where Sergeant Siffleet had his radio.

Fearful of the Japanese finding the radio, the codes and ciphers, and their operational base, Siffleet destroyed the transceiver and retreated to safety in the jungle with Pattiwael and the other

Indonesian, Private Raharing. The three made south, looking to escape, but they were followed. While they sat eating a meal, they were surrounded by locals of the Wapi tribe. Siffleet fired into the group, wounding one of them, but the three operatives were quickly overcome and handed over to the Japanese.

The Japanese were well aware of the secret operations and capabilities of the organisation, based on the intelligence gathered from captured members of the Lagarto party and others on Timor. Siffleet, Pattiwael and Raharing were tortured at Malol, near Aitape, but revealed little of importance to the enemy. On 24 October, after being held for two weeks in frightful conditions, with regular beatings and severe interrogation, the three men were taken to the beach at Aitape. Before both Japanese and local onlookers, they were marched blindfolded to a pre-dug grave and there beheaded and buried. The execution of Sergeant Siffleet and Raharing was captured by a Japanese photographer, and the photos were found by Allied soldiers in 1944 on the bodies of dead Japanese soldiers in Hollandia.

Meanwhile, the Locust party had established a base in the Torricelli Mountains south of Aitape, not far from the Lumi airstrip. Here they began observing and reporting on Japanese movements, but when they heard news of the capture of the Whiting party, they realised the Japanese were closing in and that their capture would be a matter of time. They left the area at the end of November 1943 and, from a base on the Sepik River, were returned to Port Moresby by air. Their intelligence was of limited value, as it had been from the operations around Lae, Salamaua and Madang, but unlike the unfortunate Whiting party, the Locust men lived to fight another day.

During the course of the Papua New Guinea campaign, the locals were generally supportive of the Allies, though there are a number of cases where Japanese propaganda and coercion found them actively working for the enemy. The Allies undertook great effort to ensure the local people knew the Australians were fighting to rid Papua New Guinea of the Japanese, and that the loyalty of the locals was paramount.

An intelligence report from an AIB party in the Wewak-Aitape area, dated 30 December 1943, states:

> In some of the southern areas, the native's knowledge of the 'war' is vague, but a very definite fear of the enemy exists. Other areas express a complete neutrality, but an undercurrent of treachery is always present. Two classes of natives exist – the friendly and the apparently friendly, but treacherous. Differentiation is generally impossible. On our patrol, native treachery expressed itself in theft and attacks on native labour in areas where incentive was the looting of Europeans. More serious were the attacks on Hook, Fryer and Aitken and Siffleet. Those were organised acts of treachery inspired by Jap propagandas and carried out by active Jap agents, assisted by sympathisers and viewed by disinterested sadists.[5]

The need to better protect intelligence-gathering operatives like the men of Whiting, coupled with the need to establish a line of posts to report on Japanese movements and provide detailed intelligence, saw instructions issued in mid-July 1943 for the formation of units that became known as Mosstroops. These were to be made up of white personnel supported by native police, and were to be given an initial six months' supply of food, weapons and necessary stores. The insertion of these parties occurred from mid-August until the end of the year, and would have varied success in the months ahead.

EIGHT

Increasing the Pressure and Pushing West

By late 1942, the Japanese withdrawal had begun owing to reverses at Guadalcanal and the fear the Japanese had of the landing of Allied forces in their rear. By early November, the Australians had retaken Kokoda village and were in pursuit of the Japanese northwards and pushing towards their coastal bases at Buna and Gona.

However, provisioned and resupplied from Rabaul, the Japanese were building up operational bases all along the northern New Guinea and Papuan coast, with an estimated 20,000 Japanese troops in Wewak alone. To respond and counter this build-up, GHQ needed reliable intelligence, but to get this it also needed to find a way to protect these SRD units in the field. This would then provide a springboard for further Allied advances along the Papua New Guinea coast and a new and revised role for the operatives of the new Services Reconnaissance Department.

Between late August and mid-October 1942 the initial eight parties sent into Papua New Guinea under the control of ISD had achieved little. They had focused on the main Japanese concentrations at Lae, Salamaua and Madang and on New Britain, but their offensive capacity had been reduced to reconnaissance and reporting. And so, in May 1943, a conference in Port Moresby devised a plan.

While it could be argued that ISD, and soon the follow-up organisation SRD, found it difficult to recruit suitable men for the eight operational groups, in the end they had secured many experienced ex-patrol officers, miners, plantation owners and government administrative officials, who knew the areas into which they were inserted, as well as the local people and their leaders. Yet still they were unable to establish guerrilla units, disseminate effective propaganda or build up active information-gathering groups and a communications network to support them.

However, unlike the aggressive situation in which ISD operatives had found themselves in Timor, where they were relentlessly hunted by both the Japanese and the unfriendly pro-Japanese locals, in the operational areas of northern Papua New Guinea, from early 1943, the Japanese were the ones who faced a difficult situation. They had to deal with a see-sawing war, with the Australians now pushing them back to the north coast, against the backdrop for the Japanese of strategic difficulties on Guadalcanal and the reverses at Milne Bay. As such, the Japanese were too preoccupied with their immediate future to chase small bands of enemy operatives who, for the most part, they saw as ineffective and benign.

After the Japanese capture of Rabaul in late January 1941, they had quickly repaired the damaged airstrip and built the harbour and town into the foremost staging point and supply base for their operations in the south-west Pacific. Rabaul had become the linchpin for Japanese defence and resupply and the operational base for the various landings along the Papua New Guinea coast. While the RAAF and the US Air Force continued bombing the harbour at Rabaul, GHQ in Australia looked for other ways to damage this Japanese bastion.

In late December 1942, after a discussion between General Thomas Blamey and Captain Sam Carey, a plan was initiated for a raid on Rabaul harbour, which at the time was accommodating up to 90 vessels, with the aim of sinking 15. The operation was given the codename Scorpion and planning began immediately, with the recruitment and training of a ten-man team with Captain Carey as the leader. The team was assembled at ZES Cairns and during March and April 1943 underwent intensive training, which included a simulated attack with limpet mines on 15 vessels in Townsville harbour by two-man canoe teams in folboats. However, due to the unavailability of American submarines to transport the insertion party to Rabaul, the operation was abandoned.

At this time there existed two separate 'Special' units controlled and operated by SRD. In addition to the Z Special Unit was the M Special Unit, a successor to the very effective Coastwatchers. That unit had been established in 1919, but with the growing threat from Japan was reactivated at the beginning of the war under a Naval Reserve officer, Lieutenant Commander Eric Feldt. Born in Ingham, Queensland, and graduating from the Royal Naval College in 1917, Feldt had left the Navy and become a patrol officer and then a district officer in Papua New Guinea. He was later the Chief Mining Warden for New Guinea, which gave him access to the expat population and the administrators.

This became an important attribute when, in late 1939, Feldt was asked to form a coastwatch organisation and recruit and train suitable people for the job. By November 1940, he had established an arc of 50 Coastwatcher stations in the Solomons, the New Hebrides, Papua New Guinea, New Britain and New Ireland, and a string of radio stations and low-powered radio networks to report on shipping movements back to Australia.

This network became famous, beginning with the work of two Coastwatchers, William 'Jack' Read and Paul Mason, who reported on the movement of the Japanese fleet from their position on Bougainville as the enemy prepared to attack the American base on Guadalcanal. Another Coastwatcher, Sub-Lieutenant Arthur Evans, was responsible for the rescue of John F. Kennedy, the future US president, after his patrol boat, PT109, was rammed at night by a Japanese destroyer in the northern Solomon Islands, with Kennedy and his crew left adrift. Evans sent two locals in a canoe to search for the survivors, who were only found five days later, exhausted and near death.

After Kennedy had scratched a rough note on a coconut, the two locals paddled 38 miles (61 kilometres) through hostile Japanese-controlled waters to deliver the message to Evans. He was then able to radio the Americans, who rescued Kennedy and his men. Admiral William 'Bull' Halsey, a US Fleet Admiral, is reported to have said, 'The Coastwatchers saved Guadalcanal, and Guadalcanal saved the Pacific.'[1] The famous commander of the US Air Force Black Sheep Squadron, Major Gregory 'Pappy' Boyington, said, 'If it weren't for the Coastwatchers, then we probably would have lost WWII.'[2]

After the successes of the Coastwatchers Unit, they were absorbed into SRD in June 1942 and became known as M Special Unit. Their role was surveillance, reconnaissance and the report-ing of Japanese shipping and military units, while the Z Special Unit's role was based on more aggressive, direct action involving sabotage, the capture of prisoners and the release of prisoners of war. It was the need for long-term surveillance from bases within Japanese-held territory that had led M Special to initiate the two parallel missions of Whiting and Locust.

While SRD operations in Papua New Guinea had not provided much valuable intelligence, it was found that intelligence-gathering units needed more protection, in particular in Japanese-occupied territory along the coast, in order to succeed. At a meeting attended by SRD, FELO and AIB, consideration was given to providing 'guerrilla patrols' that would be trained and operated by SRD and supplemented with the recruitment of local police. On 15 July 1943, a recommendation was drawn up and from this a plan was approved by the commander-in-chief.

The plan, codenamed Mosstroops or Mossforce, provided for three 'gangs', each of 12 whites and 20 Sepik natives; five patrols, each of three whites and 20 Sepiks; and an HQ organisation to be inserted by Catalina into the area around the Sepik River. Agreement was reached that the party had to be trained and controlled by SRD, would be made up of locals, including native police, and after insertion would operate like a guerrilla army in protecting SRD, FELO and AIB parties in the area.

It was also seen as important for operatives to restore the locals' trust in the Allies, given the involvement of Sepik natives in supporting the Australians, and to consolidate support for the Allies in the future defeat of the Japanese. The use of propaganda to retain the support of various local groups is an overlooked aspect of the work of SRD, in particular that of Z Special and FELO.

Given the size of the party, men were drawn from not only the Z Special Unit but also transferred from other units, depending upon their specialist skills and their location at the time within Australia. Along with the operational units, the 'gangs', the remaining Australians would operate a headquarters to coordinate the parties, plan the operations, gather and transmit intelligence reports and assist with the recovery of downed Allied airmen.

In early August 1943, it was decided as a first stage to insert an advance party. This was completed on 9 August, with a small party comprising Captains Neptune Blood and Des McNamara, Lieutenants Tame and Tom Barnes (who was to die on Operation

Copper in April 1945), a signaller and 13 native police. Landing on Lake Kuvinmas by Catalina, they had hardly begun their work when they were attacked six days later by a Japanese patrol of 30–40 soldiers and a large group of armed natives. They were forced to separate into two groups: one with Captain McNamara and his signaller, Parish, and the other Captain Blood and his men. McNamara and Parish were extracted by Catalina the following day, having escaped the Japanese attack. Captain Blood and Lieutenants Tame and Barnes, along with a number of their men, were able to escape into a sago swamp and hide until the Japanese left the area.

After a restless night, the latter party decided to make the very long journey to Wabag. Blood left a note for McNamara and Parish and instructed friendly locals to find them and give it to them, then set out with his group on 16 August. Between then and late September, this small party undertook an extraordinary trek of about 200 miles (360 kilometres). Along the way two locals died, one swept down a river and the other after eating wild berries. On 22 September, they met an Australian, Lieutenant Clarke, sent to find them, who brought with him a hamper of food, the first decent meal they had eaten for over six weeks.

The following day they left early and finally arrived in Wabag. The men by this time were in poor health and a state of complete exhaustion, each man having lost about three stone (19 kilograms) in weight.[3] The men had been bitten by insects until their skin was a mass of welts and open, infected sores, they had suffered from the freezing weather at altitudes of 9000 feet (nearly 3000 metres) without blankets or warm clothing, their shoes had rotted off their feet, and they'd walked much of the way barefoot. For at least the first half of their journey, they had been forced to avoid Japanese patrols and unfriendly locals.

A second party, led by Major Richard Cardew and comprising Captain John Grimson, six other ranks (ORs) and six native police, were inserted on 5 September in the Yimas River area to the north. They were attacked by the Japanese within hours of landing and, after abandoning their equipment, fled into the hills. There they remained for three weeks until they were found by search aircraft. After supplies were dropped, the men set off on a three-month march via the Karawari River to Wabag, arriving on 29 October, at which point they were finally able to link up with Australian units and were taken to Port Moresby.

After the failure of the first two parties, a third party was inserted further north, near the junction of the Sepik and Yellow rivers. The party established two posts on the river after being inserted by Catalina, but the Japanese learnt of these bases and attacked upriver. The *Official History* writes of the encounter with the Japanese:

The first attack was at East Post about the middle of October '43. Two launches carrying enemy troops came up the river approximately two or three hundred yards apart. The patrol at East Post which consisted of Lieutenant Downie, three ORs and three natives, armed with two Bren guns and four Austens, remained undercover until one launch came abreast of their position. Then they opened fire, and it is estimated that all enemy on deck were either killed or wounded, except one, the launch then turned about and made off down the stream, listing very badly. When firing started, the other launch pulled into the bank and landed its troops. These were held off until darkness, when the party, led by a native, slipped through the Japanese lines. Next morning the enemy withdrew leaving the camp intact.[4]

On 11 November, three Japanese troops stumbled upon the second post, known as Tokyo Post. They were fired on and withdrew, but two days later the Japanese sent a larger force upriver by boat, landing between East Post and Tokyo Post, but were again driven off, taking their casualties with them. The Japanese retreated, but two weeks later, the main base was attacked by Japanese aircraft, which destroyed all of the buildings with bombing and strafing. When it was found that a strong Japanese force were also moving up to attack the village, the party were evacuated over three days by 14 Catalina sorties, and the stores were destroyed and booby-trapped. After the evacuation of the Mosstroop party and the clearing of Japanese patrols from the area, ANGAU continued their patrols.

Given the absence of a Coastwatcher unit in Dutch New Guinea, a plan was drawn up to insert an SRD party onto Batanta Island, a small, uninhabited island off the north-western coast. Here they were to establish an observation post to observe Japanese shipping movements in the Dampier, Sele and Sagewin Straits, and airfields at Samate and Sorong. As a secondary task, the party were to survey potential landing beaches for a future Allied invasion should one be planned, and also send regular meteorological information to Darwin.

This operation was codenamed Menzies, and the party consisted of six AIF personnel led by Lieutenants V. D. Prentice and G. Black. After training on Fraser Island the party were flown to Darwin, where they practised stowing their folboats and stores into the US submarine that was tasked to deliver them to their operational area. On 14 June 1944, the Menzies party boarded the submarine and slipped quietly out to sea, arriving five days later off the north-west tip of Salawati Island at Cape Dadi. As they rose to periscope depth the captain checked the coastline and, after ensuring it was safe, attempted the first disembarkation. But strong currents made disembarking impossible, and it was delayed until suitable conditions would prevail.

After the second attempt the following night, the party reported by walkie-talkie that they had landed successfully. After hiding up for the day, they set out on the morning of 22 June and for three days paddled against a strong current to Cape Makoe, on the north-east corner of Batanta Island, where they established an observation post 700 feet (213 metres) above sea level. Owing to the steep climb and the rugged country, it took the party three days to collect and carry their stores up to their new observation post.

Following the establishment of a post, a series of watches were organised, but the group encountered a problem with the radio due to a defect in the set and a lack of power. When a link was finally established with the radio station on Manus Island, the signal was weak and comms were only maintained through the Dutch radio station at Batchelor, south of Darwin. Once reports began to be sent, folboat patrols were organised. The first patrol, in July, sought to observe the Japanese airfield at Samate, but after finding Japanese weapon pits and ammunition, returned to their base. Another patrol, in September, also failed due to the difficult and rugged country.

By mid-July, RAAF Liberators of 24 Squadron Darwin were successfully providing monthly resupply drops of stores at night onto signal lights laid out 300 yards apart. On each occasion, the cylindrical containers of stores with parachutes attached, known as storpedoes, were recovered, which allowed an increase in the frequency and length of patrols. By this time, the Allies had landed at Sausapor on the north coast of the Vogelkop Peninsula, and it was decided to extract Menzies as the observation post was now of limited value. The party were first taken to Sausapor for a debriefing and the Menzies party were returned to Melbourne, leaving all stores behind. Six men of the party were given extensive medical checks and found to be in good health, even after 100 days in the field during the wet season. They had provided good, consistent intelligence, undertaken patrols, tested equipment – especially the extended use of folboats – and were able to provide useful information for future patrols.

Following the withdrawal of Menzies, GHQ determined that intelligence needed to be sought from the area of the Vogelkop Peninsula, in particular Japanese air and land movements on tracks into Sorong. Codenamed Operation Perch, a party under Captain Milton Lees and three sergeants – R. Taylor, A. N. Thompson and Leo Duffus – were assembled at Fraser Island. They travelled first to Darwin and then on to Hollandia on 10 August, which by this time had been cleared of Japanese. From here they were flown to Owi Island in Geelvink Bay, north of Papua New Guinea, which was the staging point for their final insertion. From aerial photographs it was found that no suitable landing zone existed for a parachute drop, but after a reconnaissance flight on 12 August an area was found, with low trees in rainforest near the junction of two rivers.

On the following day, the parachute drop was successfully carried out, with all men landing safely. They were also able to recover their storpedoes, a couple of which were suspended in trees. Due to the amount and weight of the stores and the density of the jungle, it was only possible for the party to advance 400 yards per day. Upon reaching the foothills after four days, a first attempt was made to establish a radio link with Darwin, but due to the low altitude, the thickness of the jungle and their inability to erect a high aerial, it was not until a week later that they were able to establish a workable radio link.

On 5 September, a seven-day patrol was organised, which established that no Japanese patrols were in the area. With these observations and intelligence supplied by friendly locals, the Perch party felt safe to continue their work. They did find that Allied propaganda had promised the locals food, which meant the party needed to share their very limited supply with them. Because the first resupply drop was two weeks overdue, this caused much distress within the party, and at times they had to rely on scant supplies of local food.

On 19 September, the Perch party were ordered to withdraw and make their way to the coast for extraction to Darwin. As they moved north, they came across many signs of recent Japanese patrols that had moved along coastal tracks towards Sorong. At one point, they came across two Japanese troops, who they killed, taking from them valuable documents which were later sent to the American Division Headquarters in Sausapor. They also attempted to intercept a Japanese party but were unsuccessful, capturing just one man who they returned to Darwin for interrogation.

On 25 September, Perch were safely extracted by naval patrol boats and, like the Menzies party, were found to be fit and healthy after 44 days in the jungle during the wet season. For his work on the patrol, Captain Lees was awarded the Military Cross and the three sergeants each received the Military Medal.

By August 1944, the Japanese withdrawal from the Solomons and much of the northern Papua New Guinea coast, in particular around Lae and Madang, had cleared the area of the enemy. As a result, GHQ decided to launch Operation Cartwheel, a major military operation which had evolved from original planning beginning in February 1943 under the name of the Elkton Plan. It involved a broad offensive strategy with 13 subordinate offensive operations stretching from the Solomons to New Britain, with the main objective, Rabaul.

By this time the Allies had isolated the huge Japanese base at Rabaul and Allied air and naval operations had seriously affected and restricted resupply of Japanese forces in this area of the South-West Pacific. It was at this point, as the Americans island-hopped north towards Japan, reoccupying the territory that had fallen to the Japanese in their drive south in early 1942, that the Australian area of operations also shifted north, to New Britain, Bougainville and New Ireland. Blamey proposed 'to employ the smallest practicable military force to these operations and he required SRD to assume greater responsibilities in this area'.[5] The Chief of Army, Lieutenant General John Northcott CB, requested various elements of AIB to contribute to this new campaign, something they had been secretly doing for over a year.

A conference was held to ascertain the best way for AIB to assist. At this time, the focus of operational work was how best 'to extend partisan warfare, to sabotage important targets, to develop political warfare by denying the enemy all forms of native assistance, and to bring both the natives and the Japanese under the influences of our propaganda'.[6] To undertake this work, three units within AIB were to be co-opted and formed into one 'Special Force': SRD was to provide operatives for sabotage, NEI was to gather intelligence and FELO was to provide propaganda.

Following the submission of an operational plan incorporating suggestions from the three services within AIB, General Headquarters approved Operation Reaper. The operation was under the overall control of General Vernon Sturdee, GOC (General Officer Commanding the First Australian Army), a Gallipoli veteran, with Major R. N. Hancock appointed the commanding officer of the SRD component. SRD offered 50 men, but needed to be reassured that these specially trained operatives would be given appropriate tasks for their skills. As an alternative, SRD proposed that men from the Independent Companies, the commandos, might be sent in. SRD also offered specialist training at their Fraser Island camp, along with radios and equipment.

Major Hancock moved to Lae to establish his operational base while his signallers set up at Tabragalba, inland from the Gold Coast, Queensland, before moving to a forward base at Nadzab in the Markham Valley behind Lae. In early December 1944, the controller of AIB flew to Lae to coordinate operations and, while there, suggested an attack on the port of Rabaul using the highly secret submersible boats known officially as Motor Submersible Canoes.

These had been developed after the fateful Operation Frankston undertaken by British Royal Marines against German shipping in Bordeaux harbour in December 1942. Needing a motorised canoe to save paddling, Major Quentin Reeves designed a canoe of mild steel with an electric motor powered by four batteries, which would allow the craft to travel 30–40 miles (48–64 kilometres) and with a maximum operating depth of 50 feet (15 metres). Around 36 of the boats had been sent to Australia after Lyon's trip to England, for evaluation, training and eventual operational use at a secret SRD facility, Station XIII at Careening Bay, Garden Island, in Western Australia.

A similar plan, but without the MSCs, had been proposed and initially approved in late 1942, codenamed Scorpion, but the operation had been cancelled in May 1943 due to the unavailability of US submarines to transport the operatives to the Rabaul area. Of these MSCs, 16 were sent on the ill-fated Rimau mission in late 1944, while the remaining 20 were to be used now at Rabaul.

A plan was drawn up to use these submersible kayaks in an attack on shipping and on hidden barge hideouts in Rabaul harbour. They would be used to travel on the surface until near the target, then dive and approach the target underwater and place their limpets onto the side of the enemy ship. For this purpose, an officer, Lieutenant John Walne, and six other ranks were selected and sent to Careening Bay for both folboat and jungle training for the operation.

In early December 1944, the Controller of AIB, Commander J. G. McManus, arrived in Lae to assess the situation and take over operations. McManus stated that, in his opinion, there were no worthwhile sabotage targets left for SRD operations and that raids should instead be carried out by commandos and the partisan native armies raised and trained and now in position.

Meanwhile, planned raids on Japanese coastal positions, in particular the Japanese submarine base on Kairiru Island near Wewak and other targets of opportunity, continued to be developed. It was suggested that such attacks were not to be commando-style raids, which were generally large and undertaken at a particular time and date, but rather the deployment of small parties who, after a period of reconnaissance, would attack these targets at an opportune and carefully calculated time. These raids would also be supported by the small craft units within the Australian Army, along with RAAF and RAN units.

SRD operational planning was continually changing according to Allied priorities. Initially the priories were to capture Bougainville first, Wewak second and New Britain third, but it was realised that Wewak, now the main Japanese supply base in the area, could be captured quicker than planned, so it moved up to share equal priority with Bougainville. But it was in Bougainville that SRD assistance was the most urgent, because their training and capability better fitted the operations required. Also, Bougainville was more difficult to take, requiring suitable shallow-draft transport, so various US naval craft based on Treasury Island and barges from nearby Torokina were called in. It was also decided that operatives were to avoid offensive action where possible by placing small reconnaissance parties onto Japanese-held islands to conduct a defensive, intelligence-gathering operation only.

After reviewing the availability of suitable targets on Kairiru, Major R. Cardew, the CO of SRD in the area, cancelled the Reaper operation. Instead he suggested attacks on Kieta and Buin on Bougainville, but this was vetoed by McManus, who suggested instead that a party be put ashore onto Shortland Island south of Bougainville to capture Japanese troops for interrogation, and at the same time release a French missionary held captive there. But Flight Lieutenant Robinson, the AIB representative in Torokina, argued instead for an SRD team to be put into Abloe Island as flights over the island had encountered heavy anti-aircraft fire, which suggested the location of an important installation to warrant such defence.

After a directive from the commander, 2 Australian Corps, Lieutenant General Stan Savige, it was decided not to insert SRD parties into Bougainville, but rather use SRD experience towards the consideration and planning of other projects.

Now began a series of suggested operations to satisfy changing GHQ priorities, various Australian commanders and those within SRD. After the Commander 2 Australian Corps ordered that there would be no SRD operations in Bougainville without his approval, three other projects were considered.

The first was to attack coastal defence batteries on the Warangoi River, on the east coast of New Britain south of Rabaul, as any future landing on the island needed to be spared such heavy defensive fire. This operation did not proceed. The second idea was to insert a party into the Wewak area to capture a Japanese prisoner for interrogation, and the third to also capture a prisoner and do a thorough reconnaissance of the beach at Karawop, ready for a possible landing by elements of the Australian 6th Division.

The three operations were submitted to McManus, approved by him and sent on to the First Australian Army Headquarters for final approval as Australian Army units were pushing from Aitape eastwards towards Wewak. These are not to be confused with possible operations outlined above. The first of the three proposed operations, submitted to McManus under the broad title Reaper, was Silver (originally Oak). It was tasked with capturing a Japanese prisoner for interrogation from the Boiken Plantation area, 15 miles to the west of Wewak. However, the area was captured before the planned insertion, so the operation was cancelled.

A second attempt to extract a prisoner, Gold (originally Oregon), went ahead on the night of 8 April 1945. A party of six men under Captain H. Nicholls landed near Cape Moem, just to the east of Wewak. As the party approached the shore the men saw lights, but they were extinguished before they landed. The party then walked a mile and a half along the beach but found no evidence of any fortifications, obstacles or defences, and no potential prisoners. They returned to the launch and were extracted, as Nicholls felt it unsafe to remain in the area during the day.

During this time, a small SRD party under Lieutenant Peter Hill was moving ahead of the main 6th Australian Division advance with the idea of locating potential Japanese installations for demolition. The advance of the 6th Division was more rapid than expected and this operation was cancelled. But 6th Division HQ did request the assistance of SRD in the area of Boiken, and a base camp for SRD operations was completed in Lae, where personnel were transferred from their current base at Nadzab.

A third operation was planned, again to extract a prisoner and to recce suspected heavy-gun emplacements on Muschu Island, eight miles (13 kilometres) to the north of Wewak. While the final operational plans were not at this stage completed for the capture of the large Japanese garrison here, the Allies needed to allow for a possible landing on Muschu Island and the elimination of any heavy, long-range artillery that could also fire on the landing beaches at Wewak. This third operation would become the disastrous Operation Copper.

NINE

The Ill-Fated
Operation Copper

On 18 December 1942, the Japanese had landed 2000 troops from four ships at Wewak, after which they had established the major base, a number of airfields and extensive defensive positions. They had also occupied two large islands, Kairiru and Muschu, just eight miles to the north of Wewak. On Kairiru, the Japanese established a flying-boat base, which served as a waypoint between Hollandia and Aitape to the west and Madang to the east.

On Muschu they constructed two defensive lines along the coast and installed a number of heavy machine guns and two 140 mm naval guns that covered the approaches to Wewak harbour. Should a seaborne assault of Wewak be undertaken, these guns could fire on Allied ships and the beaches, causing considerable damage.

By early 1944, the Allied success of the grinding advance in Papua New Guinea was reflected in their broader advance in the Pacific. This became a two-pronged attack towards mainland Japan. While MacArthur cleared the south-west Pacific, the Central Pacific Offensive was continuing under Admirals Nimitz and Halsey. It was now decided that, rather than attempt risky and ultimately costly invasions on the heavily defended Japanese land bases, it was easier to simply bypass them and to leave them to wither on the vine, in a leapfrogging manoeuvre northwards. For the Japanese, the extended resupply lines and the increased Allied potential for their interdiction brought home the grim reality of taking on a populous, industrial nation like America.

As a result, the Allied control of the Pacific saw this two-pronged vanguard rapidly moving towards Japan, and as the islands of the Marshall and Marianas came under American control, Japan itself came within range of Allied air attack. This became possible with new long-range bombers like the B-29 Superfortress, with a range of 3200 miles (about 5200 kilometres) and with a ceiling of nearly 32,000 feet (almost 10,000 metres).

The advance moved relentlessly north with the destruction of the Japanese base at Truk Lagoon north of Papua New Guinea, and then in June the Philippines campaign, which included the capture of Guam, Saipan and Tinian. These Allied captures severely restricted the resupply of Japanese bases further south, including both Rabaul and Wewak.

The Australian Army, much to their disappointment, had been directed by MacArthur to 'mop up' these isolated and remote Japanese strongholds left behind in the American drive north. This was made all the more trying for the Australian Army given that the RAAF and the RAN were invited north to support the American advance in offensives across Borneo and the Philippines; the RAAF squadrons found themselves at Noemfoor, Morotai and later Labuan in Indonesia, while the RAN fought in the Battle of Leyte Gulf.

To support planned future landings, in particular in the advance on the large Japanese base at Wewak, reliable intelligence was needed on enemy strength, defensive positions including heavy artillery and on potential landing beaches. The capture of a Japanese prisoner remained a consideration, for military intelligence but also important details on Japanese morale and health issues. This type of specialist operation could only be done with elite operatives, so GHQ turned to SRD for help.

Many of the men now recruited into SRD were ex-members of the Independent Companies. These companies had fought the harassing action earlier in Timor, with the 2nd and 4th Independent Companies carrying out a successful guerrilla campaign long after the capture of the Australian, Dutch and Portuguese garrisons. A similarly successful series of actions were carried out by the 5th Independent Company in the Markham Valley behind Lae, where this small and well-trained unit had prevented the Japanese capturing Nadzab, a strategically important airfield and resupply point.

Apart from their military training in Australia, the 5th Independent Company had benefitted from jungle training provided by the men of ANGAU (Australian New Guinea Administrative Unit) and from extended periods of living and operating in the jungle.

After the successful American landing at Aitape on 22 April 1944, the Australian 6th Division had taken over from the US 31st and 32nd Divisions, who were redeployed on MacArthur's drive towards the Philippines. In early October 1944, the first elements of the Australian 6th Division began replacing the Americans with men of the 2/6th Cavalry Commando Regiment.

This unit had fought at Bardia and Tobruk in North Africa and later Syria, and after their return to Australia were reorganised and deployed into the Aitape-Wewak campaign. The unit quickly began offensive patrols towards Japanese positions to the east of Aitape, and were then tasked with reconnaissance in the remote and difficult Torricelli Mountains to the south. It was to these mountains that the Japanese had retreated and based themselves in the village of Maprik, where food could be secured for their starving army.

The Australian plan was to advance on Wewak along two axes. The first was the advance of the 19th Brigade of the 6th Division along the coast, while a second advance by the 2/6 Cavalry Commando Regiment, supported by units from ANGAU, was to move parallel inland and into the Torricelli Mountains towards Maprik. In support were the 17th Brigade, who would form a defensive perimeter around Aitape and the 16th Brigade in reserve. By mid-January 1945, the 19th Brigade had advanced about 45 miles (72 kilometres) along the coast to Wallum without any major contacts, and were relieved by the 16th Brigade. To the south, the 17th Brigade continued the advance through the mountains, continually rotating their frontline battalions between defence and attack. They constantly harassed the enemy who were also subjected to air attack.

As the advance continued on Wewak, GHQ wanted detailed intelligence on the defensive islands held by the Japanese just off the coast to the north, including Kairiru and Muschu. GOC 6th Division requested the insertion of an SRD party onto Muschu Island with the intention of capturing a Japanese soldier, doing a thorough reconnaissance of potential landing beaches and confirming the location and status of the two naval guns. The party of eight operatives were to be transferred by a Harbour Defence Motor Launch (HDML Fairmile) to a position off Muschu Island and from there paddle about five miles (eight kilometres) to a predetermined beach which they had surveyed from the air in the days prior. In all, the operation was to take 48 hours, after which time the HDML would return and collect the party along with their Japanese prisoner.

Of the eight men in the raiding party, seven had trained together previously. Three days before the mission, they undertook a training exercise, landing in Japanese territory at Cape Wom, on the mainland of Papua New Guinea south of Muschu. The following day, the party – minus two men whose jeep broke down on the way to the airstrip – flew an aerial reconnaissance of the island, where a beach for the landing was chosen and bearings taken.

The eight operatives in the party, codenamed Copper (originally Ash), had come through a range of civilian and military backgrounds. The leader was Lieutenant Thomas Barnes, who had joined the AIF in early November 1939. He had served with the Victorian 2/8th Battalion and seen action in Libya, Greece, Crete, Palestine and Syria. On his return to Australia, he joined SRD, was commissioned as a lieutenant and assigned to the Scorpion operation, the planned folboat attack on Rabaul harbour that had been cancelled after the success of Allied air raids on the base. He was then reassigned to the Copper operation.

The second-in-command was Lieutenant Alan Gubbay, who had grown up in Noumea, New Caledonia. He had joined the AIF and was initially posted to the 2/11 Australian Armoured Car Regiment, then to the 2/3rd Battalion before his posting to SRD. Also in the party were Sergeant Malcolm Weber, a Queenslander; Lance Corporal Spencer Walklate, a grocer and first-grade rugby league player for St George in Sydney, married with three children. The two signallers were Michael Hagger, a Victorian, and John Chandler from Western Australia. Finally there were two privates: Ronald Eagleton from Sydney, who had falsified his age to enlist at Paddington and had fought in the Markham Valley and at Shaggy Ridge, and Sapper Edgar 'Mick' Dennis.

The only member of the party who had not previously trained with the others, Dennis had been a member of the

2/5th Independent Company, had also fought in the Markham Valley campaign and was in the raid on Heath's Plantation and the successful Salamaua raid. It was here that a satchel carried by a Japanese seaplane pilot was captured which included the Japanese invasion plans for Milne Bay. He was called upon late in the planning for the mission and had set out from the SRD reception office at Brisbane's Milton Tennis Court, where he was told he was to be transported to Papua New Guinea as part of a special mission. He arrived in Port Moresby by ship and then was flown first to Lae and then by HDML to the staging area at Aitape, when he joined the rest of the party.

At dawn on 11 April 1945, the raiding party had assembled at Aitape. Dressed in jungle-green uniforms without insignia and wearing boots and beret, each man was armed with an Austen submachine gun. Along with a tin of rations which included dates, a chocolate bar and some high-energy Horlicks Malted Milk tablets, they carried a compass, maps, a watch, torch, grenades, a bush knife and flares. Each man also carried a pistol, with some carrying the SOE-developed Welrod, a silent, bolt-action weapon for subversive use. Three wireless sets were also taken, and each man carried a cyanide tablet in case of capture.

On Aitape beach, they loaded onto an Army 'Duck', a six-wheeled American-produced amphibious vehicle, which ferried them out to the waiting HDML. Departing Aitape at 1100, they headed east in calm seas for the 85-mile (135-kilometre) journey to Muschu Island at 12 knots. They arrived off Barabar Point at 1740 and slowly approached the drop-off area some three miles (4.8 kilometres) from the coast. Here, after a cup of tea and sandwiches provided by the crew, they assembled their folboats and slipped over the side, disappearing into the darkness at 2315.

The men paddled silently towards the dark shape of the island. They expected to reach it in 90 minutes, but the strong northerly current pushed them away from the shore. Battling the tide, it took them over three hours before the men heard waves breaking ahead on the shallow reef and saw the line of white water, fluorescent in the darkness. Suddenly the waves picked up the fragile craft and carried them across the shallow reef, but men on three of the folboats were unable to steer and their boats capsized, throwing the men into the water. They soon recovered most of their equipment, but everything was wet and they lost two paddles, a walkie-talkie and two Austen guns. While they were only in shallow water, the coral was very thick and high, which exhausted the men as they waded towards the shore.

Landing on the beach, they pushed through the jungle and moved a little way inland, where they stopped to rest. Here they discovered that the strong current had taken them to the wrong beach, but they were to find out that was a blessing, as the proposed landing spot was patrolled by the Japanese. Still, their equipment, including the radios, was now inoperable and saturated, as were their clothes, rations and stores.

After an uncomfortable night lying in the jungle, wet, cold and stinging from the coral cuts, the men considered their future. It was decided that they should continue with their mission. The camp was moved inland, where they covered the folboats and attempted to dry the wet radios, but without success.

Mick Dennis later recalled, 'The ammunition I had was in a pouch with 12 bullets for my revolver. I also had two body pouches with 100 rounds in each for my Austen gun. The rest of the patrol had about the same and we all had watches. We were all well trained and gave no thought of failure. We were all very confident.'[1]

Early on 12 April, the operatives moved north and reached Sup Point on the south-eastern corner of the island opposite Wewak, which they had paddled past on the previous night. Here they found unattended Japanese pillboxes with strong timber frames and crushed coral lining, sunk into the ground. The pre-prepared positions also contained well-oiled, bipod mounted machine guns, which the men disabled and, along with the ammunition, threw into the sea. These pillboxes were connected by a network of trenches, with well-constructed strong points every 50 yards, and based on the men's observations of footprints were obviously regularly maintained and patrolled. Notes were taken on the location and details of these defensive positions and the men moved silently on, crossing a well-used track and finding themselves in a local's garden, surrounded by scattered huts.

With Lieutenant Gubbay in the lead, the men passed through the deserted huts and came upon an old village. Here Gubbay observed a lone Japanese soldier, who was quickly captured, bound and gagged. While they had not yet made a reconnaissance of the naval guns, they had completed two of their tasks: the sketching of the coastal defences and the capture of a prisoner.

It was here that things began to go wrong for the operatives. In the maze of tracks, the Australians became confused and partially lost. They inadvertently passed the hidden folboats and emerged on a beach further down the coast. Realising their mistake, they began to backtrack, and as they stumbled along with the bound prisoner, their movement was slow and deliberate.

The men discovered a native hut, and they spread out and surrounded it. A Japanese soldier ran out and was silently shot with a Welrod. They found another, similar hut in which a Japanese soldier was asleep on a stretcher. He made a dash for the door, but was also shot with the Welrod and sank to the ground. Leaving the huts and the two dead Japanese, the operatives again came to the beach. Moving silently along in the thick foliage on the shoreline, they came upon another Japanese heavy machine gun, which had been mounted high on a rock to provide a good field of fire.

Suddenly, a Japanese soldier walked from behind the rock, and was captured and bound up. After dismantling the machine gun, the party now began to move off, but the prisoner refused to move. Instead he sat down and, even after he was threatened with a Welrod, remained seated in the sand, refusing to move or walk.

Mick Dennis recalled asking the group, 'What are we going to do with this bloke?' to which they replied, 'If he does not come with us, kill him.' 'I got my Welrod out and put it to the back of his head and pulled the trigger, but the blasted thing didn't work, so I cocked it again and it still didn't work. So I pulled out my .38 and put it to his head and shot him.'[2]

Dennis noted, 'I could only think that he could have a wife and child back in Japan, who would be waiting for him, and after I shot him, I searched his pockets and found a photograph of his wife and small child in his wallet. I still feel for him today.'[3]

Given their increasing contacts with roving Japanese, the party needed to return to the hidden folboats and try to make radio contact to organise their extraction. As they approached a clearing, they heard Japanese voices calling, possibly trying to find the prisoner, so they moved silently towards the sea. They were then confronted by a very steep incline, so they untied the prisoner's hands from behind his back then retied them in front to make it possible for him to climb down. But as they reached the top they again heard Japanese voices, at which point the prisoner ripped off his gag and shouted out.

Dennis recalled, 'One of the boys hit him over the head and another one pulled out his gun and shot him.'[4] The Australians, like the Japanese, bolted into the jungle. Having worked out the location of their folboats, the party moved towards the location, but found that about 12 Japanese with two machine guns had laid an ambush. The party quickly retraced their steps and moved silently inland to the camp where they had left the radios.

The situation was not looking good, as they'd stirred up the Japanese and lost their folboats to the enemy. At this point Lieutenant Barnes asked the party for suggestions, and a number of ideas were put forward and voted on. Dennis, along with the two signallers, suggested they move further inland and attempt to get the radios working, but this was rejected. Another idea was attacking the Japanese then guarding the folboats, but this was also rejected. A third suggestion was to build a raft and paddle out into the channel in the hope of contacting a passing HDML which the men knew would be searching for them. They agreed upon the third suggestion, and the party moved away from the Japanese and further up the coast.

It was now night, and their journey through the jungle was difficult. Under the moonlight, the operatives collected timber and debris from the beach and began binding together a crude raft with the use of jungle vines. Stacking their Austen guns on the rough deck, they pushed out across the coral shelf. Dennis had suggested they all sling their Austens around their neck in case the raft broke up, but his suggestion was disregarded. They waded out towards the shallow section of reef, but here the surging waves became rough, battering into the flimsy raft. It quickly broke up, and the machine guns were lost in the sea, sinking to the bottom.

Floundering and dragging themselves back to the beach through the bristling coral, the men realised they were in an even worse situation. The party had no weapons apart from Mick Dennis's Austen and the odd Welrod, no food or water, and wet radio transmitters. Again the men gathered to discuss options and vote on what to do next. Again they agreed on the need to get out into the strait and there signal the HDML that would no doubt be continuing their search.

Four men chose to go: Lieutenants Barnes and Gubbay, Lance Corporal Walklate and Private Eagleton. The idea was they would float out on logs and in the morning use the sun and mirrors, which each of them had, to heliograph a message to passing search planes. After an emotional farewell and wishes of good luck, the four men pushed their logs out into the rising surf. They weren't seen again, and their fate remained a mystery until their bodies were recovered in 2013. As Dennis subsequently discovered, 'The two officers drowned. They were found on the beach by a native, who buried them so the Japanese wouldn't get them. The two others landed and they were captured and executed.'[5]

Four men now remained: Sergeant Weber, the two signallers, Hagger and Chandler, and Sapper Dennis. The party well knew of Mick Dennis's experience fighting the Japanese around Salamaua and in the Markham Valley, and were prepared to listen to his advice. Dennis suggested they rest for the night and then in the morning return to the radios and attempt to get them operational. In the meantime, they placed their hopes on the four men clinging to logs and fighting strong currents in shark- and crocodile-infested waters, far from rescue, safety and home.

After a wet and miserable night lying on the marshy jungle floor, the party moved off on the morning of 13 April 1945 and headed for the rendezvous point at Cape Saum. There had been no news from Lieutenant Barnes and his party. When the Japanese had discovered the hidden folboats, they would have known they were dealing with eight highly trained commandoes. They would not have known that the party was down to four men, unless they had by then caught Barnes and extracted details of the party under interrogation and torture. As such, the four operatives still on Muschu were, as Dennis recalled, 'naturally nervous but not frightened; our tough training would pull us through, we thought'.[6]

To avoid Japanese patrols, the four men moved west and laid low in the thick jungle, where they attempted to rest. Late in the afternoon they backtracked to the east, arriving at Cape Saum, the designated pick-up point by the HDML Fairmile, at 2000 hours. But without a radio they could not contact the patrol craft, and as their torches were not waterproof, having been submerged when the folboats capsized on landing, they could not even flash a coded signal to the boat.

As Mick Dennis said, 'We all had torches, they were just ordinary torches bound up with tape, but they forgot about taping it over the switches, so water would go into the batteries. So not one torch worked and we couldn't signal the boat. So we all had to go bush again, and from then on we were just hunted.'[7]

Their HDML was in fact waiting for them out there in the darkness, scanning the shoreline for that blinking, all-important signal – but, for a wet and inoperable torch, recovery became impossible. This seems an extraordinary oversight that men on such a dangerous mission could be issued with torches that were not waterproof. The crew of the HDML remained at action stations, all eyes on the darkened shoreline, but nothing. At one point, a lantern-lit Japanese barge passed about 500 yards away. The Fairmile was heavily armed and could have quickly destroyed the barge, but it would have only drawn more attention from the Japanese on the now-missing Copper party.

After again spending an uncomfortable night saturated and bitten by mosquitos, the men cautiously moved towards the shoreline. Along the way, they came across a water-filled bomb crater and were able to refill their water bottles. The party decided this crater would be their rendezvous point for the future should they be separated, as, apart from the supply of drinking water, it was fairly easy to find and provided good cover. Considering their options, they decided to try to recover the concealed radio and other equipment and to meet back at the crater.

Moving slowly through the jungle, the party approached their hidden cache to find that the radios were still there, as were the codebooks, call signs and even a camera. The larger set could not be made to work as the Japanese had blocked the transmission frequency, but while the small radios were wet, the signallers believed they were still able to be dried out to become operable. This raised their spirits, so they set off for the return journey to the crater.

Mick Dennis was now in the lead, his Austen cocked and ready. Looking down, he saw fresh Japanese footprints 'in the wet ground, with the water trickling into the indenture'.[8] Turning to the others, he signalled to them his intention to move forward carefully. Suddenly a Japanese soldier opened fire, but Dennis quickly went to ground and returned fire on the Japanese. The other three Australians broke cover and raced back into the jungle.

The three unarmed Australians crashed through the undergrowth as the Japanese fired wildly after them. Dennis followed, and soon came upon the radio they had dropped in their flight, which he put a burst of bullets into to render it inoperable. He then stopped and waited. A party of four Japanese approached his position, and when one stopped ten yards from him to take up a firing position, Dennis 'lined him up and put two bullets into his chest. He did not utter a sound and fell face down in the bush on top of his gun.'[9] Another Japanese soldier appeared and he too was shot at close range by a burst from Dennis's Austen.

Mick Dennis now began to move in the direction of the crater when he saw more Japanese. He recalled:

> I had moved about 100 yards when I saw three people walking across, one holding the other one up, they're all limping so I must have hit one or two of them. So I opened up and I killed them. I then headed down the track and saw a Jap with a rifle. He was 15 foot from me. He fired and missed me, and I fired and hit him twice in the chest and killed him, and then I had to go for my life.[10]

Dennis quickly changed direction, making a line for the crater, where he expected to find his three operative mates. But he only saw evidence of Japanese footprints and, on testing the water, found that it had been poisoned. He moved away cautiously and crossed a local's garden. As he crept close to a hut, a Japanese soldier suddenly came around the corner, just two yards away. Dennis recalled, 'He was as surprised as me and fired at me, but in his panic his rifle was pointed skywards. I fired almost at the same time and hit him in the chest, and he fell backwards without a sound.'[11]

Fearing pursuit, Dennis returned along the track then dived into the jungle, where he stayed hidden, ready to deal with any pursuers. As none came he returned to the garden, hoping to find something edible as it had been four days since he had enjoyed the sandwiches and cup of tea on the Fairmile. As it started to become dark, he heard more Japanese voices so dropped into the jungle beside the track and waited. It was not long before four Japanese came sneaking along the track towards his hideout.

> They were talking in low voices and were close together. The first one came to the corner and would have seen me as I could not

find decent cover. I had no option but to shoot him, so I shot him twice and fired about six shots into the remainder, and heard a groan and a yelp of pain. I then took to my heels and dived around the next corner, and made good time along the track for a couple of hundred yards then went into the bush for a while until I was just about done.[12]

It was now Sunday 15 April. Again he returned to the crater in the hope of finding his mates, but again without luck. At this point, he crept out of the jungle and into a patch of kunai grass, but suddenly saw a line of 20 Japanese approaching, their bayonets glinting on their rifles. As Dennis crouched behind the fronds of a low, ground-hugging palm tree, he saw the last Japanese man at the end of the extended line pass to the other side of the palm tree and probe it with his bayonet. Dennis moved away silently. He later wrote, 'This Japanese soldier seemed to look right at me, but obviously did not see me and kept going. This was not training but plain luck for me.'[13]

The lack of food and sleep were seriously affecting Dennis's health and strength. As it was expected to be an overnight operation, he'd only been given the one 24-hour ration of the dates, chocolate and Horlicks malted milk tablets. To conserve his strength as he pushed through the jungle, he walked along tracks, searching ahead for Japanese footprints and listening actively for the sound of their voices. He believed he was fortunate, as on so many occasions their careless chatter warned him of their approach. He then climbed a hill and hid in the jungle there, trying to sleep in the rain while he was continually bitten by mosquitos that swarmed about him in droves.

As the next day dawned, Dennis realised that any chance of rescuing his mates had passed, and that he needed to look to his own plan of escape and safety. He knew his training, fitness and luck had kept him alive. As he recalled, 'When I [had run] into the Japanese [the previous day], they were shooting at me and missing, and I was returning fire and not missing. They were still reluctant to follow me into the jungle after any engagement, so I still had a chance if I did not panic and my luck held out.'[14]

Dennis continued heading west and, after climbing a high hill, he could see the Papua New Guinea coast a couple of miles away. At one point he found a small, uninhabited hut with a few beds, but did not dally. He was now close to the sea in what was the Japanese defensive zone. Here he found a heavy Japanese machine gun on a tripod. With some difficulty and a great deal of effort, he was able to push the gun over a nearby cliff and watched it smash among the rocks below with a loud crash.

He moved on, and not long after, as he stooped to check he was not leaving any footprints, he glanced sideways and saw, just across a narrow creek, a Japanese officer in full uniform cleaning his teeth. Again Dennis's luck held, but his strength was now limiting his movements and concentration. Continuing to move west, he came across a dirt road and could hear the sounds of engines, perhaps trucks or barges.

He passed through a village and came upon an amazing sight: a large pig being slowly roasted on a spit under the watchful eye of another Japanese officer, other soldiers and what appeared to be friendly locals. As Dennis recalled, 'I would have loved to have some of that pig. I thought of shooting the lot of them for that pig.'[15]

Skirting the village, he climbed another hill and saw a series of villages, where he hoped to be able to check for his mates. He moved back to the beach, and was moving a little inland when he heard Japanese voices, then a large group of Japanese soldiers heading to the beach for a swim. Dennis watched from a secure hiding place as the Japanese, on the sound of a whistle, moved away, returning along the track. Too tired to move, he lay down and rested until dawn.

The following day, he rose early and, realising he could not continue on the island, looked for a suitable log or plank he could use to head out to sea. He found a heavy hatch cover from a ship and hid this close to the beach, ready for a night escape. But the Japanese returned early that morning to swim, fish and 'skylark' around on the beach, not 20 yards from his hiding place. He was down to two Horlicks tablets a day and now had just one day's supply left, 'but the expectation of leaving the island gave me more nervous energy'.[16]

At 4 pm, a whistle blew and the Japanese promptly formed up and moved off the beach, heading back down the track to their billets. Dennis scanned the beach carefully, concerned that a Japanese sentry might have been left, but the coast was clear. Quickly he returned to his hidden hatch cover, only to find it gone. But when he explored the wrecks of four Japanese barges at the end of the beach, he found the hatch cover, which had been used by the Japanese as a gangplank. He silently dragged it across the deck and dropped it into the water. Then, stripping off his trousers and tying his Austen gun, boots and ammunition down the legs of his pants and securing them with vines, Dennis pushed out into the muddy, dark sea, the tropical moon above casting a silver glow across the water.

He had not been in the sea long when something large and ominous came close by him and circled. As he recalled, he thought, '"Oh Christ, it could be a shark." To come this far and now to lose an arm or a leg. It would mean death – I became very fright-ened.'[17] He tried to put his limbs up onto the hatch and remained still, and it was some time before he again attempted to set out for the mainland coast.

Sapper Dennis now despaired of his chances of survival. He had seen numerous sharks from the deck of the HDML Fairmile and realised the sea around him would have been swarming with both sharks and crocodiles. Fighting sleep, he thought of his mother in Sydney and his sister Clare, who had won a swimming gold medal for Australia in the Los Angeles Olympic Games in 1932. During the night, the sea was lashed by rain squalls, but they settled down and he slowly paddled on. His fear was that the strong currents would take him back to Muschu and around the eastern point then on to Kairiru Island, also held by the Japanese.

Just before dawn, after having survived on his heavy hatch cover in a dangerous sea, the tide carried Dennis to a beach near Cape Pus on the Papua New Guinea mainland, but he was still behind the Japanese lines and far from safety and Australian care. He looked up and could see above him the barrel of a large Japanese gun, but it appeared unmanned. Collecting his bundle of clothes, his webbing and his weapon, he dragged his exhausted body up the beach, hardly able to stand. As he said, 'I scooted up into the jungle and got dressed there properly.'[18]

It took Dennis 15 minutes of rubbing his legs to induce circulation before he could dress himself and move off, bidding his hatch cover a farewell thank you. Heading away from the beach, he came upon a road, but soon heard the sound of an approaching truck. He dived into the bushes and watched as the crew of the artillery piece went past on the way to their gun. Had he been an hour later landing on the beach, he would have no doubt fallen into their hands. Unlike the Australians, the Japanese returned to their billets at night, so again he had been fortunate that the gun position was unmanned.

Soon after, he saw a low-flying Australian reconnaissance aircraft and waved, but was not seen. He then moved back into the bush, but on hearing the sound of chopping and Japanese voices, he crept into deeper cover and skirted the work party. Japanese soldiers seemed to be everywhere, with footprints clearly visible on paths, and parked trucks and a steady stream of vehicle traffic on the roads.

Dennis moved into precipitous, hilly country, and was traversing a narrow track with a steep drop on either side when two Japanese soldiers appeared in front of him. In his panic, one of them swung around, knocking the other off his feet, who then fell screaming down into a ravine. The second Jap turned and fled, a very lucky escape for Dennis as his weapon had misfired.

Travelling on, he came upon another Japanese camp, where, fortunately for him, they were making a great deal of noise. He skirted the camp undetected and, realising the number of Japanese in this area, turned south and headed for the higher ground where he could get his bearings and hopefully avoid further contact. Hearing distant artillery fire, he took a compass reading and was trying to ascertain his position when a Japanese soldier suddenly appeared on his left and yelled out. Three more appeared, one crouching and taking aim with his rifle. Dennis quickly fired and the man went down. The others ran, but one fell and the Japanese tried to find shelter behind the corner of a hut. Dennis too turned and ran, downhill and away from the area. He rested in a creek bed and recovered his breath, knowing his fitness and training were paying off.

Believing the Australian 6th Division were advancing from Aitape, he continued moving west, on occasion avoiding Japanese patrols who passed within a few yards of him by the track. He came across a Japanese defensive trench system, where again he could hear their voices and spent a tense hour slowly and cautiously moving through the area. He swallowed one of the last two Horlicks tablets, had a drink and lay down for a restless night in torrential rain. As for the mosquitos, 'brushing them away was like pushing through water, they were so thick'.[19]

The following morning, Thursday 19 April, Dennis cleaned his Austen gun and set off west. Soon he heard Japanese voices and again, hiding by the track, watched a well-armed group pass close by his hiding place. He moved into a patch of kunai grass and was confronted by a Japanese patrol, immediately opening fire on them and killing one soldier, who fell with two bullets in the stomach. As Dennis raced into the high kunai grass, Japanese bullets were zipping past him, some very close. Checking his Austen, he saw some branches move and a Japanese soldier appeared. He recalled, 'I let go three shots, heard him give a bit of a groan and he fell. I turned and jumped over the side of a hill and went pell-mell down the mountainside.'[20]

Dennis was now in a very poor state, exhausted, hungry and covered in blood from the scratches and cuts he had received from the trees and vines. As he wrote later, 'I could not have looked a pretty sight as my hair was very long, tangled all over my face. I had a fourteen-day beard, no hat, torn shirt and the knees out of my pants.'[21]

But he could not stop and rest. Moving down a steep hill, he fell and slid some distance before his foot caught in a root, and he found himself hanging upside down. His movements dislodged small rocks around him, which cascaded down the hillside and landed on the roof of a hut just ten feet below him.

Fortunately it was by now getting dark, but when he looked more closely, he saw he was hanging above what appeared to be a Japanese mess hut. He had no strength to extricate himself and each time he tried to move he dislodged more stones which fell onto the thatched roof below. As he hung there, he counted over 20 Japanese enter the hut, so he remained still, hanging painfully by his foot, for more than an hour. Once the enemy soldiers all left, he was able to free his foot and move slowly away.

The moon was up so Dennis decided to continue his journey west, realising that the forward Australian lines could not be too far. He rested for short intervals and at dawn came across a wide road. While attempting to cross he was seen by what appeared to be locals in Japanese uniforms, but he again bolted into the bush and they did not give chase. Soon after, he came upon a small Japanese post with two soldiers by a hut. Figuring there would be food, he shot one and chased the other off. He did not find food in the hut, but was able to secure a Japanese overcoat, which was ideal for the cold, wet nights.

It was now Saturday 21 April, ten days since his insertion from the HDML. After cleaning his weapon and taking a drink of water, Dennis continued westwards. At one point he could see the sea and the islands and reckoned he was near Dagua, where he believed the Australian frontline was last reported to be. Following a disused track, he came upon a telephone line and just off the track heard locals' voices. He dived into the kunai and waited, fearing another Japanese patrol would come upon him. There were more voices, and he cocked his Austen as he waited. A line of locals appeared carrying water, and in the middle of them was 'a soldier walking away from me, wearing a felt slouch hat, green clothes, a cross webbing strap on his back and an Aussie rifle'.[22]

Dennis called out, 'Ahoy the patrol,' but there was no reply as this was a well-known Japanese trick. Again he called out and this time a reply came.

'Who are you?'

'Sapper Dennis from Z Special Unit. Who are you?'

'I'm Sergeant Osborne of the 2/7th Commandos.'

Slowly rising from his position, holding his Austen above his head, Dennis called out, 'Is that you, Fatty?'

'Yes,' said Osborne, surprised. Osborne had fought near Wau with Mick Dennis in the 2/5th.[23] Dennis slowly walked in, still carrying his Austen, with just two clips of bullets left, his damaged compass, water bottle, a notebook, aerial photographs and the cyanide tablet he did not get around to taking. As Dennis said, 'From then on, things looked pretty good.'[24]

The Australians came to Dennis's assistance, carrying him back to camp, where he was given a cup of tea and some bread and jam. He asked that they contact the Australian Intelligence Headquarters in Aitape as his patrol intelligence would be of great benefit. He was taken to Dagua, where he was allowed to get himself tidied up. He wrote, 'I'd showered, shaved and put on clean clothes. I felt wonderful. I can still remember that feeling today.'[25]

Mick Dennis had stumbled into the forward Australian lines and found himself among old mates, many of whom he knew from fighting with the Independent Companies. He had been on this dangerous and intense patrol for ten frightening days, many of those alone and living off his wits and his luck. Arriving in Lae, he was informed that General Sturdee, commander of Australian troops in Papua New Guinea, had recommended him for the Military Medal.

In the days and weeks after, Dennis met Lieutenant General Jack Stevens, the Commanding Officer of the Australian 6th Division, and the SRD officer, Naval Commander McManus. He was debriefed by Australian Intelligence, who were pleased with his detailed information that had been supported by accurate compass bearings. As a result of his intelligence, GHQ cancelled plans for landings on Muschu Island.

Having lost ten kilos in weight, Dennis was well fed, enjoying steak, chips, eggs and tomatoes, and had his injuries tended to. But even long after the war his mind was never far from his lost mates, and the joy of his return to Australia was tempered by their tragic loss. To honour a commitment the men had made before they left, he visited a number of families, including the wife of the leader, Lieutenant Barnes, who had only been married three weeks before his departure.

An official investigation on Operation Copper was written in 1945 by Major R. A. C. Cardew, which drew heavily on two notebooks provided by Mick Dennis, written after his return. Cardew's report was later criticised, as it is believed the information given by two senior Japanese officers, Captains Temura and Tomei, and accepted by Cardew were false and avoided the fact that the Australian operatives were executed, some even burned, to cover up their torture and mutilation. These two officers lied and were directly complicit in the execution of the Australians, who they claimed died of sickness, and hence escaped prosecution as war criminals. More recently, the graves of all the seven Australians lost in the operation have been recovered, and their bodies now lie in either Bomana or the Lae Commonwealth War Graves Cemetery.

Mick Dennis passed away in Maroubra, a Sydney beachside suburb, on 10 November 2015.

TEN

The Bite of the Sand-fly –
the Agas Operations

On 19 December 1941, less than two weeks after the bombing of
Pearl Harbor and the landings in Thailand and northern Malaya,
the Japanese landed at Miri, Sarawak, in northern Borneo. They
quickly secured Miri and nearby Seria, Brunei Town and the
northern oilfields before advancing south towards Kuching. Here
they were confronted by 15th Punjab Regiment of the British
Indian Army, who put up a spirited resistance but were driven
up the Santubong River into the interior of the island, allowing
the Japanese to secure the Kuching airfield. On 3 January, the
Japanese landed on Labuan Island off the north of Borneo, and
on 18 January at nearby Sandakan, which was at the time the
British seat of government for British North Borneo. The British
governor, Charles Robert Smith, surrendered the following day,
and he and his staff went into captivity for the duration of the
war. By 1 April 1942, all Allied resistance on Borneo had ceased.

At this time the island of Borneo was divided into five separate
territories, four under British administration and the fifth under
the Dutch. The British dependencies included Sarawak, Brunei,
British North Borneo and the small island of Labuan. But the
largest part of the island was under Dutch administration and was
known as the Dutch East Indies. Both nations had been seeking

control over these valuable trading islands, with the Dutch arriving in 1815 and a series of British incursions and acquisitions from the 1840s.

From April 1942 the Japanese quickly took control in the area, introducing the idea that all Asian people should rise up against European and Western influence, ridding themselves of the colonial yoke and becoming independent under the new East Asia Japanese Empire. This concept had been developed by the Japanese Minister for Foreign Affairs, General Hachiro Arita, from 1936, and Borneo was one of a string of countries, along with Indochina, Malaya, Sumatra, Java and the Celebes, which would form this new protectorate. Japan needed the resources of these areas, in particular the oil, resulting in Borneo becoming a prime, early target.

Under the Anglo-Japanese Alliance of 1902, Japanese companies like Nissan and Mitsubishi, as well as Japanese citizens, had been encouraged to live and trade within British North Borneo. Many Japanese immigrants arrived during the First World War and were to become agents for the Japanese Government from the early 1930s, undertaking espionage as well as providing intelligence to visiting Japanese merchant ships on British intentions, exports and military preparations.

As was the case in northern Papua New Guinea, the Allies had no forces on the ground nor intelligence sources from local anti-Japanese elements. In 1942, SRD was the only Allied formation able to operate in this area, as it counted among its operatives a number of expats who had lived and operated businesses in Borneo before the war. SRD also benefitted from previous operational experience in a range of other theatres where failures, having been analysed, were not repeated. Also, equipment, training and tactics had been developed and operational knowledge collated and

The *Krait* at anchor in Refuge Bay before the Jaywick mission to Singapore.

Above: Two operatives paddling a folboat off the secret training camp at Refuge Bay in the Hawkesbury River with the *Krait* in the background.

Right: A painting by Dennis Adams of two operatives in a folboat in Singapore Harbour on Operation Jaywick.
(AWM ART 28537)

Left: Group portrait after the completion of Operation Jaywick, showing the personnel who carried out the operation. Back row, left to right: Berryman, Marsh, Jones, Huston. Centre row: Crilly, Cain, McDowell, Young, Falls, Morris. Front row: Carse, Davidson, Lyon, Campbell (did not accompany the expedition), Page.

Major Ivan Lyon, commander of both Jaywick and Rimau operations. He was killed in a firefight south of Singapore on 16 October 1944.

Group portrait of Operation Python survivors aboard USS *Harder*. Back row, left to right: Cottee, Olson, Dodds, Neil. Front row: Jinkins, Chew, Chester, Woods. (AWM P11933.001)

Aitape, Papua New Guinea, 24 October 1943. A photograph found on the body of a dead Japanese soldier, showing Sergeant Leonard Siffleet of M Special Unit, wearing a blindfold and with his arms tied, about to be beheaded with a sword by Yasuno Chikao. (AWM 101099)

Catalina resupply, Papua New Guinea.

Two-man folboat with outboard motor.
Note the canvas splash cover.

Backpack radio as used by
Z Special Unit.

Two-man folboat with outboard motor and operational load.

The junk *Mustika* taken from the submarine *Porpoise* on the way to Singapore, as part of Operation Rimau.

A Motorised Submersible Boat (MSB) during trials in Britain.

A B-24 Consolidated Liberator as used by No. 200 Flight RAAF.

The British 98 cc Welbike designed for SOE and provided to SRD for operations north of Australia.

Operatives in lap-laps in their secret jungle camp in Borneo.

Lieutenant Colonel 'Gort' Chester and guerrillas in Borneo.

Training Dyak guerrillas in Borneo, 1945.

The local tribes in Borneo were proficient, and deadly, with blowpipes.

Australians training local guerrillas, Borneo.

Captain 'Jock' McLaren MC and Bar.

Major Gordon 'Toby' Carter, leader of the Semut II party, and a local Borneo chief. (AWM P01806.010)

Sapper 'Mick' Dennis, far right, and four members of the crew of Motor Launch (ML) 1321 in Brisbane after the failed Copper operation on Muschu Island. (AWM P03953.004)

Motor Launch (ML) 1321 at anchor after the ill-fated raid on Muschu Island, off the coast of Papua New Guinea, on 11 April 1945. (AWM P03953.007)

Corporal Roland Griffiths-Marsh MM.
(AWM P01204.004)

Major Rex Blow DSO.
(AWM 072918)

distributed to the benefit of future SRD operations. Given this experience, GHQ instructed SRD to operate independent of the AIF, and later involved SRD in operations that supported the AIF directly or indirectly.

Prior to the Australian operations, the Japanese had slowly and deliberately imposed restrictions, curfews and labour demands upon the people. They had exploited the natural resources, especially oil, and Borneo had become a major supplier of oil and lubricants to the Japanese war effort. Over the following two years, from October 1943 through to the Japanese surrender in August 1945, SRD conducted a number of operations in Borneo under the codenames Agas (I–V), Semet (I–IV), Squirrel, Stallion (I–VIII) and Platypus (I–XII) in support of AIF operations.

From the beginning, the Japanese subjected the local people to heavy influence through education, the singing of the Japanese national anthem, currency and a range of measures to ensure the population would embrace the invaders and think and act like them. The Chinese residents were most harshly dealt with, as the Japanese believed it would be from this section of the population that resistance would be organised. In fact, one of the most successful resistance movements, known as the Kinabalu Guerrillas, came under the leadership of Albert Kwok, a young Chinese doctor born in Kuching, Sarawak, in 1921.

To counteract this Japanese policy, SRD planned the insertion of a party to 'contact natives and secure intel regarding enemy movements, installations and to prepare the ground for a campaign of sabotage and underground resistance when the time became opportune'.[1] This operation was codenamed Python. The leader of the party was Major F. G. L. 'Gort' Chester, a resident of British North Borneo for 20 years prior to the war and a member of the British Army, as was his second-in-command,

Captain E. O'Keefe. Together they would draw up a plan and select and train personnel for the first of a series of operations in this important area. One of his operatives, New Zealander Graham Greenwood, remembered of Chester, 'He was as rough as sacks, his language was disgusting and we got on well. He was a magnificent leader, he treated us well. He'd talk to you, ask your opinion, none of this "sir" business, I couldn't have had a better leader.'[2]

This plan, along with the provision of a submarine to transfer the party to the landing point, was agreed to by GHQ. But Chester did not trust the security of his party and so, after an aerial reconnaissance of the coast, decided to choose his own landing spot and not tell HQ. As Greenwood later said, 'It sure saved us as we never had any Japanese anywhere around where we landed. He [Chester] had worked all his life in Borneo in a timber company and got on well with the natives, and spoke Malay like the local people.'[3]

In August 1943, these two officers plus Lieutenant L. J. Woods and two AIF sergeants, L. L. Cottee and L. L. Olsen, began training in Brisbane before being transferred to Western Australia for embarkation on a US submarine. On 24 September the party departed and, after an uneventful voyage, arrived in the vicinity of Labuan Point with 3500 pounds of stores for four months, given the extended operational tasks to be undertaken. The stores were safely brought ashore, but while the party waited for the submarine to depart, a drama unfolded before them. As Sergeant Lindsay Cottee remembers:

While we were waiting, a big tanker comes around the point followed by a destroyer and we knew the submarine was out there and we hadn't signalled them that night. The next thing we heard was an explosion. The tanker got one in the stern. The tanker stopped the engines and was drifting. The destroyer stayed still and started sending ASDIC [Allied Submarine Detection Investigation Committee – an underwater sonar system to detect submerged submarines]. It was after about 15 to 20 minutes and they started depth-charging and they did this for about an hour, all over the place. We were wondering what happened.[4]

The party then moved inland, and it took them three or four days to find a suitable position for the base and the radio. Cottee recalled, 'We found a place on a ridge and cleared the smaller trees. Made contact with Darwin and they came back immediately, and from then on we were in perfect communication with Darwin.'[5]

Once a base was set up, Major Chester contacted an American party on Tawi Tawi – about 450 miles (720 kilometres) by sea from Labuan, but only about 130 miles (210 kilometres) southeast of Sandakan – to help out with the provision of boats to allow Python to carry out a reconnaissance of Sitangkay Island, with the assistance of two members of their party, Captain Hamner and Lieutenant Valera. Valera was a former British North Borneo forestry officer who, after the Japanese invasion, had made visits to the islands and mainland ports to recruit people for an intelligence network. To help undertake this, Chester suggested that Lieutenant Colonel Alejandro Suarez, the commander of US partisans on Tawi Tawi, be appointed to liaise with Python for the collection of intelligence and for the transmission of this information to Australia.

On one occasion, Lindsay Cottee said he and Gort Chester were travelling between islands on a reconnaissance mission in a native prahu vessel, at which point he recalled the following:

We had a couple of natives with us and were coming back, and a Jap convoy was coming past and we were caught in it. We could see the Japanese, and Gort and I got under the floorboards of this boat among the stinking fish. They didn't challenge us, the natives waved to them and aircraft went over and had a good look, and we just sailed through. That was a horrible occasion too.[6]

The Japanese were conducting terror raids on villages by bombing and machine-gunning the natives, which helped to rally support for the Allies among the locals, as well as recruiting some of them. As a result, Suarez and Valera were able to establish an intelligence-gathering network stretching from Tarakan in the south to Sandakan in the north, as well as many of the islands in the area. They also met with representatives of Albert Kwok's guerrilla movement to involve them in intelligence-gathering and to see what assistance the Allies could provide with respect to arms, medical supplies and food.

The initial success of the Python party with the establishment of a radio link and the provisioning of supplies to the guerrillas, saw them further reinforced with the landing of Major Bill Jinkins and five men, all AIF, from a US submarine on 20 January 1944. While they landed with 5000 pounds of stores, they left behind the supplies promised to Kwok due to unavailable storage space in the submarine. However, it was learnt that, after a second attack on the town of Jesselton in northern Borneo, Kwok and most of his men had surrendered to prevent the massacre of civilians and were subsequently executed by the Japanese.

The Japanese now knew of the existence of an Allied party, and began landing troops in the operational area of Python in mid-February. A second party of Japanese, numbering 60 men, landed just 400 yards from one of Python's coastwatching posts, which forced a hasty retreat into the jungle. Given this increased pressure, the decision was made in Australia to evacuate the Python party by first moving them to the west coast. The initial stage of this evacuation required the assistance of Lieutenant Kwok's second-in-command, Lim Keng Fatt, but the boat to be used was intercepted by the Japanese and Fatt was killed. It was then decided to deliver the stores for Kwok's guerrillas and extract three officers – Captain O'Keefe, who was sick, Captain Broadhurst and Major Jinkins – and return them to Australia. After a confused and tense period in which the stores were being unloaded, the US submarine was approached by a Japanese destroyer. The submarine quickly took on the three officers and Lieutenant Valera, who was supervising the unloading, and made their escape.

The Japanese increased their patrolling, forcing the remainder of the Python party to stay on the run. As Lindsay Cottee related:

First a reconnaissance plane went above the beach, and I was up a tree on a small platform and I stayed very still. Then I saw the Japs land. I went down the tree quickly and I radioed the camp that the Japs had landed and they were getting close to us. We were told to meet at a certain rendezvous and two of the new fellas were told to go halfway back to the radio station and guard the track. In the meantime, they dismantled the main radio station and covered everything up, and they were to meet us at the other spot. The two guarding the track [Lieutenant Rudwick and Sergeant McKenzie] were caught by the Japanese and later executed.[7]

The Japanese landed 12 patrols in two days, during which they had found supply dumps and captured Lieutenant A. J. Rudwick and Sergeant D. G. McKenzie. The Japanese then deployed

500 troops and had 20 launches over a three-month period as they searched the coast for the party.

It was decided by SRD HQ to extract Python by submarine, and the operatives nominated a location. The first attempt failed as the operatives had no boat and the submarine left without sending one in to collect them. Then another attempt was made, as told by Lindsay Cottee:

> We organised a new pick-up and were standing in the water with our boots around our necks. We saw then the Japs, who challenged us. We all went down and the one in the front raced into the jungle. By then the Japs were shooting at us [and] I had a radio on my back, so I turned it to the direction the bullets were coming from. The sand was spitting up all around us, but we got to the jungle okay without being shot. We'd been carrying a chook with us and it would lay an egg, so we all took it in turns to have an egg. We still had this chook with us – we carried it in our shirts. Fred Olsen fired on the Japs with his Austen and ran into the jungle with Stan Neil, and it took Fred and Stan four days before they found their way back to the camp.[8]

A third pick-up was arranged, and this time a party from the submarine came into the shore. Cottee recalled

> They were almost to the beach when the Japs started firing. They must have spotted the signals and here we were on the edge of the jungle with the Japs just a bit further along the coast. The Americans had Thompson submachine guns and they fixed these Japs in no time.[9]

Again the Americans left without the operatives, but after this third failure the Americans were not keen on risking their submarines to pick up Allied operatives, and it took some talking by Major Jinkins to the American top brass in Fremantle to secure their involvement again.

By now it was early June and the Python party were weak and had little food.

> We were thinking we were not going to get rescued and things were getting grim. We were short of water as we were sitting in a mangrove swamp and we were eating dried food, which was swelling up in our stomachs. We were in our hammocks, but two stayed out and they got a signal and they said 'come on'. After Bill Jinkins had called out and identified his ex-batman [Warrant Officer 2 Alexander Chew, a labourer from Bendigo who was later awarded an MBE], we had about 300 yards to get to the shore. But it was thick mud, up to our knees, [and] we had seen how the crocodiles slid so we stripped off all our clothes and slid through the mud. Fred Olsen, who was weak with malaria, got stuck halfway, so Bill Dodds went in and dragged him out. So when we all got into the folboats, they had very little freeboard [and] we had to keep still. They had a silent outboard motor, but there were four on each of two folboats. One of the outboards wouldn't start as the petrol had leaked out, so the other one took us in tow. But it took us two hours to get out to the submarine, and they pulled us on board and gave us a shower. We got into the officers' mess and sat down to our first meal, steak and eggs and ice cream.[10]

And so Python were finally extracted on 8 June 1944, including Major Chester and five other men. As a result of the Python operation, an intelligence network was set up and a coast-watching operation established, which reported 88 Japanese shipping movements and other valuable intelligence.

But for the Python party, the danger had not yet passed. Cottee related:

> The following morning, we were on the surface charging the batteries when out of the sun comes a Japanese bomber who saw us. The submarine submerged straightaway and the plane dropped a couple of bombs near us and missed. Then a couple of days later, up near the Philippines, we came across part of a Japanese fleet at anchor. Then the captain said, 'They've spotted us and there are two destroyers heading our way, and I'm going to give them three torpedoes as they are coming towards us.' He collected the two destroyers and the nearest one to us more or less came over the top of us and blew up just as it went over us. It shook the submarine around like a depth charge.
>
> The submarine was getting away as there were more destroyers after the first two of them. I heard the pinging coming and they start depth-charging us, and they did it for four hours. These submarines were not to go deeper than 300 feet but we went to 400 feet on this occasion to try to get away from these depth charges, and you could hear the pressure on the hull and the crunching of the steel. Then he went up to a warm water layer, which deflected the ASDIC, so we waited there. I didn't feel fear, I accepted fear. I thought, *If this thing goes, we'll go with it.* After that, we headed for Darwin. We had an easy cruise back to Darwin, but I was glad to get off the submarine.[11]

The Python success led to the insertion of a larger party, known as Agas I. This operation was tasked with the establishment of an intelligence network to operate along the north-east coast of British North Borneo, the 'organisation of guerrilla forces and subsequent harassing of enemy forces with particular attention to coastwise and inland Jap L of C's [lines of communication] from Sandakan to the north and west coast' and 'obtaining information on the location and condition of allied PWs [prisoners of war] in the Sandakan area'.[12]

The initial Agas I party was led by Major Gort Chester, with Captain D. S. Sutcliffe and two Lieutenants, D. K. L. Harlem and F. G. Olsen, plus three other ranks. They departed Darwin on the US submarine USS *Tuna* on 24 February 1945 and were dropped six miles (10 kilometres) off the coast on the night of 3 March. After quickly disembarking, 'the submarine went off at full speed',[13] and the party paddled to shore in an inflatable rubber boat, towing two folboats loaded with supplies. After successfully landing at the correct location, they travelled inland for two miles (3.2 kilometres), where they set up their base on an island in the river which provided a good level of security, being surrounded by mangroves and nipa palms, a salt-tolerant type of palm common in the region.

The following morning, radio contact was established and the base laid out. In the weeks following, parties began folboat sorties along the coast, and on 1 April established contact with the village of Jembongham, which they found to be strongly anti-Japanese. This village was a collection point for refugees, and as such proved suitable for the establishment of a semi-permanent headquarters and a place to begin the recruitment and training of a guerrilla force.

The new operational orders from SRD were 'to strike vigorously at the enemy, inflicting as much damage and casualties as possible'.[14] At this time, GHQ decided to establish a second operational base at Sungei Sungei on the Sugut River, in the far north of Borneo, and this move took place on 29 May with two separate parties, one led by Major Chester and the other by

Lieutenant Harlem. While Chester reached the river without incident, Harlem ran into a Japanese patrol guarding a large stores dump. The Japanese fled, so Harlem destroyed the dump and continued to the rendezvous. Apart from a base camp, a drop zone was also prepared there, which now placed the two parties astride the main Japanese line of communication and ready to undertake offensive operations.

By early May, 150 locals were ready to begin training. It was generally found that they were keen to help the Allies as everywhere the Japanese had mistreated them, stealing food, forcing the men into labour and raping women. The health of the locals was also very poor, with malaria, TB and jungle sores needing attention. To build the support and trust of locals, two small hospitals were set up, and medical supplies and stores provided with airdrops from Australia.

The first Agas I action was an attack on the village of Aling, where 30 Japanese troops were reported to be stationed. After a recce of the area, Captain Sutcliffe and Lieutenant Harlem led 23 guerrillas into an attack on the village using three Bren guns for covering fire. The Japanese quickly responded with light machine guns and mortars, but after a firefight of nearly four hours, the village was captured, with 11 Japanese killed for the loss of one guerrilla.

However, Sutcliffe reported his reservations about the use of locals in actions: 'Guerrillas recruited in this area showed little inclination to fight when contact was made with the enemy. Desertion caused considerable delay in carrying out our plans. Four Bren guns and 20 rifles had to be destroyed after mass desertion following the action at Aling on 8 June. Estimated Jap casualties caused by our agents was estimated at approx. 50.'[15]

A report was received that 100 heavily armed Japanese troops were now searching for the Agas I party. This forced them to go off the air and undertake a hurried retreat inland. On 10 June, guards reported an unidentified prahu had anchored 200 yards off the beach a mile south-west of Jembongham Island and had ignored the challenge to identify itself. The following morning, eight Japanese were seen on board and the prahu was racked by Bren gunfire. The Japanese jumped over the side and started to swim, dragging the craft behind them, but when two boats of locals set out from the shore in pursuit, the Japanese climbed back on board and engaged them. The battle lasted for three hours, after which all the Japanese had been killed and the damaged prahu towed into shore.

While the training of local troops continued, four reinforcements were inserted on 21 June and joined two new operational sections in a new base camp. About this time, an Australian prisoner of war, Gunner Colin Campbell, was found in a very weak condition and evacuated to Tawi Tawi by flying boat. Campbell had been one of a party of five Australians who had escaped on 7 June after an Allied plane, flying overhead, had scattered the guards. During the following month, the other four Australians were to die, two from disease and exhaustion and two from being shot by the Japanese. Campbell, delirious, emaciated, starving and covered in sores, had finally been found by friendly locals and, after a time in hiding, handed over to Lieutenant Jock Hollingworth, one of the recent reinforcements.

The Agas I party split into two separate parties, one under Lieutenant Harlem and the other under Captain Sutcliffe. Harlem was planning a series of three or four quick actions and, with the help of Hollingworth, had prepared an escape route. However, a runner arrived to inform Harlem that a large prahu containing 60 Japanese troops was proceeding to Basai to attack him, so he passed this information to the RAAF at Morotai, which was the operational headquarters for SRD at this time. Immediately an air strike was arranged and the prahu and 16 enemy boats were destroyed, with 50 Japanese killed by gunfire or drowned.

As the Japanese surrendered in August, further actions planned by Harlem's and Sutcliffe's parties were cancelled. But the surrender did not neutralise Japanese activity, and one Australian party under Warrant Officer Thompson was fired on, but they were able to withdraw without casualties. Similarly, as Harlem was returning to base, he was informed by Kulang, a local leader, that the wife of a trader had informed him the Japanese had prepared an ambush, based on information supplied by her husband. This timely warning allowed Harlem's party to avoid the ambush site but the husband, a Filipino named Periong, and a Chinese man named Pang Fook, were hunted down and killed by Kulang and a party of five locals. By 24 August, all three Agas I parties had arrived safely at Bongaya, from where they were extracted, except for Lieutenant Harlem and some other Australians and local troops.

On 20 September, nearly six weeks after the end of the war, Harlem, with two other Australians and some guerrillas, guides and carriers, led a ten-day patrol which covered 180 miles (290 kilometres) into previously Japanese-occupied areas. This patrol reported Japanese movements and observed many armed Japanese parties still unaware the war had ended. They also found destroyed Japanese camps and stores dumps, mass gravesites, evidence of widespread Japanese death through sickness and starvation, and photographic evidence of the treatment of Australian POWs. As well, they found evidence of the massacre of 75 Australians by the Japanese in June 1945, just a month before the end of the war, and that some of these men had been cannibalised. At Boto they were informed the Japanese commander had stated the war was over, while in other places, 'the Japanese were quiet and were posting notices to the natives proclaiming the finish of the war'.[16]

While Agas I was continuing its work, a second SRD party, codenamed Agas II, was inserted by parachute from a B24 of 200 Flight RAAF on 3 May 1945. The party was led by Major R. G. Combe and Captain W. K. S. May, both British Army, along with three AIF sergeants, and was then reinforced by Australian SRD personnel in late May and early June.

Their task was much like that of Agas I: establish a base on the west coast of British North Borneo, establish an efficient intelligence network, secure friendly relations with local chiefs and their people and undertake sabotage. Further, Agas II were to make contact with the Chinese guerrillas and train locals for guerrilla activity and continue intelligence-gathering work. This training was quickly underway, and while 'of average intelligence and very keen to learn . . . and a genuine desire to kill Japanese, [the locals] were not of the material that could be trained quickly'.[17]

Between 3 June and early August 1945, Agas II undertook six actions against the Japanese. The first was against the Japanese-owned Borneo Fishing Company's facilities on Banguey Island, protected by 12 Japanese troops and native police. However, after an operative was sent to reconnoitre the site, it was found that the Japanese had left. The operatives searched the area and found arms and other 'booty', and departed.

On 13 June, Major Combe led two sections of Chinese troops in a simultaneous attack on a Japanese barracks containing some 18 enemy soldiers with another attack at Pitas. Based on intelligence supplied by a Japanese-employed policeman, the party approached the barracks, and when everyone was in position opened fire. It was believed about six Japanese were killed as the barracks burnt. Nearby, Sergeant Watts, with three sections of guerrillas, travelled upriver by prahu, disembarking just 300 yards from the Japanese police station at 2030 hours.

As the *Official History* relates, 'Watts and a native named Mustol entered the quarters while four guerrillas remained below to fire on any attempting to escape by jumping from their quarters. Four Japanese were killed in their quarters and two escaped. A search was made in the surrounding undergrowth and the adjacent lavatory where one Japanese was found and killed by Watts.'[18] While the operatives killed six Japanese, wounded one and took one prisoner, one of the guerrillas named Koloh was also killed.

In an action on 24 June at Tanjong Batu, two Chinese sections under Major Combe attacked a Japanese position and killed three Japanese troops with no casualties. Two weeks later, Combe and a Chinese section attempted to ambush Japanese on the well-used road. Driving into the ambush site was a large, heavily armed party of 40 Japanese who were allowed to proceed, but later a convoy of trucks was attacked and explosive materials and other supplies captured.

The last offensive action began on 2 August 1945, less than two weeks before the cessation of hostilities. Captain McLean, with Lieutenant McMaster and five sections, set out to destroy a Japanese garrison of 40 men, but en route made contact with a Japanese party of 22 men. In the ensuing firefight, 16 Japanese were killed without casualties to themselves. Two more contacts eventuated on this patrol. One was on 9 August, where the operatives attacked a well-prepared Japanese position but were forced back due to heavy mortar fire. They attacked again on 12 August, killing four Japanese before the enemy fled. On 14 August, a signal was received from Morotai to cease fire, and from that time the Agas II party was extracted by Catalina and work boats to Morotai.

In June 1945, Headquarters 1st Australian Corps sought specific information on the area around Ranau in the central north of British North Borneo. The Agas III party was formed and inserted to seek intelligence on known Australian POWs in the area, and they set up a field medical post in preparation for the release and evacuation of the POWs. The party was also tasked to gather further intelligence, investigate the availability of food in the area and report on the condition of the Japanese airstrip at Ranau.

This initial party were landed on Jembongham Island on 21 June, and consisted of Flight Lieutenant Geoffrey Ripley (RAAF); a signaller, Sergeant A. W. C. Hywood; and four native police. They were reinforced soon after by Major J. A. Forster from the Indian Medical Service, Captain H. Nicholls (AIF) and five ORs who were parachuted in on 18 August. After a difficult journey through mountainous terrain in which they needed to bypass known Japanese forces, a local named Gimbahan handed over a message from an Australian POW who had escaped the Japanese in Ranau and was hiding in the jungle to the west of the town.

The handwritten note was from Warrant Officer William 'Wild Bill' Sticpewich, a man well known as a tough and ruthless character both before and after his capture. Two trusted locals were sent with medicine to recover Sticpewich and returned with him in a very weak condition. He had escaped with another man who had subsequently died of dysentery. Sticpewich was able to report that four other Australians had also escaped before him, Bombardier Moxham and Privates Short, Botterill and Anderson, but he knew nothing of their whereabouts.

Two days after rescuing Sticpewich, Gimbahan again set out, this time to smuggle food and medicines into a POW camp where there were at least 20 Australians – guarded by 80 Japanese with another 2000 Japanese in the area – many of them sick and hungry. It was also discovered at this time that a 'Chinese half caste named Sua Nam was searching for Sticpewich on the orders of the Japanese'[19] and knew of his hiding place. A trusted local policeman was sent to find and arrest Sua Nam and he did so, returning the collaborator, who was put under close arrest.

On 24 August 1945, a party from Agas III met up with three of the Australian POWs who had escaped before Sticpewich: Bill Moxham, Nelson Short and Keith Botterill, all of whom were in 'an extremely grave condition'.[20] To extract them, a short airstrip was cut in the jungle, but this proved unsuitable, so the men were taken on horseback to Todangan. On 20 September, five Austers – British short take-off and landing observation planes – arrived to evacuate the four POWs, but the Auster carrying Moxham crashed on take-off. Although the pilot was unhurt, Moxham received head injuries and was immediately evacuated on the fifth plane, which had been sent to evacuate Major Forster.

Needing intelligence on Japanese dispositions in the south-eastern corner of British North Borneo, a further SRD mission was inserted, known as Agas IV, under the well-respected Major Rex Blow. Blow had escaped a Japanese prison camp at Sandakan, and along with other Allied POWs, had made contact with Filipino guerrilla forces. For months he had led, trained and operated among these very successful groups before being recalled to Australia. Completing the Agas IV party were Captain J. A. Halsey and WO2 (Warrant Officer Class Two) A. Campbell from the British Army, an AIF signaller, a policeman and two locals.

On 13 July, the party left Tawi Tawi, to the south-east of Sandakan, and landed from a PT boat (a motor torpedo boat) at Semporna, where, after establishing a headquarters, they made radio contact with Morotai. Here they met two local men who they immediately engaged as agents, instructing them to recruit others for guerrilla training. Blow and Halsey with others then set off to extract a Eurasian woman, Mrs Lewis, and her three children, which they succeeded in doing. The party then organised the extraction of a second family, that of Dr Blaaun, from the Mostyn Estate, inland and to the north of Semporna. The *Official History* notes:

> At 2300 hours, 2 August, Dr Blaaun, his wife and three children, with several Chinese coolies and families, walked down the main roadway, passed several Japanese-occupied houses and proceeded overland to the river, where Blaaun and family and party members embarked in the prahu and paddled down the river to the waiting workboat. All arrived safely at Semporna on 3 August. At this time, the enemy strength at Mostyn Estate was 5 Kempetai [Japanese secret police], 250 armed Japanese civilians and 500 other Japanese.[21]

Major Blow continued his active work, undertaking reconnaissance patrols and supervising stores drops. On 27 July, he sent out a local patrol under Sergeant Korun to attempt to find and rescue a downed RAAF pilot who had parachuted from his aircraft on 10 July near Kalabakan, about 80 miles (130 kilometres) to the west of Semporna. Upon landing, the patrol made contact with the Japanese, killing four and wounding eight, and again the following morning they were fired on by the enemy. Returning fire, it was later reported they killed at least 20 Japanese and wounded a further 16. They also gathered valuable intelligence on Japanese dispositions as they proceeded on their rescue mission. The following day they encountered a number of local craft, and hearing Japanese voices fired on the boats, killing a further four enemy and wounding eight.

Sergeant Korun set out to again attempt the rescue of the Australian pilot and also to organise guerrillas and his agents. But his party soon discovered that the airman had found his way to the Brantian Estate. Here he was arrested by a pro-Japanese local who tied him up and handed him over to the Japanese military police in Brantian, where he was later shot.

On 15 August, news of the Japanese surrender was reported. From this time, much of the work of this Agas party was to receive and distribute airdrops, round up Japanese units, disarm them and to pay off local guerrilla fighters. Many Japanese troops in the area were in a serious condition, without food or medicines, so managing the concentration of Japanese units and their welfare also became an ongoing role. It was not until mid-October that Major Blow and his signaller were evacuated by Catalina to Labuan.

As a further means to gather intelligence, organise the guerrilla forces and engage in ongoing raiding, the last Agas party, known as Agas V, was inserted by boat about 40 miles north-east of Semporna on 27 July. This party was led by the legendary mate of Rex Blow, Captain Robert 'Jock' McLaren. He had escaped with Blow first in Singapore and then from Sandakan, after which he had joined the Filipino guerrillas. While there, McLaren had secured an eight-metre whaleboat from Australia, powered by a 32-horsepower motor, which he named *The Bastard*. He'd armed the boat with a 20 mm cannon in the bow, and twin 303 machine guns and another gun in the stern. McLaren had begun patrolling the waters between Mindanao and North Borneo, attacking Japanese shipping and shore installations.

On one occasion, he sailed into Parang, a seaside port on the Philippine island of Mindanao, and shot up the port area, killing many Japanese who had assembled on the wharf, sinking three vessels and severely damaging shore installations, before speeding out of range. This and many other audacious actions earned him a Military Cross and Bar.

In mid-April 1945, McLaren, then at the guerrilla headquarters by Lake Lanao on Mindanao, had been ordered back to Australia, where he'd been given leave, and then posted, along with Major Rex Blow, to SRD.

Flown to Morotai, Rex Blow and Jock McLaren met with General Blamey on 22 April, who explained the upcoming operations in Tarakan and Balikpapan on the east coast of Borneo. McLaren led a number of missions, often alone, into Japanese-held areas to undertake detailed reconnaissance on potential landing beaches, enemy airfields and defensive positions. In late June 1945, McLaren, along with two AIF signallers, parachuted into Balikpapan for Platypus VI, but they missed their drop zone by three miles (five kilometres) and landed within 50 yards of a Japanese post. In the ensuing firefight, one of the signallers, who had suddenly become sick and collapsed unconscious, needed to be carried. McLaren hauled him onto his shoulders while the Japanese were hard on their heels, firing at the fleeing party. Hiding in kunai grass, the three Australians were able to evade the Japanese and, due to McLaren's skill and leadership, make their way to the safety of the Australian lines.

Next, McLaren was tasked to lead Agas V. On 29 July, his party – McLaren, two AIF signallers, three local police and an interpreter – were inserted by HMAS *Blacksnake* onto Tawi

Tawi Island. Upon arrival, they quickly established a radio link to Morotai and, because of the large number of sick local civilians, set up a hospital and dressing station at Talasai and began growing food for the evacuees in the area. McLaren also organised the making of clothes and worked with the local leaders to improve the lot of the people in the area. This work continued until the Agas V party were evacuated on 10 September, leaving a clerk and Chinese attendants in charge of the hospital.

This ended the Agas operations. But, in parallel, SRD had been busy elsewhere on Borneo with the operations codenamed Semut.

ELEVEN

The Bite of the Ant –
the Semut Operations

The advance of Admiral Nimitz across the Central Pacific had seen the capture of the Gilbert Islands, the Marshalls and Marianas (Saipan, Guam and Tinian), and along with the advance of MacArthur through PNG, Morotai and the Dutch East Indies, the prize of the Philippines was now within MacArthur's grasp. Given these military successes, a meeting of the American Combined Chiefs of Staff moved both the place and the date of the first landing in the Philippines from Mindanao to Leyte Island and up from 15 November to 20 October 1944. The pressure on Japan was increasing.

Further south, the war had moved north leaving behind the Dutch and British possessions in the Borneo and Celebes area. However, not only did large numbers of Japanese troops remain behind MacArthur's advancing front, but these islands held valuable resources for the Allied war effort. Much to their disappointment and annoyance, the Australian Army was left to mop up isolated pockets of Japanese on islands left behind. Through the interdiction of convoys, these Japanese bases had been cut off from resupply and many of the troops and the Japanese civilian population, who worked in parallel with the military, were close to starvation.

To liberate this area, MacArthur planned a series of operations collectively known as Oboe, with the first two, Oboe I and II, to capture Tarakan and Balikpapan. And as part of this and on the orders of MacArthur, the three Australia services – the Army, Navy and Air Force – were to throw themselves against these remnant outposts.

The changing strategic priorities and the success of the Agas and other SRD parties in British North Borneo confirmed to GHQ their value and capacity and the resolve of the men of the Z Special Unit. SRD operatives were also better trained and more experienced, their equipment – including radios and communications – had improved as had insertion and resupply options. Valuable intelligence had been gained, locally raised guerrilla units had been trained and deployed, and Australian casualties were light in comparison to the Japanese. Given the success of the strategic work of the operatives here, especially compared to earlier failures in Timor, it was time to call upon SRD to assist when the operational area was extended into neighbouring Sarawak, to the south.

The first stage of Operation Oboe, the Borneo campaign was to begin with an amphibious landing on the small coastal island of Tarakan, halfway down the eastern coast of what was then Dutch Borneo. Tarakan had been a port and oil terminal exporting 90,000 barrels of oil per month before the war, but the Japanese, seeing Tarakan as an important objective, had landed on 11 January 1942 and captured the island after just two days of fighting against overwhelmed Dutch troops. Quickly repairing the Dutch sabotage on the oil refinery, the Japanese had increased production to 350,000 barrels per month by 1944.

The refinery became a strategic target for the Allies, but by early 1944, with interdiction strategies, minefields and air attacks,

Japanese exports of oil virtually ceased, with the last tanker leaving in July. This reduced Borneo's strategic importance to the Japanese, and by early 1945 only an estimated 2200 Japanese infantry and naval personnel remained, along with radar installations, naval gun emplacements and defensive positions.

It was not only the oil resources that the Allies wanted, but also the airstrip in Tarakan in order to launch offensive operations north in Sarawak, Brunei and the island of Labuan. By late 1944, the *Official History* recounts, 'Tarakan held first place on the GHQ priority list of intelligence targets,'[1] and in December SRD developed a plan, codenamed Squirrel, for the insertion by Catalina of an eight-man patrol to remain there for a period of three months. A party was organised and began training near Melbourne in mid-December 1944, then flew to Morotai on 20 January.

In the days after, an aerial reconnaissance was undertaken and preparations made for the insertion of the party two days later. But the operation was cancelled when they heard news of the failure of a Dutch party called Apple, which had been inserted on 15 January and found enemy patrols vigilant and locals pro-Japanese. The Squirrel party returned to Darwin to await new instructions.

Planning for the large amphibious landing on Tarakan began in March 1945, but details of Japanese defences, potential landing sites and the state of Japanese morale needed detailed intelligence. As a result, a new plan was developed for the Squirrel party comprising 'a series of short-term kidnapping raids by Catalina to obtain intelligence before the main operation could be carried out'.[2] This involved two phases: 'the first was to extract natives from prahus for interrogation and the second to insert a small party a few days prior to D-Day'.[3]

The first mission, on 3 April, failed after a Catalina strafed a Japanese lugger then returned to Morotai. Two days later, a second party set out. They made landfall and went ashore in a rubber boat, but after searching the nearby coast returned to the seaplane. After they continued the aerial search they sighted a prahu, landed and took on board nine locals. One stated that his cousin wished to be extracted as he had information, having worked as a clerk for the Japanese, 'who apparently trusted him'.[4] This triggered the third mission, to extract the cousin, which was done successfully four days later. The man was returned to Morotai, where, as the *Official History* states, he provided 'valuable information'.[5]

The second phase of Squirrel came at the request of 1st Australian Corps to provide specific intelligence on the number, composition and movement of Japanese forces at Djoeata, the oilfields on the north coast of Tarakan Island. Also required were details of the defences, the deployment of artillery, and the condition of the roads and the oil installations. The party was led by Captain V. D. Prentice, a Queenslander, along with Lieutenant P. W. Beiers and four sergeants.

The Squirrel party were inserted by Catalina at dusk on 25 April and paddled their rubber boats into the delta area. When they'd reached about one mile inland, they established a base. But they were unable to make radio contact with Morotai, and attempts to repair the set in the days after were not successful. While a number of patrols were sent out and intelligence gathered both on the oilfield and the defences, this could not be relayed to Morotai, as their radio was still not working, and the party were evacuated by Catalina and patrol boat in early May. As an outcome of the basic failure of the Squirrel party to recce the oilfields and complete the tasks given them, Brigadier David Whitehead, CO of the 26th Brigade, while expressing his thanks, 'declined to use the Squirrel party again, even when it returned. He stated that he would prefer to use his Cav Regt. [Cavalry Regiment] required for any further reconnaissance at this juncture.'[6]

The focus for SRD now turned to the planned Allied operations on the north-western side of Borneo, in Sarawak and Brunei, and the need for reliable intelligence, local resistance and a population sympathetic to the Allied cause. Plans for SRD operations in Sarawak, codenamed Semut, had begun in early 1944 and were submitted to GHQ in May of that year. Sarawak had been a low Allied priority, compounded by the unavailability of submarine and flying boat transport. At this time in the war, countries and objectives within territories were given a priority, but this changed with successes and failures and upon the direction of MacArthur. Sarawak and Brunei rose up the priority list and became strategically more important, which in turn impacted on SRD. Then, with the planning of the Oboe operations, and as this area came within range of Allied aircraft, the option of aerial insertion – in particular into the unexplored and mountainous central region – gave the Semut operation new life.

Work began on a revised plan, which was completed on 11 November 1944 and submitted to GHQ. This called for the insertion by parachute of SRD units into the hinterland of Brunei Bay and the fertile, productive interior, with the final plan submitted to GHQ on 24 November and eventually approved early in the following month.[7] The revised plan initially envisaged two parties: a reconnaissance party followed two weeks later by what was termed 'a main body'. The first party was under the command of Major Tom Harrisson. An English anthropologist and explorer, Harrisson was a well-known eccentric who would later find fame as a journalist, broadcaster and filmmaker, being honoured with a DSO (Distinguished Service Order) in

1947 and an OBE in 1959. He died in 1976 in a road accident in Thailand.

This operation became Semut I, while the second party, under Major Greg Carter, became Semut II. Two further parties would be established, known as Semut III and Semut IV.

In January 1945, Major Harrisson flew the first of two reconnaissance flights to locate a suitable drop zone, the second, in March, with RAAF 200 Flight. An eight-man party comprising Semut I under Harrisson and his second-in-command, Lieutenant Rick Edmeades, was assembled, trained and made ready. On the morning of their departure, the radio operator, Jack Tredrea, remembered:

> We lined up beside our planes and Tom Harrisson took out a tin from his pocket, opened it and handed us all a rubber capsule. I remember someone asking Harrisson, 'What's this?'
>
> Harrisson said, 'It's an L-pill.'
>
> 'What's an L-pill?'
>
> 'It's a cyanide pill. If you're caught by the Japs, bite it and you're dead in three seconds.'
>
> Freddy looked at me and said, 'Tred, what the hell have we got ourselves into?'[8]

After four unsuccessful insertion sorties, the first group of operatives were dropped by parachute from two B-24 Liberator aircraft from RAAF 200 Flight into the mountainous central area of the Borneo hinterland on 23 March 1945. Tredrea recalled of the drop:

> We had two planes. Arrived over the DZ [drop zone] at 7.30 am and you could not see the ground because of the heavy mist and

cloud. They dropped Harrisson and the others and the storpedoes, which all our gear was packed in. Then we circled but couldn't find a hole, so Edmeades got on the intercom and said, 'The next time around, drop us where you think it is.' Around we went and when we came out of the cloud, all we could see was jungle. He'd [the pilot] missed the DZ by at least five miles and we were heading into the highest jungle I have ever seen. Once we got to the ground we took a compass bearing and it took us from about 8.30 am until midday to find the DZ, where we were welcomed by Harrisson, who was very happy to see us.[9]

Unfortunately, one of these two aircraft crashed on the return flight, leading to the loss of the crew. The pilot was Squadron Leader Harold Pockley DFC and Bar, who had made a name for himself hunting submarines in the Atlantic as the commander of a Sunderland flying boat and was at the time commander of 200 Flight. His aircraft was never found, nor his body recovered.

The operatives and their stores were spread over a large area, and although some storpedoes were recovered during the following four days, a large proportion were not. But the Semut party were fortunate in another regard. Prior to their insertion, they had no idea if there were Japanese in the area and if the local inhabitants were pro-Japanese or otherwise. As it turned out, as noted in a report written by Harrisson, 'within five minutes of landing, one party was met by a native carrying a white flag. The moment they saw we were whites, they sent runners to villages for 20 miles [32 kilometres] round, and by nightfall over 500 people had come in to help us find storpedoes.'[10] The report goes on to say, 'The people were absolutely delighted to see us . . . [but] at the same time were nervous about Jap reprisals if they helped us. Already 14 natives in North Sarawak had been taken prisoner or killed by the Japs for helping shot-down Americans.'[11] Harrisson also met with and reassured the local chief 'from an area three days walk around . . . and we received unlimited native support in this area, without any further misgivings on their part'.[12]

A later operative on Semut I, Corporal Roland Griffiths-Marsh – who had joined the AIF at 16 and fought in North Africa, Greece and Crete before finding himself in Borneo – mentioned in an interview, of the locals:

> When they [the Japanese] first came, they would say to the
> native chief, pointing to their skin, 'Look, we are the same colour.
> Let us get rid of these white men.' But they abused the people,
> who soon realised how well off they were and wanted the British
> to come back. They [the Japanese] took what they wanted, and
> that included the women. One of my guerrillas, his sister was
> taken by a Jap officer of the Kempei-tai. He used her for about
> six weeks then he handed her over to his soldiers. They used her
> for about the same time then killed her. That man [the guerrilla]
> hated them, and he would never dob me in to the Japs.[13]

With an operational base established and a radio link with Darwin opened, Major Harrisson began a series of patrols to ascertain likely penetration routes for a Japanese attack and held ongoing meetings with native chiefs and villagers. This Allied unit were the first white people seen since the Japanese landings four years before, and with their delivery of medical supplies, Harrisson was able to change the ambivalent view of these people into an antipathy for the Japanese, something that increased as Semut II was inserted with more men and more valuable supplies.

Harrisson had on side a large number of Dutch-educated, Christian locals who had a deep hatred for the Japanese. They lived remotely, had gardens that provided a reliable food source and were potential fighters, guides and porters. By the end of May, Major Harrisson was able to consolidate the Kalabit Plateau, and by blocking all approach roads and paths could receive early warning of any Japanese penetration of the area. He also moved his headquarters to an area on the Sarawak–Dutch Borneo border, where deputations of locals from as far as 12 days' walk away were arriving to offer their support and intelligence. By this time there were six SRD parties in the field, including Harrisson's own, plus a roving doctor who provided medical assistance.

The next task was to train and arm the local people and begin attacks on the Japanese. After their insertion over a number of weeks, each group were given a separate territory to control and rarely had contact with each other or with Harrisson. As Jack Tredrea related, 'My area was the Kallob kampongs [Malay word for enclosures or villages], and it took me six weeks to cover all of them, giving them medical assistance and so forth and recruiting people. They came back with me and I began training them in our weapons. The natives still preferred to use their parangs [swords carried by the guerrillas] as their main weapon to shooting guns.'[14]

The Dyaks – one of a number of local tribes – were also very proficient with blowpipes. These were about two metres long, generally made of ironwood or another hardwood, into which was inserted a small dart about 30 centimetres long with a poison tip. The blowpipes were very effective in the jungle, as explained by Jack Tredrea: 'At one point Lieutenant Edmeades had no ammunition and so, hearing a Japanese patrol was approaching, organised his boys with blowpipes and took out the lot. Once the dart went in, within five paces you were dead. The dart was more like the bite of an insect and the Jap, before he knew what hit him, was dead.'[15]

During April and May 1945, SRD supplied 300 rifles, and by the end of July, Harrisson had over 1000 men under arms. This distribution of arms further increased the locals' loyalty to the Australians, though the locals needed to be carefully watched so as not to take offensive action themselves. As was noted in a report, 'They observed excellent discipline in this respect once the need for co-ordination with sea landings was clearly understood.'[16]

Harrisson then established an armed party under a white officer, with Malay and Chinese NCOs, in each of the approach valleys. With each officer were 20–30 permanent guerrillas, while further part-time guerrillas returned to their village ready for action. What was amazing was that these armed groups under white leaders did not become known to the Japanese, and 'of the tens of thousands of natives who knew of our activities, not one had given us away'.[17]

Typical of Semut I operations at the time was the one led by Roland Griffiths-Marsh. With his band of about 30 native guer- rillas, he fought a lonely war, far from any assistance or support, certainly none from Harrisson. At one point he received a report that a band of Japanese had landed in a nearby part of a river in his area. He recalled:

We went down into the mangroves and tracked them down. There must have been about eight of them. As soon as they saw us they started to shout and scream. One fellow raised his rifle, fired a shot at me, he missed me. I shot him, then I shot the second man. We attacked the Japs with the parangs and they were obliterated. From that day on I had nightmares. After the firefight they [the locals] took the heads, as it was part and parcel of their rite of passage . . . I never allowed them to kill a live prisoner, but after a firefight it was their privilege to take a head and they proved that they were a warrior by having a head.[18]

The issues of the taking of heads was a vexed one. The practice had been banned by the British Administrator or Rajah, Sir Charles Vyner Brooke, but, said Tredrea, 'Harrisson restarted it to put the fear of God into the Japs . . . He offered the natives five Dutch guilders for a Jap head, and this was very successful.'[19] Tredrea recalled:

> The first occasion it happened to me, I'd taken out half a dozen Japs and I told the [local] boys to burn the small house they were living in. I went back to the prahu and when they came back, they were carrying six heads. I think they [the Japanese] deserved it.
> I came across one kampong where a missionary, his wife and three children had lived for years, and the Japanese had decapitated the whole family.[20]

Jack Tredrea's guerrillas were also hitting the Japanese hard. As he said, 'The Japanese had no idea we were there. We would hear of a Jap patrol coming, set up an ambush, kill the lot, get rid of their bodies and the Japs would not know what happened to them.'[21] On another occasion he remembered, 'The Japanese were coming up the big tidal river behind Tarakan on rafts. One had four on, one had six on, another had four on, and they were easy target practice for my boys. Soon after, my best native, Mulca, and I circled around the Japanese, who had a woodpecker machine gun and came in from the back. I tossed a grenade and we went in and were able to clean up the six of them.'[22]

In late April and with days to go before the Australian landings at Tarakan, attempts were made to find a suitable seaplane landing area, but without success. Instead, Harrisson rounded up 300 locals to quickly clear, drain and level a short runway, laying down more than a thousand split bamboo lengths, 35 inches (89 centimetres) long. Soon after, two Auster aircraft landed but the first one, taking off with Harrisson, crashed. Immediately the runway was extended a further 80 feet (24 metres), and the following day Harrisson was flown to Morotai in the other aircraft. After this, the bamboo airstrip, probably the only one in the world, became an important service point for returning downed airmen, intelligence, prisoners and captured documents.

Key to the success of the Allied landings was intelligence. Semut agents had penetrated all of the coastal areas and returned accurate information. To greatly enhance this, a senior Malay official working for the Japanese would provide daily reports on troop numbers and movements, conversations and wireless traffic, which provided the RAAF with precise targets. One important success was the cutting of all Japanese radio and telephone communications before the landings, along with destroying a sawmill, Japanese barracks and other important facilities. Also, by the time of the landings, the supply of rice, meat and vegetables from the interior to the coast had been halted by Harrisson, and when Japanese patrols were sent into the interior to find out why, they did not return. Adding to the Allies' promising position were Japanese deserters, mainly auxiliary troops and police, who brought with them valuable information and swelled the ranks of the guerrillas.

A series of small-scale attacks continued on isolated Japanese units. As Tredrea said, 'I always felt I had to lead. On one occasion it was 3 am. I took out the sentry with my cosh[23] and then tossed a grenade into the hut, and the boys finished the work off then.' On another occasion, Harrisson had located a Japanese unit he wanted attacked and ordered Tredrea to 'get rid of them'.[24] Tredrea recounted:

> I worked out a plan that if I could get a strafing raid on the Japanese that were occupying six houses in this town, maybe my group could handle them. Harrisson arranged an attack by two Lightnings at 5 am,[25] which strafed the six houses with the Japs sleeping in them. After, we counted 38 Japs who had been killed, and the rest took to the boat. They were heading upriver towards Pensiang and I was able to ambush them from the banks of the river on two occasions.[26]

With Major Harrisson hard at work and now receiving regular airdrops and reinforcements, it was time for Semut II to be inserted. While Semut I was in the north around Brunei, Semut II was inserted further to the south-west along the coast, in the hinterland of the Miri-Seria region, a swampy, thick jungle area some 80 miles (129 kilometres) from the operational area of Semut I. As for Semut I, this party's tasks included the securing of naval and military intelligence, and locating missing Europeans and organising their evacuation. The party were also tasked with investigating the local population: their situation with regards to Japanese propaganda, their relationship with the enemy and whether they had been denying or would deny the Japanese food, labour and information. The Semut II party were also to train and equip local guerrilla units and prepare for the postwar return of the colonial powers. It was believed that the presence of this party would show the locals some visible signs of the restoration of the stable prewar British and Dutch administrations.

The Semut II party comprised 24 operatives under the command of Major Gordon 'Toby' Carter. The first party of eight operatives departed on 16 April 1945 at 0400 hours from Mindoro in the Philippines in three Liberator bombers, a journey of about 950 miles (1500 kilometres), arriving at 0830 to find the drop zone covered in low cloud. But the party and storpedoes were delivered safely after a hair-raising flight through dangerous, narrow valleys. Once on the ground, they were met by porters and a mass of people who welcomed Major Carter, having known him prior to the war when he had worked for the Shell Oil Company as a surveyor.

By early May, the Semut II party had established themselves in the old abandoned government fort, where Carter had been given a rousing welcome by the local people. He met the area chiefs, who, after talking through the likely problems, offered their unconditional support to the Allies and his operatives. The only glitch was the loss of long-range radio equipment when the party were first dropped in, until a relay was established via Semut I to the SRD base in Darwin.

Meanwhile, planning was being finalised for the landing at Labuan and Brunei Bay as Oboe VI,[27] beginning 10 June 1945. Now, once radio communications were established, resupply could begin in earnest. To equip the guerrilla force that was assembled required large quantities of arms and ammunition, medical supplies, clothing and other stores. After a major drop on 30 May, less than two weeks before the invasion, regular and frequent supply drops became possible, and at this time, a dangerous stretch of river – due to shallows, logs and Japanese along the banks – was found potentially suitable for Catalina operations. This made possible preliminary attacks upon Japanese troops and positions, and ensured the preparations necessary for the upcoming landings. It also established a mode of operation which included the elimination of Japanese wherever they could be found, the destruction of radio stations, the capture of food reserves, plans and intelligence, and to completely hamper any Japanese movement.

While little information could be found about missing Europeans, reports were received of the harsh treatment of Indian POWs in the Miri-Belait area. In fact, the flow of valuable intelligence was far greater than expected, with locals travelling miles to report enemy concentrations and movements, which allowed Semut II to travel in relative safety, knowing as it did all enemy movements, defences and preparations in the area.

Major Carter now had three bases: his headquarters with five personnel, an outstation with two personnel and a third party of two personnel at Lupu Luji on the Tinjar River. As the *Official History* notes, 'These personnel were supported by a motley band of guerrillas, partially and newly trained, wildly enthusiastic, but woefully lacking in training, mostly gun-shy, and bridling with inter-tribal jealousy.'[28] While the Japanese 'did not intend to put up much of a fight on the coast',[29] they were collecting inland, and if they were to attack the Semut II bases, there was every chance these would be overrun and eliminated. If Semut II could control Marudi, some 25 miles (40 kilometres) inland from Miri, the movement of Japanese into the interior would allow for the continual harassment of their lines of communication.

Yet there was deep discontent in the Semut I party. Major Tom Harrisson was never liked, had little real military training and was seen as a typical British officer, arrogant and opinionated. Some, like Sergeant Jack Tredrea, liked him: 'Harrisson was a very unusual man. He was one of those well-educated, posh-speaking gentlemen who you couldn't act like with an Australian officer. He cared more about the natives than he did about us. His methods worked and he was a terrific organiser.'[30]

Others, like Roland Griffiths-Marsh, hated him: 'I personally despised him and I think he knew that as he was incompetent, which he was. I did not have open confrontation, but I was prepared to kill him, murder him if ever he came down to my area. By that time I was a very sick man, I had malaria, malnutrition, I had no medication whatsoever. Harrisson kept the lot.'[31]

Tredrea confirmed this claim against Harrisson: 'Tom himself ate very well in Belawit, where local food was plentiful and where the Australian food parcels were dropped. Tom helped himself to food dropped in for Semut I, while he made his operatives "live off the land". This is undoubtedly the single biggest grievance his subordinates have held against him.'[32] Tredrea further recounted, 'Another operative, Charlie Hardy, actually pulled a pistol on him and threatened to shoot him for keeping the rations for himself. I think he [Harrisson] was a sick man mentally.'[33]

With events developing rapidly and the number of operational armed parties increasing, Harrisson again moved his headquarters, to a more central location, to manage them. To ensure continued local support, a civil administration was quickly created, while other areas were handed over to the AIF and to the Dutch administration.

Following several weeks of intense naval and aerial bombardment, on 10 June 1945, the Australians came ashore in two separate landings. Two battalions, the 2/28th Battalion and the 2/43rd Battalion of Brigadier Selwyn Porter's 24th Brigade, came ashore on Labuan Island and quickly secured both the airfield and the harbour. The Japanese retreated into the interior, into a fortified position called the 'Pocket', which, after heavy bombardment, fell to the Allies, securing the end of resistance and the capture of the island on 21 June.

The second Allied landing, again on 10 June, was at Muara on the mainland, north of Brooketon, by two battalions, the 2/15th and the 2/17th Battalions of Brigadier Victor Windeyer's 20th Brigade. A further landing was made at Weston on the north-eastern side of Brunei Bay by the 2/32nd Battalion. By this time, Semut had 32 operators controlling 2000 armed and trained guerrillas, and the Japanese found themselves under simultaneous attack from the inland by SRD units, taken completely by surprise.

Prior to March 1945, the Japanese had not attempted patrols into the interior. When they did, they found they were facing hostile locals, and later well-armed guerrillas under white officers. With pressure from the Allied landings, the Japanese made four attempts to move inland to establish a strong garrison to contain the invasion. One Japanese patrol of 200 men was forced to return to the coast with only 80 survivors.

The natives removed all food supplies to secret jungle store-houses, blocked tracks and hid in the jungle on the approach of the Japanese to deny them manpower. They also hid canoes and prahus, removed bridges and signposts, and carried out ambushes and harassing tactics along these routes inland. 'As a result, no Japanese reached within 4 days of the fertile centre from March '45 onwards, and at no time was there any serious probability of any large force getting inland except at extreme cost of themselves.'[34]

As the Australians closed on the Japanese in Brunei and along the immediate coastal areas, the enemy continued pushing inland in an attempt to escape and join up with Japanese forces in British North Borneo. One large group of 500 Japanese troops under the command of a general moved towards Tenom, about 30 miles (48 kilometres) inland, but they were continually ambushed and harassed, and over the following three weeks some 320 were killed or captured for the loss of only two local guerrillas. They were also continually attacked by the RAAF, and those who finally arrived were starving and in little condition to fight. Many more were left behind, lost in the jungle. As the *Official History* notes, 'If it had not been for Semut I activities, it is likely that those forces, which had already evaded the AIF patrols on the coast, would have had no difficulty in reaching Tenom in good order.'[35]

Skirmishes and harassment drove the Japanese further inland, increasing their casualties, but the Japanese began undertaking reprisals, killing locals, burning longhouses and stealing food. They had also received information on the whereabouts and strength of Semut II, and sent a heavily armed party of 70 to eliminate the SRD operatives. Major Carter heard of the Japanese advance and set an ambush, with eight Europeans, four Bren guns, 40 armed locals and a further 100 armed with parangs and spears. The leading two boatloads of Japanese were attacked and 18 of them were killed, but they pressed on, forcing the Semut party and the locals to retreat. Again the Japanese took reprisals on the local people, killing 18 Malays and Chinese. But the locals continued to harass the enemy, taking their heads if they killed them, and provide valuable intelligence for the Australians.

After Carter was extracted by Catalina for discussions with Brigadier Windeyer, it was decided to provide a company from the 2/17th Battalion to assist with the consolidation of the area around Marudi and to establish the military administration in the district. This began a special relationship between the battalion and the SRD operatives, who were able to procure guides, porters and fresh food for the battalion. While this added to the Allied strength, along with an estimated 150 guerrillas under European command, the Japanese still had a well-armed force of 1500 to 2000 under Colonel Aikyo Masao. (Aikyo was to be later captured and charged with the massacre of POWs, but he hanged himself on 23 October 1945 at Labuan before he could face a court for war crimes.)

The Japanese had dug themselves in at Beluru, 30 miles (48 kilometres) south of the coastal town of Miri, and prepared to make a stand. To remove the irritation of guerrilla harassment, the *Official History* recounts that Colonel Aikyo 'attacked in well-organised parties of 100 or more. The natives would not hold, they broke and ran, leaving the few operatives often surrounded and in extreme danger.'[36] The *Official History* continues, 'The Iban [tribe] had shown that he was only good while winning and that he was no good at all unless the advantage lay definitely with him. Their success had lain in trickery, when they could decapitate the enemy while asleep or drunk. Against organised resistance they were useless.'[37]

By early August, the Japanese had been completely driven from Brunei, Sarawak and the northern areas of Dutch Borneo. But considerable numbers remained around the bordering areas, so Major Harrisson planned offensive operations against these Japanese positions. In the first attack, on the Sapong Estate, a force of seven white operatives and 160 local troops were assembled, while for the attack on the garrison on Pensiangan, Harrisson assembled four white operatives and 200 local troops. Before these operations could be launched, the Japanese surrender was announced.

What was not expected was the continuing resistance put up by the Japanese after the official surrender. As Semut was ordered to cease further offensive action, the Japanese took advantage of this, pushing towards the Semut base, stealing locals' food supplies and firing upon unarmed locals, even ignoring leaflet drops to come in and surrender. It took a letter on 29 October from Lieutenant General Masao Baba, the Japanese General commanding the

37th Army, for nearly 600 Japanese troops to finally surrender, of whom over 200 were collected by SRD operatives.

Along with the substantial success of Semut parties in providing intelligence, training and controlling local units, and killing the Japanese enemy, Semut I controlled an area of approximately 16,000 square miles and 250,000 locals. During this time, they inflicted over 1200 casualties on the Japanese, including over 1000 killed, with 14 locals killed and no casualties among the Australian and European SRD operatives.

It might be timely to pick up the operational work of the Semut III party, led by Major W. L. P. Sochon DSO, British Army. He was inserted on 6 April 1945 at Bario in Sarawak and was followed by a large party comprising AIF, local prewar police and militia, and Chinese operatives. In a report written by Major Sochon, he stated, 'In London, April 1942, I met Lieutenant-Colonel D. L. Leach of the Sarawak government, and we discussed the position of Sarawak . . . and realised that something had to be done . . . we formed a plan.'[38]

Sochon was transferred to SOE in May 1944 and, after training in Scotland and parachute training outside Manchester, he received orders to proceed to Australia. Here he did further training on Fraser Island and a parachute conversion course at Leyburn in Queensland. Following his insertion at Bario were a series of Catalina and parachute insertions that brought his force to more than 40 operatives.

After information was received that the Japanese were planning to cross Borneo to reform on the south coast, it was decided to organise locals to close the tracks likely to be used by the Japanese. Upon receiving a signal that the remainder of the Semut III party would be inserted in early June, Sochon and a small patrol made a difficult inland trek to Belaga, at one point using a wide Japanese track of 8.5 miles (14 kilometres) which had been made just three weeks earlier by the forced labour of 1000 locals. The Japanese track reduced a three-day trek to just seven hours, but along the way they risked meeting the Japanese, who were preparing a secure track across the island and sending patrols out at regular intervals.

The *Official History* recounts that, along this journey

> a tremendous reception awaited the party at every village. The local population was not only willing to help, but eager, though emphasis was always placed on the lack of arms which prevented them contemplating any offensive action against the Japanese. They compromised by agreeing to dispose of any odd Japanese who appeared in the area, and were advised, should they take such action, to make certain that the corpses were well buried in the jungle.[39]

These instructions also ensured that locals' patrols were sent ahead to each village, and that they provided sufficient warning on the presence or otherwise of Japanese patrols. At this time Major Sochon was required to report to HQ following an extraction by Catalina, but he had no radio communication with Morotai or Darwin, which, with the difficulties he was experiencing in using a signalling mirror on passing Allied aircraft, confounded his plans.

Things began to deteriorate for the Australians. Along with their lack of radio communication and the failed Catalina extraction, the Japanese presence was intensifying against the local guerrillas, who were lightly armed and had few stores or supplies of ammunition. This translated into low morale, and it took some effort to persuade the locals that the Australians were there to stay and to continue the fight. Other Dyaks were divided between fighting the Japanese and running, many fearing retribution on their villages and people. With the seeds of doubt growing and the absence of visible support through airdrops and Catalina extractions, the decision was made to attack small Japanese patrols, collect their weapons and increase active guerrilla activity across the region. The operatives realised they needed to remain in the area, as a retreat would increase the locals' doubts about the Allies' intentions.

In a typical small action, the locals reported the approach of three Japanese troops. An ambush was quickly arranged 'and their heads were taken'.[40] Then, on about 10 June, reports came in of the approach of a large Japanese party assisted by 50 or 60 Baleh Dyaks as porters. Various Dyak groups with the Allies argued over whether to attack, fearing reprisals, or to ambush the Japanese before they passed into other Dyak territory. While plans were being discussed,

> . . . at about 7 o'clock that night a party of excited Dyaks arrived
> at the camp carrying two or three Japanese heads and announced
> that the Japanese had been killed about 10 o'clock that morning.
> The Baleh Dyaks, seeing a favourable moment, attacked and
> killed the Japanese as they were loading their stores into prahus.
> Unfortunately, there were a number of hot-blooded youngsters
> among the Dyaks. And a number of Chinese prisoners who were
> with the Japanese were also killed.[41]

After Semut III had no radio contact for a month, a small group of operatives reinforced Sochon's party, bringing with them new radio equipment which allowed contact with Labuan.

From this time, continual contacts, ambushes and firefights were common. For example, at 1 am in the morning of 26 June, a Japanese launch arrived at the wharf at Kapit and was ambushed. Three Japanese were killed, while the survivors, in their sinking boat, limped off down the river. Soon after, another boatload of Japanese arrived, but as the ambush party did not know the enemy strength and were short of ammunition, they slipped across the river in the low fog and disappeared into the jungle.

The increased Japanese activity also increased the frequency of Japanese reprisals, which drove the locals to look for revenge and for heads. After a resupply of weapons, two operatives began training and arming Dyaks and a solid blockhouse with views of the Balleh and Rajang rivers was constructed. On 3 July, a well-armed Japanese patrol came upriver on two large launches, machine-gunning villages, houses and any locals they saw. They believed the Semut party consisted of 200 Europeans and were falsely led to believe there were up to 4000 armed guerrillas, having been informed by an ex–Sarawak Ranger, Sergeant Embah, who was working with the Australians. After looting the government station they retreated down the river after only 18 hours, but this increased attention by the Japanese into areas they had never ventured in before 'again put the [SRD] party into a precarious position'.[42]

With further insertions of SRD operatives, stores and weapons drops, the local Dyak people became more confident to take on the Japanese using their own methods and weapons. In a report written after the war, Major Sochon noted one particular method used: 'on crossing streams, it was the usual practice for the Japs to take the hand of a native for assistance when crossing logs used for bridging. At a given signal, if the drop was sufficient, they would let go of the Japs' hands and they would fall into the stream below, generally landing on rocks or hard riverbed. The natives would then jump down the bank and attack them.'[43]

Sochon continued:

> Another method successfully employed was to take three trees growing closely together along the side of the track and cut two-thirds through them close to the ground and tie them back with a length of rotan rope and on the approach of the Japanese party the rotan attached to the rear-most tree would be cut and one tree would bring the others down on top of the party. The best method of all for ambushing we discovered to be by persuading the Japs when in longboats to tie their weapons to the thwarts of the boats [struts placed crosswise to brace the vessels] and on approaching rough water or rapids, a boat would pull into the bank and the paddlers of the boats occupied by the Japs would, when in rough water at a given signal, upset the boats and the Japs would either drown or be caught in the water by the boat which had been left to follow up. By these various means, in the course of a week or so a great quantity of arms were captured, and we were able to attack many small parties of Japs which happened to make it in from the coast.[44]

The Australian operatives too were more confident in taking on larger Japanese patrols. In one incident, on the night of 24 July, they ambushed a large launch carrying about 60 Japanese reinforcements from Kanowit to Song. The *Official History* notes, 'As the launch was passing Kearny's party, someone on board lit a cigarette and the deck was seen to be full of troops. The party opened fire with two Bren guns, using eight magazines each. It was learnt at a later date that 57 out of the 60 troops on board were killed and that the launch was subsequently sunk.'[45]

The increased flow of accurate intelligence resulted in follow-up air strikes to be called and these further shook Japanese morale, in particular that of civilians. By now, RAAF bases at Morotai and Labuan allowed the deployment of a range of aircraft as part of the Australian First Tactical Airforce and units of the US Thirteenth Air Force. This included Spitfires, P-40 Kittyhawks, P-38 Lightnings, Beaufighters, B-24 Liberators, B-25 Mitchells and Austers, as well as amphibious aircraft like Catalinas. It was at this time that a programme was introduced whereby Catalina pilots would be inserted and join SRD parties on the ground to get firsthand experience of the conditions, the terrain and the work of the SRD operatives.

The pressure on the Japanese from all sides was now intense, and by 21 July, apart from sporadic, small contacts with elusive Japanese units, operations ceased because the Japanese were dispersed, devoid of material support and completely cut off. While they were continually confronted by major Allied landings, in particular those of the Australian 7th and 9th Divisions, and harassed by SRD operatives and local guerrillas, their supply lines were also interdicted by RAAF air strikes, which left Japanese forces starving and debilitated by disease.

On 11 August, a surrender ultimatum was sent to the Japanese commander at Sibu, some 40 miles (65 kilometres) inland from the coast, but he refused, instead beating the emissary and throwing him in gaol. Major Sochon again sent an ultimatum, to expire at midnight on 16 August. Skirmishes with Japanese patrols were ongoing, with the operatives continuing their policy of hit-and-run, striking and disappearing into the jungle, which, as the *Official History* notes, 'began to tell on the Japanese morale and from intelligence reports received, the party learned that the ultimatum had been discussed and the majority of the enemy were in favour of surrender, but that this would not be considered by the CO and the Kempe-tai'.[46]

Before the ultimatum ran out the official Japanese surrender was announced, and Allied offensive operations ceased. As was experienced by Semut I and II, this news did not prevent continued Japanese actions that led to the deaths of a number of Australians and their allies after the surrender. Having still received no reply from the Japanese military, Sochon sent a letter to the head of the civilian Japanese, at the same time instructing the Japanese military that any movement outside a defined perimeter 'would be treated as an aggressive one'[47].

The *Official History* notes that 'Up until 31 August [more than two weeks after the surrender] all patrols were reporting continual Japanese aggression in the Sibu area',[48] and even by mid-September, Sochon was still despatching letters to the Japanese area command ordering them to meet and surrender their forces. Finally a response was received from the Japanese, allowing the surrender to take place on 17 September 1945. The *Official History* entry states, 'The enemy had three courses open to him; to stay, dig in and be strafed, to move into the jungle and be ambushed by our patrols and Dyaks, to withdraw. He always took the easy way out, and withdrew.'[49]

Also operational in Sarawak at this time was the Semut IV party, who had been inserted in varying-sized groups from 2 August through to the end of the month. Their role was to report on Japanese movements through an intelligence network of locals, to establish a new administration and to locate the Europeans who were known to be held by the Japanese. It was seen as important to ascertain Japanese attitudes to the idea of surrendering and, with the assistance of the Japanese High Command, to contact remaining enemy parties with regard to the surrender. This work continued, parallel to similar operational work of the other Semut parties, until early October, when the Semut IV party were withdrawn.

At the time of the surrender, there were 23 officers and 59 other ranks in the field as part of the Semut operation, along with an estimated 2000 armed local guerrillas. By this time, Semut controlled the whole of Sarawak, excluding some parts under the AIF, along with the southern part of British North Borneo and half of Dutch Borneo. This operation had not only confined the Japanese to coastal areas but also prevented their penetration inland to seek food that was now not arriving from Japan. The *Official History* notes, 'The casualties inflicted on the enemy were 1486 Japanese killed, 37 prisoners, 36 auxiliaries killed, 204 auxiliaries prisoner, a total of 1736 casualties inflicted at the cost to Semut of approximately 390 native troops killed.'[50] There were no Australians killed during this time.

The Japanese had little knowledge of the Semut operation or the parties involved, due mainly to the loyalty of the local people and their hatred for the enemy. The Japanese did learn of the insertion by parachute of Semut I in May 1945, but rightly concluded that this was in preparation for the expected Allied invasion and so no action was taken to find them, as the Japanese considered their activity 'could do little harm'.[51] They also had a vague knowledge of Semut II and Semut III, but again saw little problem with them and basically ignored their presence in the interior. Any intelligence that was gained on the Semut parties was not passed on to Japanese 37 Army HQ, so no effort was made to eliminate them. As a consequence, SRD control was uninterrupted, and the recruiting of locals and the organisation and arming of a guerrilla army was allowed to proceed unhindered.

None of these operations in Borneo and Sarawak would have been possible without the loyal and continued support of the local people. As Roland Griffiths-Marsh said, 'We operatives would not have lasted one day if it was not for the loyalty and the assistance and the courage of the local indigenous people.'[52] To this, Jack Tredrea added, 'The Semut operation would not have succeeded without those natives. They were wonderful. In all of the inland natives you could trust them. Down on the coast, where the Japs were in occupation, a lot of the Malay people did help the Japs. To this day, the Australian people are the most highly thought of over there.'[53]

By the time the four Semut parties were extracted, they had provided valuable intelligence to both the Australian Army to assist the invasion planning and the RAAF for target indication. The enemy were denied movement inland and hence food supplies, which in turn spared the local population, at least in the inland areas, the severe treatment inflicted by the Japanese on Borneo locals elsewhere. The imposition of strict discipline by SRD operatives prevented inter-tribal fighting, and allowed for the return to a strong civilian administration after the war. These victories, coupled with the fact there were no SRD casualties, mean that the series of Semut operations must rank as some of the most successful the SRD organisation undertook during the course of the war.

TWELVE

The Secret War in the Spice Islands

The areas known during the war as the Celebes and Moluccas today form part of Indonesia and are known as Sulawesi and Maluku. This area, which included an array of islands between Dutch New Guinea in the east, the Philippines to the north and the large island of Borneo to the west, had a turbulent colonial history. The islands of the Celebes, Halmahera, Morotai, Ceram and the small island of Ambon had been, since the early 1500s, known as the legendary Spice Islands, important sources of nutmeg, cloves and other sought-after spices for the tables of Europe. After numerous wars of conquest, it was the Dutch who were finally victorious, but by the end of the 18th century, with the market for spice in decline, the islands became largely forgotten.

After the Japanese quickly overran the islands south of Singapore, across through the Philippines and on to Papua New Guinea, on 12 January 1942 they landed troops from Davao in the Philippines on the north-eastern corner of the Celebes at Manado. From there, Japanese paratroopers captured the airfield of Langoan just to the south of Manado, then on 24 January made landings at Kendari and Macassar in the south of the Celebes to secure the whole island.

To the east, Ambon, with its airfield, had been identified in late 1941 as a strategic target and a potential base for Japanese bombers to fly from and bomb the Australian mainland. On 14 December, the Australian 2/21st Battalion of the 8th Division, known as 'Gull Force', sailed from Darwin, arriving on Ambon on 17 December. Comprising 1090 men along with artillery and other elements, they joined a Dutch force of 2800 men, known as the Molukken Brigade of the Royal Netherlands East Indies Army (KNIL), and stood in readiness to defend the island.

Having secured the Celebes and increased their air attacks, the Japanese landed on 30 January. They quickly overcame the defending Dutch and Australian units, who were forced to surrender, and the Japanese executed more than 250 Australian and Dutch prisoners in the days after. As a result, from early 1942 until the return of the Allies in late 1944 and early 1945, this area was under Japanese control. The Japanese found themselves with 1100 Dutch POWs plus some 1800 Australian, British, American and Dutch sailors, so that by April 1942, some 2870 POWs were held across the area. Many were sent to work in the interior, some to build airfields and defensive positions, while others were shipped to the Chinese island of Hainan and mainland Japan. Many remained in various military and civilian camps across the archipelago, and by war's end a number were to unfortunately die in Allied air raids.

For the remainder of 1942 and well into 1943, the Allied focus in the South West Pacific Area was on defending Guadalcanal and recovering Papua New Guinea. As the front moved to the west, towards Dutch New Guinea, and plans were drawn up for the Celebes and Moluccas, so too did SRD become drawn into a new operational area. At the headquarters of SWPA, the area was now divided for operational purposes among a number of units. SRD was allocated the south-eastern area of the Celebes, with a focus on the area around Kendari on the eastern of the two prominent peninsulas. While the Allies were still moving towards Hollandia in Dutch New Guinea, planning began after May 1944 for both SRD operations and then large-scale invasions by the Allies into the Celebes. For SRD, the main tasks for operations in this area were principally reconnaissance and the location of POW camps believed to be in various parts of the archipelago.

While the Japanese had taken control of the area in early 1942, they had not established permanent garrisons nor developed the islands until early 1944, when it became important as a focus for the defence of the southern Philippines. By this time, General MacArthur was also seeking a base for operations for the liberation of Mindanao. MacArthur preferred Morotai to the nearby Halmahera Island, as Morotai had serviceable airstrips and the island was not heavily defended by the Japanese, so both US and Australian forces landed there on 15 September 1944, with a simultaneous landing on Peleliu to the north-east.[1] Outnumbering the Japanese defenders, they quickly secured Morotai, leaving any remaining Japanese forces confined to the rugged interior covered by thick jungle and cut off from supplies from the sea.

Given its strategic importance, Morotai was quickly developed. Two airstrips were ready for operational use within weeks of the invasion, as were port facilities, stores dumps, a headquarters and communications centre. Yet while all this went on, the Allies continued to resist a number of Japanese attempts to retake the island between September and November. Along with this development, in October 1944, SRD appointed Major Ambrose Trappes-Lomax as the SRD liaison officer, who was tasked with training members of FELO for a mission, codenamed J Mission (Crab), which never eventuated. Lomax had been with SRD from the beginning, and was, as Des Foster, a member of SRD, remembered, 'a lovely man, no affectation, unassuming guy and everyone had a great respect for him'.[2]

However, there were difficulties with shipping and supply and the fact that, apart from the continuing operation to find and extract POWs, this area was seen to be of reduced strategic importance given the movement of the war northwards towards mainland Japan.

Due to the number of potential operations in this area, two groups were established: Group A, which was to cover Borneo, and Group B, which covered the Celebes and the Moluccas. This second group was further broken down into two groups, one headquartered in Morotai and another on the island of Noemfoor further to the east. The first of these sub-groups was to develop operations in the Celebes (Giraffe, Crane, Shrill, Magpie, Raven and Garfish), while the second sub-group was focused on operations in the Moluccas (Opossum, Swallow, Swift and Finch I–IV) and led by Major Trappes-Lomax, who flew into Morotai on 4 March 1945. Having been separately tasked, each group was to develop guerrilla attacks and spread their offensive operations to a range of other islands within the outlying area.

To limit the movement of Japanese troops and to cut off their resupply lines, the task of SRD was first to deny the enemy the use of native prahus and luggers by capturing and then sailing them to Morotai, and second to destroy any vessels under construction and extract the local boat builders, then also return them to Morotai. Secondary tasks included the removal of parts from downed aircraft, including radar and radios, and their destruction at the crash site.

The first series of operations were confined to the Celebes, while a second series were undertaken as part of the defence of Morotai.

The Celebes operations, which included Giraffe I–III, Crane I–II, Shrill, Magpie I–III, Raven and Garfish, sought to gather intelligence from Manado and Minahassa at the northern end of the island and to secure or destroy water transport, built locally and available to the enemy. The Morotai operations, which included Opossum, Swallow, Swift and Finch I–IV, were tasked to assist NICA (the Netherlands Indies Civil Administration) and the US Morotai PT (Patrol Torpedo Boat) base in gathering intelligence, collecting and interrogating locals and assisting in the erection of navigation lights.

The first operation, codenamed Giraffe I, was led by Major Trappes-Lomax. A party of nine were inserted by Catalina onto Tahoelandang (now Tahulandang) Island in the Sangihe Group, some 40 miles (64 kilometres) from the north-eastern tip of the Celebes, on 17 March 1945. Their objectives were to 'deny the enemy the use of native luggers by removing them to Morotai, to evacuate native boat builders and to remove or destroy parts of a US naval aircraft which had been forced down on the island'.[3]

After landing and transporting the party and stores to the shore in an inflatable two-man boat, they were informed that the locals were too afraid to assist, as the chief of police and the local police force were all working for the Japanese. Major Trappes-Lomax took four men to arrest the two Japanese-appointed 'quislings'[4] – the police chief and an administrative officer – and three native police, with the aim of returning them to Morotai for questioning, but the two main suspects had fled.

Meanwhile, the remainder of the party set about establishing radio communications with Morotai, but they needed to move to a new location before this link could be secured. While the base was being prepared, Trappes-Lomax and a Dutch colleague, Lieutenant Brunnings, made a reconnaissance both east and west along the well-paved coastal road by Welbike – a small, collapsible single-seat motorbike made in England for special operations and parachute units. The two men stopped at villages along the way to interview locals and seek information on the Japanese.

The party split up and embarked on other tasks. Major Richard Hardwick, a Dutch interpreter, collected and sorted useful documents from the police files, including some from the Kempeitai, and these were returned to Morotai. At this time a captured Japanese cutter was modified with a 9-horsepower outboard motor by Captain V. D. Prentice and Lieutenant H. E. Josselyn (RNVR) with the help of a local shipwright, and a trial was run satisfactorily. Meanwhile, two US naval ratings (junior ranks) paddled out to a downed American aircraft, where they destroyed both the radar and the radio and threw the parts into the sea.

Keen to undertake a reconnaissance along the coast, Trappes-Lomax set out with three others in the outboard-powered Japanese cutter, but a short time later the motor broke down and the party transferred to a prahu to continue their patrol. But word was received that a large party of Japanese were heading for the island and were expected that night or the following morning. Having found no suitable vessels to sail to Morotai, the party requested a Catalina extraction and this was completed, along with a prahu-load of locals. But this vessel did not arrive as expected, and an operation was mounted to find and return it. This became Giraffe II. In the meantime, and as a result of intelligence sent to SRD Morotai, RAAF Kittyhawks were able to sink five two-masted Japanese vessels south of Siaoe.

On 24 March, Major Lomax led a second operation, this time to not only find the missing prahu, but to provide protection for a NICA operation to extract locals from Majoe Island who he feared had been compromised by SRD operatives. Inserted on the island by Catalina at 0930, they soon found the missing prahu, and the women and children in the party were flown back to Morotai by the US Catalina. After other locals had been questioned, a number were selected to be returned to Morotai, but when the Catalina was taking off, it crashed and sank, taking with it all the stores. However, those on board were rescued by other locals and transported to shore, where they were later extracted by a US Army crash boat.

Having failed to extract the local vessels on Majoe Island, another operation was mounted, Giraffe III, which sailed under Major Tony Gluth on HMAS *Blacksnake*. Its aim was to deny the enemy the use of local luggers by removing them and local boat builders to Morotai. The Giraffe party departed Morotai at dawn on 26 March 1945, arriving at 0400 the following morning off Majoe Island. A party under Major Gluth went ashore, where they inspected the boats spread along the beach before heading along the coast in search of further boats. On the way, they landed at a village, where they provided much-needed medical atten-tion to the locals and left them a gramophone and Dutch flag. The Dutch were of course keen to retain the support of the local people and keep their influence and control apparent, ready for the expected departure of the Japanese and the return of their colonial possessions to them. After returning to *Blacksnake* for the night, the following day the party again inspected local boats, in particular one they considered the most important, but it was found rotten and unseaworthy.

On the night before their return to Morotai, the locals gave the operatives a party and organised a dance, such was their appreci-ation, in particular for the medical help the crew had provided. The following morning, after a fond farewell by the villagers,

Blacksnake set off for Morotai with a local boat in tow, arriving at 1430 on 30 March.

On 9 May 1945, a US B-24 Liberator bomber was shot down over the Togian Islands in the Celebes. Of the 11 men in the crew, six were subsequently rescued, but five landed and their fate was unknown. Responding to a request by 13 Bomber Command USAF, SRD were requested to carry out an operation, codenamed Crane I, to locate the five missing crewmen. A Catalina was despatched from Morotai with Captain Keith Stringfellow and Flight Lieutenant Geoffrey Ripley. Departing on the morning of 11 May, the aircraft flew over the area at 0915, conducting a low-level search at 100 feet (30 metres) along the shoreline, before landing at the village of Kaboetan, which was at the southern entrance to the Benteng Strait. The two Australians, accompanied by two members of the Catalina crew, then went ashore, where they interrogated the village *kepala* (Japanese-appointed headman), but he could give no information about the fate of the American airmen. Stringfellow's report of the operation recalled, 'The natives were very friendly and promised to hide the downed airmen. This promise was further strengthened when we issued them with cigarettes.'[5] The operatives returned to the aircraft and flew back to Morotai.

On the following day, a similar search-and-rescue mission was flown, but the sea was unsuitable for the Catalina to land so it again returned. Then, on the evening of 13 May, 13 Bomber Command USAF requested yet another search be made, this time with the assistance of SRD. To undertake this operation, a party of six operatives under Major Gluth were assembled. Leaving Morotai by Catalina the following morning, the party landed at Kg Katoepa, one of the largest villages in the area, which they found deserted. Soon a group of six locals arrived and were put to work helping to erect the aerial, but four of them fled, escaping in a prahu. The remaining two, when interrogated, said they had heard there were five American airmen in the village of Tobili but had no detailed information.

Another local arrived and was interrogated. He stated that the Americans had collected at Tobili but had been betrayed by the headman, sending a message to the Japanese in Oena Oena. The Japanese had then sent a 12-man patrol to ambush the Americans, who, having trusted the villagers, had been armed and had boarded a prahu in the hope of escaping. But when they were off the coast opposite the Japanese, the locals upset the boat, throwing all into the sea and quickly swimming away. The Japanese then opened fire, killing four and capturing one, who was tied up and taken back to Oena Oena. A captured document recording Japanese actions stated, '. . . on the 9 May, five enemy paratroopers were dropped near Tobili village. Four men of these paratroopers were killed and one was captured by the Japanese.'[6] The search-and-rescue patrol was extracted by Catalina on the morning of 15 May and returned to Morotai.

The question of local loyalty was always difficult and risky to judge. Within the Celebes, like many places under Japanese control, the people suffered badly. Food was scarce, but the most serious problem was the shortage of cloth, with the people resorting to wearing clothes made from hessian and bark. Village chiefs took the majority of the rice along with fowls and eggs, leaving many starving. The two main diseases were dysentery and malaria, for which there were no medicines except native cures and herbs.

The village *kepala* were also often very harsh on the local people. They wore Japanese clothes, had a bad reputation for brutality and were feared by the people. As a result, the locals were afraid and apprehensive about assisting the Allies in any way or accepting gifts 'until the Jap flag was pulled down and the Dutch flag hoisted. The natives expressed a desire to fight for their homes.'[7]

Yet another attempt was made to find the surviving American airman, who had been captured by the Japanese. On 24 May, a small party under Major Gluth, Crane II, departed Morotai by Catalina for a reconnaissance of Oena Oena Island off the north-west coast of Togian Island. After paddling ashore by inflated boat, they landed about 500 yards from a village, where, apart from an old local brewing *sogoya*, an alcohol, the village was empty. He was interrogated along with some other locals who happened to arrive, but they had little useful information on the fate of the American. Later in the morning another local appeared, who said he did know of the capture of the American: after being taken to Oena Oena, he had been transported to Poso on the Celebes coast, some 70 miles (112 kilometres) to the south-west. With the party unable to do anything further with regards to locating the downed Americans, and after burning their remaining stores and trade clothes, a Catalina arrived to extract them and return them to Morotai.

Having failed to find the missing airman, SRD moved to undertake a search to ascertain the fate of another downed American, this time a pilot from a P-38 Lightning, and to collect intelligence. The operation had a party of three, under Major Gluth, and was codenamed Shrill. They left Morotai on 19 May by Catalina and flew to Katatoeng, where they briefly undertook some intelligence work before flying on to the island of Merampit. Here they found the P-38 clearly visible on the beach, but were informed by the locals that the pilot had been captured by the Japanese and taken to Boe. After further attempts to interrogate locals in the area, the Catalina returned to Morotai.

In response to GHQ's request for intelligence in the upper Celebes and Moluccas, SRD submitted a plan, codenamed Snipe, in April 1945. This plan proposed a force of 70 Europeans and 200 Sangirese locals to establish a base in the Sangihe Island stretching north from the Celebes, and from there to conduct operations to cut the Japanese line of communication between Manado in the Celebes and Mindanao in the Philippines. This plan was rejected by GHQ, but the changing strategic situation and the need for detailed intelligence saw it resubmitted under the codename Magpie.

Following the success of the Giraffe and Crane operations, SRD was notified of the priority for intelligence on the town of Manado on the far-northern coast of the Celebes and on the likely Japanese escape line from Mindanao through the Sangihe and Talaud Islands to Manado. For this, SRD needed to establish an intelligence network, extract and interrogate locals, undertake short-term raiding and build a forward base from which further operations could be launched against Manado. SRD divided the operation into three phases: the first was reconnaissance, the second the establishment and provisioning of forward bases, and the third the building of a local intelligence network. As the approach to the operational area was from three directions, the north, south and east, there were to be three separate Magpie operations: Magpie I, Magpie II and Magpie III.

It was decided that since previous operations had provided the preliminary reconnaissance, the first of the three phases was not to be undertaken. SRD was tasked to insert a party to recce both Majoe and Tidore Islands and establish a stores dump on Tidore, as well as make a hydrographical survey of Laboehan Bay and provide medical assistance to the locals. The leader was New Zealand Major J. L. K. Brown plus eight members, mostly AIF, who left Morotai aboard HMAS *Blacksnake* on 28 June 1945. After landing the following day, an extensive patrol of Tidore Island was undertaken, and a number of locals were interrogated and useful intelligence gathered. Over the following two days the survey work was completed, as was the provision of medical aid to the locals, and the party returned to Morotai.

After the completion of the Crane mission it was found that the necessary intelligence was at hand, so the southern approach as part of the Magpie operation was cancelled. Intelligence was still required from the northern approach, in particular for Siaoe, Biaro and Tahoelandang islands, plus the capture of a Japanese lugger that was being constructed at the village of Mala on Siaoe Island. A combined SRD and NICA party under Lieutenant Frank Lambert (AIF) departed Morotai on board *Blacksnake* on 9 June and landed at 0900 on 11 June. In support were two PT boats with a support barge carrying fuel being towed behind *Blacksnake*. Corporal Henry Fawkes, one of the Australian operatives, recalled, 'On the way down we struck a terrible storm and the barge we were towing broke adrift and that was full of fuel for the PT boats. So we had to run around in circles to catch up to the barge, and [lost] time.'[8]

On arrival the operatives were broken into two groups, one to destroy the Japanese lugger being built at Mala on Siaoe and the other to rescue a pro-British Chinese doctor from the hospital on the hill. Operative Des Foster remembered seeing the hospital, which he noted was 'what I thought was a sultan's palace . . . there was this impressive building in this quite primitive area'.[9]

Henry Fawkes told the full story of the operation:

On the way up [to the hospital] a boy of 10–12 years of age comes running down this path, shouting, 'Nippon, Nippon, Nippon' [to warn the Japanese], so [the locals] were sensible enough to wake up the Japs [who] were there in the bushes beside the path, so they started to withdraw. We joined up with [the Japanese] and got into a bit of crossfire with them. But when we got into the boat, the bloody outboard motor wouldn't start, would it! So we tied both [of the PT support boats] together and we were paddling out. There's 20 of us. The Japs started to come down to the foreshore and they were firing across the bay to us in inflated boats but I still couldn't swim. One shot ricocheted across the bow of the PT boat and Trappes-Lomax, who was on the PT boat, ordered they open up with the Oerlikons [20 mm cannons], and once they did that the Japs got back into the scrub.[10]

Before they departed, the PT boats fired on the shoreline. Fawkes remembered, 'There was a three-storey building there of brick and concrete, right on the foreshore, that the Japs used as a HQ. Bullets were going into this building and big holes were appearing – who was going to stay in there? We eventually got away and got onto the *Blacksnake*.'[11] While the operatives had destroyed the Japanese lugger, they were unable to extract the Chinese doctor from the hospital, and the party returned to Morotai on 12 June.

On 11 June, a small SRD party, codenamed Raven, under Captain Keith Stringfellow as planning officer and Lieutenant Scobell McFerran-Rogers as party leader, were tasked to assist in finding a lost US Navy Martin PBM Mariner flying boat, which had been forced down on 4 June in the Rando area in the north-west Celebes, and to undertake intelligence-gathering on the same mission. The request for the mission had been authorised by General MacArthur on 11 June and simply read, 'Regarding rescue mission US airmen action approved.'[12]

At hand was a report on the loss of the aircraft with 14 crew members, which in part stated the following:

> At 1305 on 4 June, while on a regular sector patrol, the PBM contacted an enemy convoy. Two ships were sunk by bombs on two separate runs. On the third strafing mission this plane suffered 3 hits by medium A/A, one bursting in the forward bunkroom and the third between the port engine and the hull. As a result of the hits, the gas line was severed and the hull was holed. Through loss of gas the plane was unable to reach base. Since one of the passengers, R. B. Jegewski, had a foot blown off by the shell which burst in the after station, the crew decided after discussion over the intercom to beach the plane instead of landing at sea and taking to the 3 life rafts because they thought the injured man could be better cared for.[13]

The 14 men made it to shore, including the injured man who died soon after. Here they met a local who promised to seek assistance, but the following morning a large Japanese patrol estimated at 75 men arrived in the area, and after machine-gunning the plane from the beach the Japanese captured nine of the survivors. The other four hid in the water until dark and then tried to make a raft to head out to sea. But the raft soon broke up, leaving the men clinging to logs. One of the four offered to go ashore to collect coconuts, but soon after he left, gunfire was heard and he was not seen again. The rest paddled further out to sea and the following day were picked up by a rescue aircraft. The captured crew were never seen again.

The operation was to be broken into two phases. The first was 'A short-term insertion of the party for the purpose of interrogating and extracting native informants', while the second was 'a 24-hour insertion of a greatly reinforced party with the same objects in view'.[14] To undertake the mission, a Mariner seaplane was despatched from Tawi Tawi in the southern Philippines to pick up the party at Morotai and fly them to Tawi Tawi on 11 June. The following day, Captain Stringfellow and Lieutenant McFerran-Rogers flew an aerial reconnaissance, during which they collected a local from a prahu off Tarakan for interrogation.

On 13 June, the first attempt was made to insert the party, but this failed as the pilot of the Mariner, no doubt anxious to take off, swamped the inflated boat by 'starting his motors before the boat was clear'.[15] The full story of this incident was told by Corporal Gordon Philpott:

> When we were getting out of the flying boat, the bloke at the back door of the plane told the pilot we were all clear and we weren't. So the pilot went to take off and the tail of the flying boat swung around and overturned the boat we were in and we all sank to the bottom like stones, although we didn't reach the bottom it was so deep. We had to get all our weapons and ammunition off us to get back to the surface, which fortunately we succeeded in doing.[16]

The following day a second attempt was made, this time landing two parties: one north of Rondo and the second beside the wreckage of the crashed aircraft. Here the party learnt that one of the aircrew had died of his injuries and was buried, the grave being later found and confirmed. Once this news was transmitted to the US HQ, the request came to determine what happened to the nine men still not accounted for and hopefully still alive.

Returning to Morotai, Stringfellow attended a conference where plans were drawn up for a larger party of ten to be inserted under the experienced leadership of Major Gluth. The party left

Morotai by RAAF C-47 Dakota and arrived in Tawi Tawi, where they transferred to a US Mariner flying boat. On 19 June they departed and landed at their insertion point on the north-west coast of the Celebes. They quickly paddled ashore and undertook a local recce while the flying boat stood by. The operatives came upon 12 locals, who, after questioning, could provide very little information. The locals were asked to return with the flying boat to Tawi Tawi but refused, 'and on a show of force by the party they immediately burst into tears, and for security reasons party leader allowed them to return to their village'.[17]

The party now moved north, having gained no intelligence about the fate or whereabouts of the missing Americans. Underfoot the ground was sandy and soft and the undergrowth made progress difficult, but they pushed on until they came to the small village of Sodi. Again they questioned the locals, who appeared very frightened of Japanese reprisals. Out at sea, the party spotted the patrolling aircraft, a reassuring sign should they require a quick escape. When they arrived in a larger village, Lalombi, their interpreter was able to reassure the locals of their intentions and they were served tea and provided comfortable mats to sit on.

While the party were enjoying the village hospitality, an ox cart was seen on the opposite side of the river about to cross. When the locals with the cart saw the operatives, they quickly turned around and made off, but not before it was observed they were wearing 'what appeared to be American shirts'.[18] Major Gluth and Private Whitworth and a local named Roestan swam across the river and searched the village. The inhabitants had gone, but the party found Japanese occupation money and a pair of US-issue sun goggles before they returned across the river.

After an uneventful night, Major Gluth decided that further time in the area was unnecessary, and so would wait for extraction with the return of the seaplane. But just after 0900 Gluth heard voices down the beach and a party of six Japanese appeared. Henry Fawkes recalled, 'We didn't see them until they started shooting . . . there was a drop of about four inches on the beach side, so we went for that for cover.'[19]

Immediately the Japanese opened an intense fire, killing Lieutenant McFerran-Rogers and the local, Roestan. As the remainder of the party dived into a 'shallow tidal wash'[20] on the edge of the beach and began withdrawing, Corporal Fawkes crept up to Lieutenant McFerran-Rogers' body, where he collected his identity discs and Owen gun. As Fawkes remembered, 'When he got hit, I ducked out and grabbed him and pulled him into shelter but he died in my arms.'[21] As they crawled away and returned fire, the remainder of the party were able to slow the enemy attack by 'the judicious use of grenades and Bren gun fire'.[22]

After pulling the officer into cover, Fawkes joined the rest of the party. He recalled, 'The major said to me, "What do you reckon?" and I said, the best place to go is into the scrub. He said, "I agree. You're first across." I said thanks and away I went, zig-zagging across. Fortunately not a shot was fired at me. But on the way across, I could see a bloke, he appeared to me to be wounded, he was holding his hip.'[23]

After a withdrawal of 500 yards, Major Gluth ordered the operatives to move into the thick undergrowth skirting the beach, but Private Whitworth, who was ahead leading the withdrawal, did not hear the order and continued on. He was not seen alive again. The remainder of the party, now missing McFerran-Rogers, Whitworth and Roestan, collected in the undergrowth before moving quickly south along the coast, leaving the Japanese still searching for then, to a point where they were able to signal the rescue seaplane, which had been flying overhead.

After circling, the plane landed just off the point and taxied in as close as could be safely navigated. With the engines still running, the party were forced to wade out 100 yards from the shore in full view of the enemy across the shallow, uneven coral reef. Fortunately they were not seen and, after being quickly hauled aboard, the aircraft took off after a few minutes. Henry Fawkes remembered, 'I asked them why they were late and got some rubbish story but I know the true story now – a bloke slept in before they left to pick us up.'[24]

A brief aerial search was made of the beach, but the party saw no sign of Private Whitworth and returned to Tawi Tawi. In an interview with Captain Keith Stringfellow, who flew on the rescue mission, he told his part of the story:

> We flew down and as we got close to it [the beach] I saw this group of our fellows out in the water, about 200 yards out in the bay, so I said to the pilot, 'Get down there quick and get those blokes off.' He got down there quick and we launched a rubber duckie and got them onto the plane and I said to Tony [Gluth], 'What are you doing?' and he said, 'The Japs surprised us this morning and we have lost three of our men.' So I said, 'How did you get out here on the reef?' as I couldn't imagine a group of people standing up in the water and a machine gun [not taking] the lot out. There was no firing from the Japs at all and our plane came down as close as possible to them, we put the rubber duckies out, picked them up and then did a flight over the beach to see if we could see anybody, but couldn't see our people in the water or on the beach.[25]

Henry Fawkes noted, 'We flew back over the place and he [Whitworth] was gone. He was taken back to Dongala and taken out and shot.'[26]

In the subsequent report on the operation, it was estimated that as many as 12 Japanese had been killed from the enemy party of 25. It was also noted that with the deterioration of the Japanese strategic position, they were inflicting more severe control on the locals, and that SRD operations had to be aware of this and prevent where possible action against the local people. The report also noted, 'It is considered that the sound and simple plan adopted by the leader and the skill at arms of the party prevented its complete destruction by the superior enemy patrol.'[27]

With each operation, SRD and the operatives of Z Special were proving their effectiveness, generally succeeding in their tasks and continuing a war of fear and attrition on the besieged and starving Japanese forces. But right up to the very end of the war, and even in the months after the end of hostilities, they were called upon to undertake extraordinary and risky operations, something others had failed to achieve, but something their training and daring well prepared them for.

Thirteen

In Support of Oboe II – Balikpapan

After the successful landings at Tarakan and Brunei Bay during June 1945, attention turned to the port and oilfields at Balikpapan, in the south-east of Borneo, so important to the Japanese war effort. This was the third and final stage of Operation Oboe, the Allied plan to invade and liberate both the British and Dutch sections of Borneo. Balikpapan had been in Japanese hands since their landings on 25 January 1942, when they had overwhelmed the limited Allied resistance.

Prior to the war, the Balikpapan oilfields, under Dutch control, were producing about 1.8 million tons of oil annually. This output was refined and pumped into 40 storage tanks then exported from a modern port with connecting roads and infrastructure. When the Japanese invaded, the Europeans, mainly the Dutch, were able to sabotage much of the oil-producing facilities and other valuable port infrastructure, which resulted in brutal reprisals from the Japanese, with about 100 European civilians executed. The Japanese were also able to quickly restore production, and by 1943 were producing nearly 4 million barrels annually, with Balikpapan becoming one of the major sources of Japanese crude oil.

The Allies had started strategic bombing of the refinery facilities in October 1943, but this involved long flights and a 17-hour round trip from airfields around Darwin. RAAF Catalinas also undertook mining operations along the coast, which, along with the bombing, nearly halved the Japanese oil output. As the war moved north, the United States Air Force initially began bombing operations from the island of Noemfoor and from airfields on Morotai, and later from Labuan and Tarakan with USAAF units flying from Mindanao. After suffering heavy losses in the first two raids due to inadequate fighter cover, subsequent raids completely destroyed the facilities and oil production ceased. Along with the successful interdiction operations, the facilities were never repaired.

Well before the Australian 7th Division landings on 1 July 1945, a request had been sent from Headquarters 1st Australian Corps to SRD to provide two broad areas of assistance. The first was to attack both the port of Balikpapan and the oil storage facilities at the Pantjser Tank Farm, and the second to provide information necessary for the planning of Operation Oboe II, comprising the Balikpapan landings.

For the first stage, SRD planned two operations, both of which were cancelled. Operation Toad was to be an attack on Japanese shipping in Balikpapan Harbour on small, submersible boats by operatives flown in and released from Catalinas, but this did not go ahead due to the anticipated early success of the Balikpapan landings and to the timings for the actual invasion. The second was Operation Vulture, an attack on the Pantjser Tank Farm and the nearby airfield. Air raids throughout 1943 and 1944 by Allied bombers operating out of Darwin on long-range missions had been unsuccessful, particularly after the loss of 50 Liberator bombers. It was then realised that the destruction of the tanks by SRD demolition teams was the only option, however the lack of available submarines prevented this operation proceeding.

Instead, SRD focused on their second area of assistance to 1st Australian Corps: securing intelligence as part of Operation Oboe for the planned landings at Balikpapan. This was given the codename Platypus and was to comprise a number of sub-operations. On 3 March 1945, as a first step, an order was received by SRD from General Headquarters SWPA to provide a reconnaissance party to be landed in the Balikpapan area. This party, codenamed Robin, was to be the first of 12 parties, all under Platypus, that would be inserted in and around Balikpapan, both before and after the invasion. Platypus I–VII would be inserted prior to the July landings and Platypus VIII–XII in the period after.

The objectives of the Robin plan (aka Platypus I) were broad, and included the establishment of a local intelligence network to gather information on Japanese defences, units and troop movements; the likely escape routes of the Japanese into the interior; the attitude of the local people to the Japanese and the British-Dutch administration; and, most importantly, where Allied POWs were held. The intelligence gained by this party would establish an operational base for further SRD parties to be inserted to undertake more varied intelligence tasks, establish armed guerrilla bands and begin subversive work on Japanese military targets.

The Robin party left Perth on the American submarine USS *Perch*. Because of the large amount of stores (6492 pounds) on board and very limited space within, the folboats and the inflatable rubber boat were secured to the outside hull of the submarine, and were assembled and tested on the voyage to Borneo. After an uneventful trip, the *Perch* approached the Borneo coast some 35 miles (56 kilometres) north of Balikpapan on the night of 20–21 March 1945.

The plan was for a party of two folboats under Major D. J. Stott to recce a landing area for the insertion of the Robin party the following night. The two folboats departed the submarine at 2200, one containing Major Stott and another New Zealand officer, Captain M. T. McMillan, with the second folboat containing Sergeants Bruce Dooland and W. Horrocks. But the small outboard motor on Stott's folboat would not start, so he and McMillan began paddling towards the shore and in the darkness the two folboats became separated. As Sergeant Horrocks later reported:

> Our motor started, but the other motor didn't and Major Stott gave orders to paddle . . . in the event of our getting separated, we were to make contact by walkie-talkie. Shortly afterwards we were separated, but were unable to contact Boat No. 1 or the submarine. We persevered with our course and when about 400 yards from the shore we grounded. At 0130h we heard a Japanese voice (muffled) on the walkie-talkie: at 0145h we heard two English voices loud and clear checking frequency. It was 0200h when we grounded and went ashore.[1]

The USS *Perch* now put to sea, fearing that the loss of the two operatives may have compromised their mission. But the decision was made to proceed with the mission, and on the night of 22–23 March, the *Perch* again approached the shore. At the proposed drop-off point it came across a Japanese oil lighter of about 700 tons, which was attacked by gunfire and set ablaze before it sank. This created another problem: the attack compromised the first party – Stott and McMillan – who it was believed were still alive. As the commander was now keen to clear the area, the main party of seven operatives (Sergeants Dooland and Horrocks had already landed) set out for the shore.

With the burning Japanese vessel lighting up the area, the rubber boats headed for shore at 2230 under Lieutenant R. M. Morton, but again there were problems with the outboards. The operatives finally landed at 0100 and worked until 0630 to carry the stores inland, where they met up with a local who fed them and hid them in the nearby jungle to give them a chance to sleep. The following day, led by this friendly local, they moved further inland, set up a temporary base and tried to make radio contact with Major Stott. But the batteries were unserviceable, so at 1500, Lieutenant William Dwyer set out alone to try and find his party leader. Instead he came across a lone hermit, an old local named Pa-Man, who agreed to warn the operatives of any Japanese approaching their position.

The following morning, Pa-Man reported the presence of an approaching Japanese patrol, which was on the way to investigate the loss of the oil barge. They discovered the party's main stores hideout and to secure it they had placed it under heavy guard then set off to hunt the operatives. The Robin party now split up, carrying their remaining stores to a new locality, but New Zealander WO R. G. Houghton did not make it. Soon after, WO L. Farquharson and a Dutch soldier were thought to have been killed in contacts with the Japanese, and Lieutenants Morton and Dwyer and Sergeant R. L. Dey were forced to retreat into the jungle.

After dark, they silently returned to their last stores dump, which fortunately had not been discovered by the Japanese. Now without help from locals, they could only carry the necessities, a few tins of rations and their personal stores. They had to leave behind their steam generator, among other equipment, and at 2000 moved off to a new base located two miles away. Out of the original party of eight, only three remained. While attempts were made by Lieutenants Morton and Dwyer to find the lost members, the heavy presence of Japanese patrols severely limited their search area.

Continuing their search over the following days, they located two of the local troops, Dua and Satu, suffering from shock, exposure and malaria, and learnt that both Farquharson and Houghton had been captured. The Australians were now surrounded by an estimated 250 Japanese troops, still actively searching for them, which made contact with Allied aircraft sent to search for them impossible. During this time, the men survived on the four tins of rations salvaged from the last camp, and a little rice provided them by the hermit Pa-Man.

On 20 April, two Australian sergeants joined the small party after 'having spent four weeks getting through the Japanese cordon',[2] bringing with them valuable intelligence which needed to be quickly transmitted to Morotai. As they didn't have a radio, it was decided to steal a prahu and escape, but this proved difficult as all vessels were held by the Japanese. One was eventually secured by natives working for the operatives at a cost of 1400 Dutch guilders, but before the party left they continued their reconnaissance patrols, obtaining in the process up-to-date intelligence and information.

At 8.30 pm on 1 May, the small party set out, heading due east in the hope of signalling a ship or rescue aircraft, or island-hopping to reach Morotai. When they were well out to sea, the party saw a number of Allied aircraft, some flying directly overhead, but they were unable to contact them with the small mirror Lieutenant Dwyer had from his Mis-X escape kit (which contained various small pieces of equipment like maps, compasses, fishing line and a mirror). Still rowing north-east on a calm sea, they finally succeeded in signalling a Catalina early on the afternoon of 3 May, which landed alongside the prahu.

Together with some local natives, the men were flown to Morotai. The party included Lieutenants Morton and Dwyer,

Sergeants Dooland and Horrocks, Sergeant Dey and the two local privates Dua and Satu, plus six locals they had extracted for interrogation. At Morotai the men learnt that Major Stott and Captain McMillan had most likely drowned after their folboat capsized and that both WOs, Farquharson and Houghton, had died of wounds, the probable results of torture while in Japanese hands.

A subsequent review of the operation concluded that, for future operations, the equipment carried by parties inserted into unknown and heavily patrolled Japanese territory was to be minimal and lightweight, containing only the bare essentials. Food would therefore need to be purchased, and for this a cache of currency must be distributed among the party. Radio equipment also needed to be lightweight, and steam generators should be replaced by hand or pedal generators. Finally, the men had been wearing boots with the Australian jungle pattern, which left a distinctive print. To get around this, it was suggested to remove boots and only use bare feet when crossing exposed ground, or to even have a fitted sole with the Japanese split-toe design attached.

Planning immediately started on the next three Platypus operations (II, III and IV), which were to be carried out by the same small party under New Zealand Lieutenant R. Tapper. Each operation had a different task. Platypus II was tasked with the capture and interrogation of locals taken from prahus. Between 20 and 24 June 1945, four missions by Catalinas from the US 7th Fleet were carried out and 11 locals brought back to Morotai. An intelligence report dated 24 June stated that some fishermen collected from their prahus were interrogated and could provide little information apart from the fact that the Japanese were short of food and medicines, the Balikpapan hospital had been destroyed by bombing and many Japanese were sick:

The following is a result of the preliminary interrogation of
11 natives taken from the Balikpapan area. They were extracted
on 22 June 1945. SEMBODJA. At kilometre 1½, near the
school, there are 40 Japanese. At kilometre 3 there are 10 Japs,
about 300 Balinese and 4 Kempei. At TIRAM there are more than
100 Japs. At MOEARA there are 50 Japs. The bridge at TIRAM
has been cut through ready to collapse if used. At kilometre 7 from
KLANDASAN there are four dugouts about 2½ metres deep,
3 metres wide and 25 metres long, constructed of wood and
covered with earth, overgrown with grass.[3]

While these reports seem very basic, it explains the distribution of
Japanese forces which in turn can be extrapolated to understand
enemy dispositions even better. Details about sickness, available
food, morale and fighting fitness are all important in ascertaining
the likely success or failure of a mission and what resources and
men should be applied.

An important element of the orders given to Platypus III was in
spreading false rumours that an Allied landing would take place in
the Sambodjalama-Tambangongot area, some 30 miles (48 kilometres) north-east of Balikpapan, on 4 July 1945. These rumours
were spread by local operatives, but the Allies also undertook
low-level recce flights over the area and even dropped a marked
map on the beach where it could be found and handed over to
the Japanese.

Platypus IV had two tasks: first, to extract a number of informants from Balikpapan who could then be reinserted in the area to
spread cleverly crafted disinformation on the upcoming Australian
landings, and second, return them. A party of local operatives
were inserted at last light on 16 June, and after six days had collected a further seven operatives. This larger group paddled out

to sea, where they were picked up by Catalina and flown back to Morotai for interrogation. This ruse proved successful after these locals were returned and interrogated by the Japanese, and 'warned' them of the fabricated plans and landing places for the Australian invasion. It was later seen that local troops loyal to the Japanese were sent to the areas of the anticipated landings, proof of the success of the operation.

The next phase of the operation, Platypus V, involved SRD operatives liaising between the Australian 7th Division and Platypus operatives then in Balikpapan once the invasion had taken place on 1 July. This group, a party totalling 14 men under Captain Murray Drew, embarked with the assault convoy from Morotai on 23 June, disembarking at Balikpapan on 30 June. They set up their camp close to the Australian HQ and immediately established a radio link to SRD Morotai. It was this unit that provided the contacts and coordination of the subsequent Platypus parties until after the surrender.

Having now established a base and a dedicated and reliable link to SRD HQ in Morotai, the next step was the insertion of reconnaissance parties to obtain intelligence for further operations in this part of Borneo. The first operation became Platypus VI and involved the insertion of a party to secure intelligence on the Riko River bridge area, inland about 15 miles (24 kilometres) and north-west from Balikpapan, and to ascertain the best line of advance for the Australians.

On 30 June at 1930 hours, a small party under Captain R. K. 'Jock' McLaren and three ORs were inserted from a Liberator by parachute, but partly due to wind overshot the drop zone, with two operatives landing in a village and another two in the jungle: 'One pair landed on the NE bank of the Riko River, one mile from the DZ [drop zone] and 50 yards from a Japanese guardhouse.'[4] Their aircraft then returned for a delivery run with the storpedoes, but dropped them not only over a mile from the drop zone but also 150 yards from another Japanese post. Given the darkness and the proximity of the Japanese, the party, along with local supporters, hid in dense jungle.

While there were no casualties, this was not a good start to the operation, with all storpedoes missing and the party now totally reliant on local support. The following day, the locals again searched for the storpedoes, but the Japanese were active in the drop zone and eventually found some of the dropped stores. Given the increased threat, natives guided the party out of the area to a better defensive position, allowing them radio contact to aircraft overhead. To add to their problems, WO A. I. Sullivan became ill with a high temperature and diarrhoea, and needed to be evacuated. The decision was made to head towards the coast and Balikpapan, and, after requesting a local guide, one was quickly supplied.

Setting out just before dusk, the party entered open country, the local guide leading. Suddenly a whistle blew and shouts were heard to the front and the flanks. Captain McLaren immediately ordered a retreat back along the jungle path, and when they had gone 50 yards, they disappeared into the jungle and lay still. But Corporal M. Sarif ran into the ambush, taking with him one of only two Austen guns and one pistol. He was never again seen alive. Japanese and local troops raced past their hiding place and took a position in their recently evacuated camp, where they formed a defensive perimeter and waited for the operatives to return.

Unsure whether their guide had in fact led them into an ambush or he had been followed, they made the decision to now head for the Riko River. All night they crawled through a swamp, finally having to abandon some of their heavier equipment, including three small radios known as S Phones. Hungry and thirsty, the three men found rainwater in fallen leaves and slept. The following morning, 5 July, they trekked downstream, finally coming to the Tawai River, which at this point was about 25 yards across. They had to swim four times to get their remaining equipment across before setting out for the Riko River. Pushing through the jungle on the edge of the river, the ground muddy, soft and strong with the stench of mildew, they next came to the Riko River, which again forced them to swim.

The men were exhausted, hungry, covered in scratches and bites, without communications and had lost their remaining Austen gun while swimming the river. Fortunately, a local sampan owner noticed their plight and, after dropping off the women and children on board his boat, returned at 1830 hours. He collected the party and proceeded downriver to the sea and then to the Australian base area at Balikpapan, arriving at 2 am the following morning. While the men were now safe, the reality was that the mission had failed, due mostly to the badly placed initial dropping of stores.

From the same Liberator of 200 Flight, and half an hour after Platypus VI had been wrongly placed on their drop zone, a four-man party, Platypus VII, under Flight Lieutenant A. R. Martin, found themselves in a similar predicament. The party had already lost one of their storpedoes, which had been mistakenly dropped with four others to the previous party. When Flight Lieutenant Martin requested they fly over the drop zone so he could observe it, he was told to return to the back of the plane and harness up. The party were then dropped ten miles from the designated DZ. During the descent, Martin lost sight of his three companions, who were close together, and also his storpedoes. Looking down, he saw he was heading for two well-lit huts, obviously Japanese, so quickly steered himself into nearby trees. Caught upside down, he hung suspended, then saw two Japanese with torches run past below him. He realised he was quite high from the ground when he heard nearby rifle fire.

Using as much cord and the harness of his parachute as he could, he dropped to the ground but still fell 50 feet (15 metres), landing heavily on his shoulder on the edge of a crevice, then tumbled a further six feet onto the rocks below, whereupon he lost consciousness. The *Official History* notes, 'When he came to, it was bright moonlight and everything was quiet. He was unable to move immediately as he had injured his left side. The equipment on his belt had been forced into his body and he was incapable of moving his left arm. He was bleeding from the mouth where he had broken a tooth and opened the gums.'[5]

This was only the beginning of a nightmare journey for Martin. Covered in blood, his clothing in tatters and without a weapon, he found himself a sheltered spot where he dropped his webbing and again lost consciousness, staying hidden until the morning. Unsure of the fate of the rest of the party, he moved off silently down the rock crevice, but he again heard rifle fire so slipped into the jungle, where he remained in hiding for the rest of the day and night. The following morning, he lay down by a river. Emptying the contents of his Mis-X kit, he found he only had a broken watch, a compass, a sovereign and his emergency rations.

While attempting to collect water, Flight Lieutenant Martin saw barges on the river and heard more rifle fire, quickly forcing him back into the jungle, where he hid beneath a fallen tree and remained there until nightfall. Knowing the coast and Balikpapan was only 18 miles (29 kilometres) away, he moved south by compass bearing until morning, when he again hid. He came across a friendly local named Jawa, who offered to help, stating that he hated the Japanese for what they had done. Jawa said he could not provide food or information, instead offering to hide the exhausted Martin for the night. Martin was keen to keep moving, but suddenly found himself in a Japanese garden. He hid upon hearing Japanese voices, but was seen by two soldiers who were patrolling the area. Racing into the jungle, he hid beneath the roots of a large tree and waited until dark before again heading south.

Racked by hunger, Martin now decided he would open his emergency rations, but the clip broke and all attempts to open the tin were unsuccessful. As the *Official History* goes on to state, 'Before proceeding, he mislaid the tin, having by this time become delirious.'[6] On the morning of the fourth day, he continued his journey south and again met up with Jawa, who provided him food and lit a small fire so he could dry himself. While Jawa was unable to guide Martin south, he did direct him to a track that he said would lead past the Japanese and to safety. Martin gave him the sovereign and headed in the direction indicated, but just before midday 'walked into a group of about six Japanese who appeared to be unarmed. He immediately retreated and swam a river which appeared to run east to west. Completely exhausted, he hid in the undergrowth at the edge of the river till late afternoon.'[7]

Martin was found by another group of friendly locals, who told him he was near Semoi, about 16 miles (28 kilometres) to the north of Balikpapan, and that the Japanese were patrolling the area. They gave him food 'resembling omelette'[8] and hot water, and a pencil and paper so he could scribble a note which they said they would deliver to the Allies. The locals took him south, again directing him to a safe track heading in the general direction of Balikpapan.

Exhausted and hungry, his clothes hanging off him in rags, Martin continued this desperate, lonely journey for six days as he stumbled and dragged himself southwards. He was found by more locals, who again provided food and shelter, and also the grim information that he was probably the only survivor of his party, the rest having been captured and shot by the Japanese. On 23 July, more than three weeks since Martin had been inserted, they hid him in a hut for two days, before putting him on a prahu and setting off for Balikpapan on 25 July. Twelve miles (19 kilometres) north of the city, the prahu was intercepted by a canoe, the crew of which were operatives from Platypus XI. The men arranged for the exhausted Martin to be collected and evacuated to Balikpapan.

The return of Martin was something of a surprise to SRD Morotai, who had heard nothing from the party since their insertion on 30 June. He was immediately admitted to hospital before being flown to Perth, where he was to remain until early 1946, such was his condition. The three other members of Platypus VII, Sergeant J. J. O'Dwyer, New Zealand signaller E. H. Myers and Lance Sergeant Ma'eroff bin Said were posted as missing, believed killed, and were never found. It was later reported that the mission had failed due to the dropping of the operatives and the storpedoes well away from the designated drop zone.

The assault onto the beaches of Balikpapan was virtually unopposed with a beachhead secured within half an hour, and by 1400 the Australians had captured the high ground, Hill 87, known as Parramatta Ridge, after heavy fighting. With the aid of tanks, flamethrowers and massive naval fire support, they had extended their line north along the coast and inland, holding an extended front of 1.2 miles (2 kilometres). The following day, the township and harbour were secured and the airfield was reached, providing an extended perimeter of 5 miles (8 kilometres). Pressure was kept up on the Japanese forces, and by 21 July they began to withdraw, some across the island to Kuching.

With the landing at Balikpapan successful and a solid base and perimeter established, it was now necessary to halt the movement of Japanese forces escaping into the interior, as had happened on the northern coast of Borneo near Labuan. To undertake this, the next phase of Platypus was launched, codenamed Platypus VIII. Prior to the party's insertion, the leader, Captain V. D. Prentice, flew two aerial reconnaissance missions by Catalina beginning 24 June to find a suitable landing area and drop zone. During the second mission, it was decided to extract some locals from Lake Melintang on the Mahakam River to obtain intelligence, but when the Catalina landed on the lake, it hit a log and was holed, forcing the aircraft to immediately become airborne.

The 16 men of the Platypus VIII party were broken into sub-parties, which began being inserted by Catalina on 3 July. The first sub-party landed safely and made contact with the locals, finding there were no Japanese in the immediate area. They then began a search for a suitable drop zone for the second sub-party and marked out an area 700 by 400 yards for this purpose. The following day, on 6 July, the second sub-party were flown in successfully with stores and maintenance equipment for 21 days. A radio link with Morotai was established and the party spread out, visiting local villages to begin the recruitment of guides and intelligence agents.

After an arms drop, a group of 30 locals were trained and armed to form a protective squad. The *Official History* notes that the men 'were keen to learn and showed distinct promise of becoming efficient soldiers'.[9] Ready to move against the Japanese, the locals asked if they could attack a nearby Japanese garrison of 13 men, and an assault was launched on 22 July, with four Japanese killed. The following day, the Japanese barracks were strafed by RAAF Spitfires and a further five were killed, forcing the few remaining enemy troops to evacuate to Samarinda.

As the men in the field required further personnel, the third sub-party left Balikpapan on 23 July, but the pilot of the Catalina failed to land in the carefully marked area of the lake and, as in the case of the earlier accident, the flying boat hit a submerged log and was badly holed. The crew, operatives and the stores were all safely recovered, and the Catalina was later repaired and flown back to Morotai. On the same day, the fourth sub-party were also inserted by parachute, with all men and stores successfully recovered. However, a flight of Spitfires that flew in protection of the drop inadvertently strafed a village, killing seven locals and wounding a further six. They were extracted and taken to hospital in Balikpapan.

Between late July and early August, a further 60 locals joined the operatives. They proved valuable as guides and intelligence-gatherers, in particular providing bombing and strafing targets for the RAAF. They were able to eliminate Japanese posts, capture enemy troops and cut off the supply of food to the Japanese, especially supplies of rice and fish. In turn, the Japanese began aggressive patrolling, burning villages. On 7 August, a large, heavily armed patrol of 45 Japanese troops attempted to land and eliminate a small outpost comprising Sergeant S. J. Taylor and four locals. Holding their ground, the small party engaged the Japanese with Bren and rifle fire, driving them back and inflicting a number of casualties.

Further small contacts and firefights developed. On 10 August, after driving off a small Japanese patrol at the mouth of the Kahala River, another party under Captain F. Horstick were later attacked by nine prahus laden with 50 Japanese troops. As they approached the shore the prahus were fired on, with all being sunk and many Japanese killed. As the *Official History* notes, 'The survivors made for the headland where they were detained by the party until the arrival of 2 Spitfires, which strafed the area thoroughly. A total of 30 Japanese were killed in the area by the party. Pte. W. Wilkie was slightly wounded.'[10]

As a result of this operation, further areas came under Allied control. The headquarters of Admiral Saburo Nomiya were completely destroyed by bombing, food supplies were cut off from the enemy and valuable intelligence was collected and radioed to Morotai and Balikpapan, providing targets for Allied fighters and bombers now operating freely in the area. With the insertion of Platypus IX, the four-man patrol set up a watching post to observe enemy barge traffic at the upper end of Balikpapan Bay, and as a result, aircraft strikes totally disrupted the movement of enemy troops and supplies to the point that they virtually ceased.

Having pushed the Japanese inland, SRD was now called upon for intelligence on Japanese troop movements and numbers further inland. Platypus X, a small patrol of four AIF operatives under Lieutenant Cresswell Chalmers, was assembled at the 2/9 Infantry Battalion headquarters to move to the area of the Riko River bridge, where they could observe and report on the Japanese withdrawal inland or the flow of reinforcements towards Balikpapan.

At 1930 hours, the party proceeded by prahu up the Riko River, disembarking at 2300 and returning the prahu with the local crew, but retaining one local for assistance. They had just landed when they heard Japanese voices close by, so retreated into the thick jungle by the track, but not before finding a wounded Japanese soldier. Given they were on a well-used thoroughfare, the party moved deeper into the jungle, but due to the weight of their stores and radio left behind Corporal Pannan and the local to establish a base camp, and proceeded on towards Riko.

Pushing through the jungle and keeping away from tracks, the party finally arrived at a clearing with a village. After speaking to a local, Lieutenant Chalmers was informed that a large party of 60 Japanese under a captain had left that morning for Riko. To reach their objective, the operatives again pushed on into the jungle.

After interrogating further locals, the party found that the Japanese were indeed assembling at Riko. The men obtained the services of two local guides and walked on to Soetek, where they had been told there were no enemy troops. However, upon arriving, they were informed that the Japanese were heading their way, and soon after a party of four Japanese were seen approaching, 'driving 4 natives, heavily laden with food baskets, towards Riko'.[11] Then followed two more parties of Japanese. Realising the numbers of Japanese in the area, Chalmers decided to return to their base and Corporal Pannan. Setting out again at dusk, the men found the track active with Japanese parties of up to ten men. When they reached the location of their stores dump and Pannan, they could not locate him, but they had previously agreed he would meet them at the appointed time and place at the prahu, so they set off to their rendezvous.

But the corporal had experienced his own problems. Not long after Chalmers and the party had left him, he was discovered by a local who reported him to the Japanese. Quickly burying the stores, he hid in the jungle and later observed a Japanese party prodding the ground with bayonets in an attempt to locate his hidden cache. They were followed by a larger party, who again undertook a search, but failed to find the buried stores and went away. Sneaking back to the river, Corporal Pannan was able to pick up a passing prahu and return to the 2/9 Battalion lines and report in. Similarly, the main party was able to secure a prahu, which returned them back to the battalion.

Given concerns about the possibility of Allied POWs being held to the north of Balikpapan, an operation was mounted codenamed Platypus XI to check this and obtain further intelligence on Japanese movements and troop numbers. A party of four operatives under Lieutenant R. Tapper set out on the night of 22 July 1945 in two folboats. Heading north into Japanese territory under a full moon, but fearing Japanese machine-gun positions along the bank, the men began a series of short, silent paddles, close to the bank and under the overhanging jungle.

By stealth and with the aid of native guides, Lieutenant Tapper located Japanese defensive positions, in particular machine-gun posts that were then engaged by artillery fire. Locals, some recently escaped from the Japanese, were also able to provide the location of other Japanese strategic targets, which could then be eliminated through bombing and artillery strafes.

While they were not able to confirm information on Allied POWs, the penultimate Platypus party did discover the location of 63 Indian POWs, including three officers, who were subsequently rescued. It was also this patrol that found the debilitated Flight Lieutenant Martin, the leader of the ill-fated Platypus VII party, who had been missing since the end of June, in a prahu in Balikpapan Bay. The men continued their patrol, interrogating other locals who provided valuable intelligence on Japanese strengths and dispositions, before returning to Balikpapan on 6 August.

A similar patrol, codenamed Platypus XII, of three men under Private J. Briggs of the 2/1 Australian Pioneer Battalion, made a one-day reconnaissance of an area north of Balikpapan, setting out at 0500 on 28 July 1945 and returning at 1330, reporting no sign of POWs but verifying enemy defensive locations and troop movements. This was the last SRD operation in the Balikpapan area, before the end of hostilities in August.

FOURTEEN

The Rescue of the Sultan

In early April 1945, SRD were called upon to undertake a very special operation: the extraction of the Sultan of Ternate, who was then under house arrest on his island of Ternate, off the west coast of the Moluccas. The original kingdom was established in about 1257 and adopted the Muslim faith, possibly from the many Arab traders who came and went. The island had a long history of exporting spices with traders from China, India, the Malay Archipelago and the Arabs, before the arrival of the first Europeans on Ternate in 1506.

In 1511, the Portuguese colonised the island, but were expelled by the local Sultan after a war of five years. In 1606 the Spanish arrived, but they were displaced by the Dutch in 1607. The spice trade was beginning, and certain spice products were more valuable by weight than gold. The Dutch saw a great future in these exotic products and sought to dominate the market in cloves and other spices by expanding the territory under their control and limiting spice production to these areas. Dutch control continued, hand in hand with the Sultan, until the Japanese invaded the island in 1942, placing the pro-Dutch Sultan, his family and retinue under house arrest.

The Japanese administration of Ternate was harsh, with the Kempeitai dealing summarily with all police offences 'and the culprits either beaten or tortured according to the seriousness of the offence'.[1] The Kempeitai had a long and shameful past. They had been formed in 1881 under the Meiji Council of State to bring discipline and rigour to the Japanese military, but also to deploy a range of espionage skills and torture techniques on both civilians and captured prisoners of war. While part of the Imperial Japanese Army, they operated as an adjunct or semi-autonomous unit, and their power increased in the 1930s under Hideki Tojo, the General of the Army, who had at one time been the commander of the Kempeitai in Manchuria.

Tojo become infamous as the wartime Prime Minister of Japan from October 1941 until July 1944, during which time he encouraged and endorsed the ill-treatment, torture and starvation of civilians and captured prisoners of war. The Kempeitai, with their notorious reputation, were given control of military discipline, civilian jurisdiction, prison camps and comfort women and were feared everywhere they went.

By early 1945 the morale of the Japanese was very low, given the success of the Allies as they moved towards mainland Japan. One Japanese officer, S. Matsuda, the Japanese Civilian Governor of the Halmaheras, stated at the time that 'the fate of Japan depends entirely on that of Germany'.[2]

The morale of the local people was also very low. They suffered at the hands of the Japanese from starvation, disease and lack of medical supplies. Australian SRD medical units found that tropical ulcers were common in the locals, in addition to cases of malaria and even one advanced case of leprosy, but there were no cases of beri-beri or yaws. While the food situation was determined as satisfactory, there was no material, cloth or clothing, and people, as with those in the Celebes, were found to be dressed in bark. It was noted that this type of clothing caused the spread of disease, in particular skin infections, and soap was required to prevent these.

The people maintained their trust and faith in the Sultan, Iskander Mohammed Jabir Syah, a man of culture and education who had refused to bow to Japanese authority and control. He spoke a number of languages and, during the course of the Japanese invasion, had maintained his allegiance to the old Dutch administration. The Sultan, with the help of his people, had also kept up a supply of intelligence to the Allies, all the time fearing the Japanese would take serious retribution on his family should this become known to them through the spies and traitors on Ternate. The influence of this allegiance was also felt in the local population, who had gone from being initially pro-Japanese to being pro-Allied after experiencing firsthand the harsh and punitive treatment of the occupiers.

The Japanese of course had their suspicions about the Sultan's allegiance. He was suspected of being pro-Ally, even of passing information to the Allies, and at one point was given a grilling by the Kempeitai. But after this the Japanese seemed partly satisfied that their suspicions were ill-founded, and the Sultan was permitted to return to his mountain home on Ternate under house arrest. The Kempeitai had up until this time lived in the old Fort Oranji, but they moved to an inconspicuous local house and converted a nearby building into a gaol, no doubt to avoid Allied air attacks.

NICA (the Netherlands Indies Civil Administration) had been aware of the Sultan's interrogation and imprisonment in his palace. The Dutch were keen to use the Sultan after the war to regain control of their colonial possession, but also to gain intelligence on Ternate and other neighbouring islands for potential landings later in 1945. NICA was able to report on the location and number of Japanese troops on Ternate:

> TERNATE TOWN, approx. 30 Jap Marines in the old fort area,
> 10 Japs in vicinity of the W/T [wireless transmission] station,
> TARAOE village approx. 20 Japs, TADOEMA village approx.
> 10 Japs. It is reported there are machine guns mounted on the
> four corners of the fort. The Japs have constructed A.R. (air raid)
> shelters inside the fort and the natives report that all Japs shelter
> in air raids, including the machine gunners.[3]

Among these NICA intelligence reports from Ternate is also mention of a captured RAAF pilot: 'In mid-January, a Spitfire was shot down to the south of the island and was rescued by friendly natives. However, a neighbouring pro-Jap village betrayed the pilot who was captured by the Japanese and incarcerated in the northern portion of the fort, together with a pro-allied native Chief. It is reported that the pilot is receiving fairly good treatment.'[4]

The rescue of this pilot became one of the objectives of the Opossum operation, along with the location and destruction of the radio station and the capture of one or two Japanese prisoners for interrogation. But it was soon found that the downed Australian pilot had been moved to an unknown location, so the initial operation was dropped. New plans needed to be drawn up, aerial and ground reconnaissance undertaken and the necessary personnel assembled. Initially NICA had planned and even attempted the extraction of the Sultan and his family, but with the limited resources available to them turned to SRD for assistance.

Planning began for the operation in late February to early March 1945 after detailed aerial reconnaissance photographs of Ternate were supplied by the RAAF. It was proposed to carry out the operation in two phases. Phase 1 would involve a four-man recce, to be inserted four days ahead of the main party. Phase 2 would see the insertion of this main party by Catalina five miles (eight kilometres) north of Ternate town, after which the party would paddle down the coast in folboats to a position south of Doefa Doefa. After hiding the folboats, the party would undertake the necessary reconnaissance. The purpose was to locate the Japanese wireless station and any sentry posts or defensive positions in the vicinity in and around the old Portuguese fort. This recce would be undertaken during the night, after which the party would return to their folboat hideout and rest. After laying up all day, during the following night they would complete the return journey by folboat to the insertion point, where they would be extracted by Catalina.

Following the return of the recce party, it was proposed that a larger party of about 15 operatives could be inserted, broken into two separate sub-parties. The first would deal with the radio transmission station, while the second would deal with the Japanese defences at the old fort. The plan was for the two parties to be deployed near the two objectives, and at dawn on the day of the action, the RAAF would stage heavy strafing runs to distract the Japanese. The first party would commence their assault on the wireless station before retiring to a prearranged rendezvous. The second party would attack the fort in the hope of finding the pilot and other Allied prisoners, and if possible capture one or two Japanese for interrogation. Then both parties would meet up and return to their insertion point, ready for extraction by Catalina.

In further intelligence collected for the original Opossum operation, the Japanese troop numbers on Ternate were given at only 50, but there were an estimated 25,000 from a variety of Japanese army and naval units on the large neighbouring island of Halmahera. An intelligence report about the Japanese Administrator, S. Matsuda, states:

> He previously lived in Kaoe, but has since moved to Laboeha on Batjan Island. He wears civilian clothes but in each lapel he has a badge with three stripes, as well as another on which is three chrysanthemums. Matsuda is a very humane man with a western outlook, having been educated at an English school. He is a gentleman in his actions, manners and dealing with natives etc. He intervened on behalf of the Australian pilot in Ternate in an endeavour to have him treated better. He is accompanied by 13 Japanese guards when on his rounds.[5]

Also included was intelligence that the Japanese piers were wired with demolition charges, although the firing method and sequence were unknown. As well, the report stated that there were no radar installations on the island, and that instead warnings of imminent Allied air attack were provided by the ringing of a bell.

Gradually these plans and the operational orders changed. The listed priorities became first to 'Assist NICA to withdraw an important person and his followers', second, 'Assist NICA to arm 70 guerrillas at Hiri', and third, 'Procure the fullest intelligence relating to the pilot located in Fort Oranji'.[6] It was at this point that SRD was asked to 'ensure protection and establish W/T communication with HQ',[7] given NICA was unable to undertake this patrol alone. It was also at this time discovered that the 'important person' was none other than the Sultan of Ternate, along with his two wives and eight children plus a house retinue of about 15 people.

At 1730 hours on 8 April 1945, the party under Captain Kroll, the Dutch Army leader of the mission, along with the SRD leader, Lieutenant George Bosworth, seven Australian operatives, two NICA representatives and 20 armed guerrillas, left Morotai in two Australian-crewed PT boats. They travelled through the night and landed at 2245 on the tiny island of Hiri, just to the north of Ternate, after a sea journey of about 150 miles (240 kilometres). Here they came ashore and, after setting up a secure camp, despatched a messenger to the Sultan on Ternate a few miles across the water to the south. The following morning, Captain Kroll and a party including Lieutenant Bosworth and some Australians walked down the eastern side of the island to the village of Dorari'isa, where they found the locals were holding nine local traitors, after one had escaped and another had been shot.

After landing more members of the party along with stores and ammunition, the complete SRD party assembled, ready for the extraction operation. At 1930 on the night of 9 April, word came from the Sultan 'to say he would try to come out, but that he was surrounded with traitors and would find it difficult'.[8] In response, five prahus of local guerrillas set out for Ternate, landing on the south-eastern coast to provide protection and undertake the transfer of the Sultan and his family to Hiri.

Here he was met by his worshipping people, a welcome described by Major Hardwick, the NICA representative, as a very dramatic show of loyalty and affection. There was great excitement among the people, as at last their Sultan was free of the Japanese and about to be taken to safety in Australia. Some of the elders in the crowd kissed his feet while the remainder squatted on one knee, their hands covering their faces in a traditional expression of respect, reverence and homage.

The following morning, 10 April, a four-man party led by WO Richard Perry, along with Hardwick, Private Robert Higginbottom and a local, left their base camp to check on a report that a local traitor was living in a house at the top of the volcano which dominated the island of Hiri, but the man was not there. They searched the house and found various documents of potential value then returned to the camp.

Meanwhile, the Sultan had crossed from Ternate to the southern end of Hiri Island in a rainstorm, evading the Japanese and meeting up with the SRD party. That night, a close watch was kept on the Sultan's party and a guard mounted. At 0200 hours, Corporal J. Kearns, who was on watch, reported lights and unusual activity on the northern shore of Ternate, just over one mile away to the south. At 0700 hours, a local rushed into the camp to explain that a party of Japanese had left by prahu and were now making for the island.

The SRD party split, some moving to Trafaka, at the very southern end of Hiri, to find the Japanese had already landed and were questioning the locals. Then another prahu was seen approaching the shore, with an officer and two Japanese soldiers paddling. At this point, WO Perry ordered the Bren gun to fire on the prahu, spraying the craft with accurate fire that killed the two paddlers. The officer survived and later paddled alone to Togolobe, where the rest of the SRD party were. Coming ashore, he was ordered to surrender, but remained stationary, a grenade held in his hand, whereupon he was shot and killed.

Meanwhile, of the nine Japanese in the first prahu at Trafaka, six, in fear of their lives, tried to swim out to sea. They were pursued by locals in a prahu, who shot them all in the sea, but the three others reached the beach and became engaged in a firefight with Lieutenant Bosworth. He shot one enemy soldier with his Thompson machine gun then ran forward in order to take him prisoner. At this point, 'the Japanese who was only wounded, raised his rifle and shot Bosworth in the head, killing him instantly'.[9]

This Japanese soldier was then shot, along with another, but the third escaped in the thick undergrowth bordering the beach and evaded capture.

Private Higginbottom, noticing that the Japanese landing party had now been dealt with, and ignoring an order from WO Perry, stripped off his clothes and swam out to secure the Japanese prahu still floating unattended off the beach. As he climbed aboard he was shot by one of the local guerrillas, who mistook him for a Japanese soldier. He fell into the prahu, which was dragged ashore, but died soon after. An operative on Opossum, Gordon Philpott, recalled, 'He was a blond bloke so I don't know how they took him for a Jap. They were the two blokes we lost [this operative and Bosworth].'[10]

With the beach now secured, the party returned to Togolobe, where contact was made with the PT boats waiting offshore. Philpott noted, 'We sent a signal to Morotai and in no time we had a flight of Kittyhawks over the strait to make sure no more Japs came over.'[11]

Prior to leaving, the operatives distributed the captured weapons to the local guerrillas, including a Nambu 6.5mm LMG (similar to a Bren gun), and some rifles and ammunition, to help them continue their fight. At 1145, the PT boats arrived off Hiri Island and the SRD party, along with the Sultan, his wife, children and their retinue, were loaded aboard and returned to Morotai, arriving late on the afternoon of 11 April.

For his leadership and bravery on the Opossum operation, Perry was awarded a Military Medal. His citation reads:

While 2I/C [second-in-command] of a patrol in the Moluccas
from 8 to 11 April 45, W.O. Perry displayed exceptional leadership
and courage. On 11 April 45 when attacked by a superior Jap

patrol landing from canoes, W.O. Perry ran to the endangered point with an LMG where he engaged the enemy, both afloat and ashore. When the officer commanding the patrol was killed, he assumed command and largely through his skill and initiative the entire enemy party was killed. On many occasions this W.O. has displayed courage and leadership of the highest order.[12]

After their extraction from Ternate, the Sultan and his family were flown by Catalina to Brisbane to start a new life in the small Queensland town of Wacol, between Brisbane and Ipswich, which was where NICA had their headquarters and where his rescue had been planned. At war's end, the Sultan and his family returned to Ternate to regain his power and authority.

By then, the Dutch East Indies was in a tumultuous state. The Dutch had been increasingly concerned about the future of the colony and the rise of an Indonesian independence movement. Two leaders of the movement, Sukarno and Mohammad Hatta, who they had imprisoned prior to the Japanese invasion, had been released by the Japanese and both had gone on to collaborate in exchange for Japanese support for their moves to establish an independent Indonesia at the end of the war.

On 17 August 1945, two days after the Japanese surrender, Sukarno and Hatta declared the Republic of Indonesia, with Sukarno as president. After a protracted struggle, the Dutch formally recognised Indonesian independence in 1949. Although the Sultan considered Sukarno a communist, he joined him as Minister of the Interior.

After the rescue of the Sultan, SRD had not concluded their operations in the Celebes and the Moluccas. By mid-1945, both NICA and the US Task Force Command on Morotai needed detailed intelligence on Japanese positions and future plans to ensure that the SRD-supported guerrilla operations in the area were not compromised.

On 19 June, a Japanese patrol boat had intercepted a prahu with eight locals travelling between Misool Island and the small island of Friwen (only 1.25 miles (two kilometres) long and half a mile (800 metres) wide), off the west coast of West Papua. The Japanese confiscated their cargo of sweet potatoes and bananas, beached their prahu and detained the men for ten days.

After his release, one of these locals was picked up by NICA guerrillas on the island of Gebe and sent to Morotai for questioning. Here he 'was able to supply useful intelligence on the strength of Japanese garrisons on various islands, the resupply arrangements of the Japanese and the condition of the Japanese troops'. In part the intelligence report dated 19 July 1945 states, 'Food was grown in a garden on Jaffari Island. The Japanese were very short of supplies, food and clothing. They were shooting wild boars and birds to supplement their diet. No medical supplies are available. Those Naval troops appeared very young, many were sick, suffering from tropical ulcers and itch. They were using herbs to cure themselves.'[13] The report also provided details of Japanese weapons, signals and housing, including the absence of navigation aids and minefields, even the results of Allied air attacks.

A subsequent report on Japanese troop deployments noted, 'On 1 July 1945, 11 Japs came to Friwen Island from Waigeo. They were all killed by the natives. On 5 July, 30 Japs invaded Friwen driving the natives out and destroying the village.'[14] The Japanese also destroyed and drove the population away from nine other villages in the area. This aggressive action by locals encouraged NICA and SRD to assist them and to use these guerrilla units for further offensive action.

To undertake the request by NICA and the US Task Force Command to gain intelligence in the Celebes and Moluccas, SRD planned four operations codenamed Finch. The first operation (Finch I) comprised a patrol of five PT boats, each one with an SRD operative on board, which set out from Morotai just after midnight on 7 July 1945. The party travelled south from Morotai along the north-western shore of Halmahera until they arrived at Hiri Island.

After refuelling, they split into two parties, with three PT boats heading south and two remaining at Hiri. At midday, two RAAF Spitfires and a Mosquito flew overhead, and further south the PT boats and the aircraft strafed a village where there was believed to be a Japanese wireless station. The strafe fell on village houses, on prahus and usable boats on the beach, and the village area, including a number of houses, was set on fire. The PT boats then continued south through the narrow Sambaki Strait, at times only 50 yards from the shore, but no enemy activity was seen. The five PT boats joined up and proceeded further south, firing with the aircraft on another village. Here a party went ashore and found various items, but were informed by an old woman that there were no Japanese in the village.

As the party returned to the PT boat tied up alongside the wharf, they were engaged by two Japanese machine guns. Immediately the PT boats returned fire, knocking out the Japanese guns and destroying a house. As Gordon Philpott related, 'A group of Japs came down to the jetty where the PT boat had pulled up. The Japs charged down the jetty and the Yanks on the cannon, blew them up and put them out of action.'[15] The PT boat ceased firing, but still tracer and machine-gun rounds came from the shoreline. Returning fire, the two PT boats withdrew and returned first to

Hiri Island, then, after taking on board a local for interrogation, returned to Morotai early on the morning of 8 July.

At this time, RAAF aircraft, in particular Beaufighters, P-40 Kittyhawks and three Spitfire squadrons, were operating out of Morotai. But the pilots were having great difficulty finding targets, and any intelligence provided by such sources was quickly acted on. Much of the time Allied aircraft were tasked to interdict Japanese barge traffic between the islands, in particular those that contained food and medical supplies.

So rare did the targets become that there was a protest by a number of senior RAAF officers, eight in total, including the famous ace, Group Captain Clive 'Killer' Caldwell. Later to become known as the 'Morotai Mutiny', this group – which also included Squadron Leader 'Mick' Grace, the son of one of the original Grace Brothers of retail store fame – tendered their resignations. The mutineers believed that the cost of men, aircraft and ordnance was not justified by the results and the losses sustained.

The mutiny resulted in an official investigation which saw Air Commodore Harry Cobby – who had been Australia's highest-scoring ace in the First World War – relieved of command. The incident was summed up in the *Official History of the RAAF* as the product of 'the conviction of a group of young leaders that they were engaging in operations that were not militarily justifiable – a conviction widely shared also by many Australian soldiers and political leaders'.[16]

The day after the return of Finch I, another fighting patrol, Finch II, under Captain Stringfellow as leader, set out by PT boat from Morotai to Hiri and Ternate islands off the west coast of Halmahera. Arriving at Hiri, they took on board some local guides and were joined, as was the previous operation, by two Spitfires and a Mosquito. As they proceeded south along the coast, the local guides pointed out the location of Japanese positions, which were fired on by the PT boat and strafed from the air. The locals were later to report that 16 Japanese had been killed and a number of enemy-occupied buildings destroyed.

The PT boat resumed the patrol, crossing to the mainland and arriving at the town of Koesoe. Tracking down the coast of the island of Tidore to Bobo, they fired on 15 large prahus, which were destroyed or seriously damaged. Continuing their rampage, they crossed back to Tidore Island, just south of Ternate, where, as the official report states, they 'destroyed or damaged another 30 or 40 prahus and some large godowns [warehouses or other storage buildings] reported by the natives to belong to the Japanese'.[17] On 10 July, a party under Captain Stringfellow went ashore on Hiri, where clothing, arms and documents were discovered and returned for assessment to Morotai. After collecting the sister of the Sultan, three months after he had been rescued, her retinue and three wounded locals, the party left Hiri and returned to Morotai, arriving at 1430 hours on 10 July.

Two days later, a small party under Stringfellow and Lieutenant Van Wyck, of NICA, set out from Morotai on Finch III, this time to find suitable sites for the erection of navigation lights on Jiew and Boo-besar Islands and to undertake intelligence-gathering. A party went ashore on Friwen Island to make contact with the local guerrillas, who it was understood held two Japanese prisoners, but they found the village destroyed and no locals or Japanese prisoners in the area. They did, however, receive intelligence from the locals about the Japanese wireless station on Jaffari Island off Batanta, after which time they returned to Morotai.

Having established the sites for the erection of the navigation beacons on Jiew and Boo-besar Islands, on 23 July a follow-up party under Stringfellow, codenamed Finch IV, left Morotai on

HMAS *Hawkesbury*, an Australian-built River Class frigate. The SRD party of seven operatives provided security for the naval party who erected the navigation beacons, and also sought intelligence on these and other islands along the way. On this patrol, the Japanese wireless station was destroyed by naval gunfire, along with a Japanese camp in the same area, where, it was later reported, a number of Japanese had been killed. The party returned with valuable intelligence, all in one day and without casualties or damage.

The Finch operations concluded the work of SRD in the Celebes and Moluccas, which had dramatically reduced Japanese offensive capabilities in this area. As SRD operatives had cut off the resupply of food, medical supplies and stores, the Japanese forces in these areas fell to sickness and starvation, which took a higher toll than Allied military action. But the final surrender and the disarming of Japanese forces, and their repatriation to Japan, would take many months, with isolated hostile actions continuing into late 1945.

FIFTEEN

The Audacious Disaster of Rimau

By late 1944, apart from the loss of life on Lagarto and the ill-fated Copper operation, and the odd few casualties, SRD had been operationally successful. Perhaps it was this ongoing success, in particular the outstanding Jaywick mission in September 1943, that imbued a level of confidence and bravado that would lead to the most disastrous and costly operation to be undertaken by SRD during the war – that of Rimau.

The operation that became Rimau had its origins in January 1944. After Jaywick, another even more audacious mission developed in the mind of the operations leader, Lieutenant-Colonel Ivan Lyon. Lyon was from a strong military family: his grandfather, Colonel Francis Lyon, had fought in the Royal Horse Artillery in the Indian Mutiny in 1857–58, while his father, Brigadier General Francis Lyon, fought in the Royal Artillery in the Great War. Young Ivan attended Harrow before going on to the Royal Military College Sandhurst, where he was commissioned into the Gordon Highlanders. In 1936, he was posted to Singapore, and it was here he met his wife, Gabrielle Bouvier, the daughter of a French prison governor in Indochina. In July 1939 they married in Saigon and their son, Clive, was born in September 1941.

After the fall of France in June 1940 and the formation of the Vichy regime under Marshal Philippe Pétain, French Indochina was occupied by the Vichy French, as were other French territories and colonies. Ivan Lyon, then an intelligence operative in Singapore, secured a job for his wife as an interpreter in the local office of General De Gaulle's Free French organisation. He also secured intelligence on the activities of the Vichy French in Indochina from his father-in-law and passed this on to London. On weekends, he went sailing among the islands south of Singapore, keeping an eye on known Japanese agents and their contacts, and collecting valuable local knowledge that would inform his work in the years ahead.

By early January 1944, just four months after his return from the Jaywick raid, the idea of a larger, more devastating and ongoing attack on the Japanese was on Ivan Lyon's mind. He was keen to repeat the success of Jaywick and felt that, with the support of SRD, Allied GHQ and the men available through the Z Special Unit, he had at hand the means to undertake a daring attack. He also knew that somewhere in Malaya – or in the immediate area around Singapore – were his wife and child, who had been caught, unable to evacuate Singapore in the days before it fell. Or so he thought. What he did not know was that his wife did get away, but the ship she escaped on was captured by a German raider and the passengers and crew handed over to the Japanese and placed in internment.

Lyon began work on the massive operation, codenamed Hornbill. It was focused on Singapore, which was at the time the GHQ for the Japanese military and the control point for military and naval units from Burma and to the east across the South China Sea. It was also a major supply depot and port, with a convergence of shipping bringing everything from rice and rubber from Thailand, oil from Sarawak and Borneo, and supplies and personnel from Japan. Given the concentration of Japanese military power at Singapore, it was well protected from attack, and the shallow seas around the island reduced the possibility of submarine attack. Another broad operational plan needed to be devised, based on commando tactics and the arming and training of local guerrilla groups capable of attacking multiple targets across a vast area.

Given the proposed number of Hornbill raids that were planned over an extended period, stage one was to find and establish an operational base as close as practicable to Singapore and launch these raids from effectively behind Japanese lines. A secret memo dated 23 June 1944 stated, 'Hornbill is the code name given to a series of operations in the South China Sea to be undertaken by SRD. The principal targets are Singapore and Saigon for actual strikes against the enemy, but in addition S.O. personnel are to be inserted into the Malayan peninsula and Hong Kong.'[1] The memo also noted as an objective 'the infiltration of men and materials for intelligence parties and resistance groups in Malaya, Siam and Indo-China'.[2] The proposed base for these attacks, possibly for as long as nine months, was the Natuna Islands off the west coast of Borneo and to the north-east of Singapore, from where small, annoying, pin-prick raids could be undertaken as well as the insertion of Allied agents into Malaya and the establishment and resupply of Coastwatch posts.

A Trojan horse was needed to insert operatives into Malaya, some kind of vessel that would pass as Japanese, or alternatively Chinese or Malay, much as the *Krait* had served this purpose as an unsuspecting fishing boat for Jaywick. The answer lay in what became known as 'Country Craft': specially constructed vessels, to be made in Australia that would outwardly look like the junks operating at that time in the South China Sea. However, their construction was stalled by union stoppages and they were never delivered – as a result, Hornbill was postponed until 1945. Needing a rethink, Lyon looked for the next possible alternative and found this in an unexpected way.

In March 1944, Lyon returned to England to discuss future SRD operations with SOE. While there he was shown three small submersibles: the Welman four-man submarine, the Welman one-man submersible and the newly developed and smaller Motorised Submersible Canoe (MSC), invented by Major H. Quentin Reeves. (It is believed he was the inspiration for the Ian Fleming character 'Q', who provided James Bond with so many gadgets.)

The MSC, nicknamed 'Sleeping Beauty' – after the inventor was found one day asleep in one – was originally designed for SOE to deliver a single diver-operative on a reconnaissance mission or to attack enemy shipping. The craft was just 12 feet eight inches (3.86 metres) long, made of mild steel and powered by a five-horsepower electric motor from four six-volt batteries carried in the bow. This gave it a cruising range of 30–40 miles (56–74 kilometres) at a maximum speed of 4.4 knots (5.1 miles/ hour or 8.1 kilometres/hour) on the surface and about 3.5 knots (4 miles/hour or 6.5 kilometres/hour) submerged, and a diving depth of 50 feet (15 metres). The operative would wear a rubber suit and breathe through either a re-breather or from tanks built into the vessel. Through a manoeuvre called 'porpoising', the operative could rise to the surface with just his head above the waterline to check his direction and then dive again, continuing this until close to the target, when he could move in to attack underwater.

This small, sturdy submersible impressed Ivan Lyon as a possible delivery vehicle for his return attack on Singapore, and a number were subsequently sent to Australia for testing and training. It was found that they were difficult to control and, with a battery life of just two hours, would have operational limitations. While the Motorised Submersible Boats were not ideal, Lyon found they could be paddled and fitted with a sail, which made them attractive should the motor fail or should his operatives need to cover long distances to get away. He believed they had a place in the operational plans that were now taking shape in his mind.

Lyon developed a new plan comprising four major stages. These were, as noted in a report:

(a) The recce and provisioning of a base (to be known as Base A) at a distance of about 70 miles from the target area.

(b) The seizure of a junk and transhipment of stores in the lee of a selected island.

(c) The sailing of the junk as a depot ship to a forward R.V. [rendezvous] from which a carefully timed and co-ordinated attack by 15 S.B.s [sleeping beauties] will be launched on six target areas.

(d) Finally a planned withdrawal to rear R.V.s and a dispersed getaway in five groups in kayaks back to the provisioned Base A.[3]

At this time, Merapas Island, just south of Singapore, was 'provisionally selected'[4] as the site for Base A and a schedule developed. It was planned that a suitable junk would be boarded and captured near Borneo and taken to Penjantan Island, between Singapore and Borneo, where the SBs, folboats, stores and weapons would be transhipped to the junk. It would then sail the 250 miles (400 kilometres) to Labon Island over six days, allowing a speed of only 1.8 knots (2.1 miles/hour or 3.3 kilometres/hour) to get there.

The coordinated attack by the 15 SBs would be over six objectives in Singapore Harbour: the Man-of-War and Eastern Explosives anchorages; the Mosquito Fleet; Examination, Western Explosives and Quarantine Anchorages; Keppel Harbour and Empire Dock; Bukum Wharf; and Sambo Wharf. The intention was to sink 30 ships and damage another 30. Each of the attacking crews would 'carry 2 lots of four linked limpets [mines] and two single limpets',[5] allowing them to sink two ships and damage a third. The actual raid would begin at 1900, with the anticipated return of the last craft to the rendezvous before the timed explosions began at 0600 the following day.

Once the SBs had returned to the rendezvous, ten would be recovered by the junk, four would go to Subar Island and the final SB would go to Dongas Island, which had been the launching point for the Jaywick attack. At each rendezvous, the SBs would be scuttled and the men would depart in five groups, each under an officer, for the 70-mile (112-kilometre) paddle to Merapas over a 14-day period, covering an anticipated five miles (eight kilometres) each night. From there the party would be extracted by a British submarine and returned to their base near Perth. In all, the mission – to be called Rimau – was expected to take two to three months, depending on the final rendezvous and pick-up: from the departure on 11 September until the anticipated pick-up on 7–8 November, before a 14-day return voyage to Perth, arriving sometime in late November 1944.

Training started on 19 July, but not before much work had been undertaken on the building and preparation of the secret camp at Careening Bay on Garden Island in Western Australia. Initially 52 men began training, in particular in the operational use of the SBs, but these were reduced through medical discharges and 'other reasons', with the aim to finally select 26 to be ready for the operation.[6] The classes were divided into three groups, some using the SBs during the day, another group at night, and a third doing 'static dives beside the jetty'.[7] A report notes, 'As soon as night diving started further weeding out became possible, and a steady trickle of bodies returned to Melbourne.'[8] The report goes on to say, 'We concentrated entirely on the handling of SBs in the last stage of an attack on ships or jetties.'[9]

A memo dated 19 September notes, 'SOA have now five of these craft in operation. A further 15 are enroute and were due during the current month. I am informed that the ship carrying them has been damaged by enemy action, but not sunk and I will notify you further of the availability of these craft for operations.'[10]

The planning and requisitioning of equipment and stores for the mission was worked out in detail, down to the last pound in weight. Detailed lists of every conceivable item were compiled and prepared into four 'tables' (separate packages or categories) 'to conform to the various phases of the operation'.[11] For example, the first category 'contained details of food, equipment and water to be off-loaded at Base A, on a scale sufficient to maintain 22 men for three months',[12] while the second category 'contained details of stores to be off-loaded from the submarine into the junk for use on the voyage'.[13] Also included was a signal plan, the frequencies and prefixes to be used, call signs, message encryption and a separate signal plan for the walkie-talkies that would be taken.

At this time, the problem of the stowage of the SBs into the HMS *Porpoise* – the submarine that would transport the men from Western Australia to the base – was also resolved, and a series of deep dives and trimming manoeuvres accomplished. After a thorough dress rehearsal had been completed and the loading of *Porpoise* finalised, Lieutenant Lyon and his Rimau party were ready to set out on their audacious and ambitious mission.

At 1220 on 11 September 1944, HMS *Porpoise* sailed from Careening Bay Camp. On board were 22 operatives, with Lyon and the second-in-command, Lieutenant Commander Donald Davidson, both men from the Jaywick mission. The passage to Lombok was uneventful, with the submarine surfacing 15 miles (24 kilometres) south of the Lombok Strait, after which it 'steamed at full speed through on the surface [the] whole way. Kept about 3 miles from Lombok Island. Full speed 13½ knots.'[14]

After the Lombok Strait the *Porpoise* remained submerged through the dangerous Karimata Strait before arriving at Merapas Island on 23 September. Here Davidson and Corporal Clair Stewart went ashore after a difficult paddle through a strong current, wind and breaking surf. They found the island an ideal base as it was uninhabited and had good cover and a clean water supply. They slung their hammocks between two fallen trees, a position they named 'Hammock Tree'. Davidson's diary notes, 'Spent a cool night. Slept none too well. The change from close quarters in the *Porpoise* to the scented peace of this island was too abrupt to sleep. The scent of the flowering trees and lily palms more delicate than any that ever came out of Paris.'[15]

Given the island met all the requirements of a forward base, on the following night, the stores destined for Base A were taken ashore and Lieutenant Walter Carey was left behind to ensure they were not disturbed.

Having completed the first stage of the operation, *Porpoise* departed Merapas on the night of 24–25 September and proceeded to Penjantan Island, 130 miles (215 kilometres) from the west coast of Borneo. After a periscope reconnaissance of the island it was determined to be uninhabited, with good jungle cover and numerous suitable protected anchorages and sandy beaches. *Porpoise* then travelled east in search of a suitable vessel and on the third day stopped and boarded the junk *Mustika*, which was travelling along the Borneo coast from Pontianak to Ketapang. With no resistance from the crew, who were taken aboard the submarine, the *Porpoise* then set out, with the junk in tow, for Penjantan Island.

The submarine released the junk just before dawn and it continued the journey under sail. The following night, 29–30 September, after the party had again briefly checked the island, the stores, including 15 SBs and folboats, were unloaded from the submarine and stowed in the junk. While this operation 'caused the submarine captain some extreme rage',[16] being tasked to undertake these insertion missions, but also because it put his submarine in danger, it marked the successful ending of stage two of the operation. This transfer was helped by the *Mustika* crew, who were quite happy to assist and were later cooperative in providing information and intelligence when interrogated back in Perth, where they were integrated and remained for the rest of the war. The *Porpoise* departed Penjantan at 2200 on 31 September and returned safely on 11 October after a mission of 27 days, three days shorter than the anticipated voyage.

The report by Lieutenant Commander Donald Davidson and a second technical report written by Major W. W. Chapman (the operation's technical officer) – dated 12 December 1944 and titled *Report on attempted pickup of 'Rimau' Party by HMS* Tantalus[17] – are the last official documents detailing Operation Rimau. The Rimau party did not have further contact with SRD HQ, and the details of the party and its ultimate fate have been pieced together since the war from various sources, including surviving Japanese records. Much of the forensic research has been completed by historians like Lynette Ramsay Silver, who has travelled to the islands, interviewed eyewitnesses and carefully analysed available data.

Following the departure of the *Porpoise*, the Rimau party began their journey from Penjantan to the operational area off Singapore Harbour. It is believed they sailed to Temiang Island and then turned north through the Sugi Straits to the vicinity of Labon Island, about 11 miles (18 kilometres) south-south-west of Keppel Harbour, Singapore, arriving on 6 October. On the way, the white men dyed their skin and donned sarongs, but their builds, larger and taller than the average Malay, and their blue eyes would have been giveaways. When they arrived, Lyon divided the party into two groups to undertake the raid, leaving four men to remain on the junk.

In the four days after they arrived off Singapore Harbour, Lyon and Davidson observed the transit of shipping in and out of the harbour, and discussed the likely targets and a plan of attack. Lyon sent out two recce parties under Lieutenant Harold 'Bobby' Ross, who paddled north as far as Labon Island then closer to Singapore Harbour, spending a day exposed on Sambu Island, just across the water from the harbour, before returning. Concerned by the constant enemy shipping movements, the *Mustika* then threaded its way north-east to Kusa Island on 10 October 1944, just three miles (five kilometres) off Keppel Harbour. It now began to rain, and with no wind, the prahu found itself becalmed off a waterfront village of thatched houses, many on stilts over the water. Slowly drifting, and without an engine, the *Mustika* was just 25 yards from the long jetty extending out over the mudflats, where, unbeknown to the operatives, they were under close observation from a local water police post halfway down the jetty

From this moment, everything went wrong. Inside the post, the native police, known as *heiho*, decided to investigate this mysterious prahu. Clamouring into their old motor-driven launch, they headed towards the junk, the operatives now at action stations watching as the *heiho* launch quickly closed on them. Suddenly a burst of fire from the prahu ripped into the launch, killing three of the four native police. The launch skewed around and returned to the shore, running aground with the fourth man, not a *heiho* but a translator they had taken along, clinging hidden in the water.

The reasons for the junk being approached by the patrol boat are unknown. Perhaps they noticed the larger non-Asian crew, badly disguised as Malays. Perhaps the *Mustika* was flying the incorrect identification flags for the area, or the junk's location, anchored for four days off the entrance to Singapore Harbour, had aroused suspicion. Perhaps the Japanese were far more wary and careful with respect to security, with increased patrols, following the Jaywick raid.

This investigation by the native police was a massive disappointment and completely blew apart their plans. This was just three hours before the Rimau party were to launch their 15 submersible boats on a major raid against Japanese shipping, in an operation so long in the planning. Lyon realised he had to sink the *Mustika* and disperse the operatives in folboats for the long paddle back to Merapas Island, ready for the submarine pick-up. But first there was one thing left to do – attack, with what limited power he now had, those tempting targets that were so very near, just across the water in Keppel Harbour. While Lyon had no time to plan a revised attack, he had well-trained, reliable men, some of whom had already been on Jaywick and had the experience and capability to pull off the attack.

Lyon's first concern would have been the anticipated arrival of Japanese harbour patrols in response to the gunfire and the explosion. Estimating he had three hours, he ordered six folboats to be assembled and 12 men to set off immediately for the Merapas rendezvous point. This left himself, Lieutenant Commander Davidson, Corporals Campbell and Stewart and Private Warne, plus Lieutenant Ross and Able Seaman Huston, who were still on Subar Island. He also had a good supply of limpet mines, which he likely did not want to go to waste.

Just after midnight, after Lyon had collected Ross and Huston from Subar, they headed for the collected Japanese shipping lying in and around Singapore Harbour. By this time in the war, Singapore was within range of American bombers and the heavy presence of both American and British submarines in the South China Sea caused a back-up of shipping. By 0300, the three double kayaks had successfully attached their mines, but the single folboat paddled by Warne could not make headway against the tidal currents. He along with the others returned to Dongas Island, where they knew they could hide their folboats and disappear into the thick cover on the island to watch the aftermath.

The damage caused by the explosion of the limpet mines generated a vicious response from the dreaded Kempeitai. Just as they had done after the Jaywick raid, the Japanese launched a bloody series of reprisals on the local population, with many being shot and beheaded, their heads displayed on stakes for all to see.

Meanwhile, Ivan Lyon, instead of heading for Merapas, decided on a further series of attacks on Japanese shipping he knew were anchored off Pangkil and Mantang Islands, 50 miles (80 kilometres) south of Singapore. After arriving on Pangkil early on the morning of 14 October they hid out for the day, and, after a brief exchange with the local chief, the party split into two groups: Lyon, Ross and Stewart, who paddled north, and the second group of Davidson, Campbell, Huston and Warne, who paddled the three miles to the southern end of Pangkil Island. Here Davidson met with the local headman, who, in exchange for small gifts, provided information on more Japanese shipping anchored just to the north-east. At the northern end of the island, Lyon's party met with another local headman, Raja Mun, who, unbeknown to them, was a secret Japanese agent and quick to report them.

Feeling confident, Lyon realised he needed a better observation point and so, on the night of 15 October, paddled to a small, circular island called Soreh, just two miles to the north-east of Pangkil and closer to the target areas. Arriving on the white sand beach which encircled the island, Lyon found it was devoid of vegetation, with only palm and tropical fig trees but no ground cover. While providing no secure observation points, it did provide a clear view of the Japanese anchorage to the east and south-east.

Meanwhile, Davidson's party had been warned they had been betrayed, so early on the morning of 16 October, he and Campbell paddled to Soreh to warn Lyon, while Warne and Huston, with a rubber raft in tow, paddled for Tapai, nearby and within sight of Soreh. Concurrent to the Rimau attack, an American B-24 Liberator bomber was seen circling Bintan Island off Singapore, and this had triggered a separate search by the Japanese for downed American airmen, who on capture were executed. Between this, the mysterious explosions and the report of white men, Pangkil Island was quickly swarming with Japanese troops, and another Japanese barge landed on Soreh about to confront five very smart fighters.

Upon landing earlier in the day, Lyon's party had met up with and spoken to a coconut-grower named Abdul Latif, who lived with his wife and child in a small hut on the island. Later in the day, when the two barges full of Japanese arrived, led by traitor Raja Mun, he questioned the young coconut-grower, threatening and later torturing him to betray the Rimau party, who were at that time not far away, hidden and ready for the attack. While Latif was being interrogated back at the beach, a sudden burst of gunfire at about 1500 ripped into the Japanese and local troops, killing and wounding a number of them. Under the concentrated fire, the Japanese fell back to the beached barges and one barge left to encircle the island to cut off any retreat.

Meanwhile, Latif's young wife, clutching her baby, had left the hut and found the five Australians, three of whom were now wounded. Davidson and Campbell had serious wounds to their upper arms and chests, and Lyon had also been wounded, but less seriously. The decision was made for Davidson and Campbell to get away and for Lyon, Ross and Stewart to remain behind to give the other two time to paddle to Tapai. Creeping off, Davidson and Campbell launched their folboat and without looking back, or being seen by the Japanese, set off south in the hope of meeting Huston and Warne.

As darkness settled over the island, the Japanese moved cautiously inland from the beach. Suddenly the night was lit with accurate, deadly fire and exploding grenades which tore into the Japanese lines. Illuminated by the explosions, they were cut down by the silent Sten guns of Lyon and Ross, who were hiding above them in the trees. Pinned down and firing wildly, the Japanese had no idea where the deadly fire was coming from. However, the high position of Lyon and Ross was finally discovered by the muzzle flash of their weapons and the Japanese quickly turned their fire upon them. A grenade lobbed into the treetops blew Lyon and Ross from their position, killing them both instantly. Meanwhile, Stewart remained hidden and was not discovered by the time the Japanese left the following morning. Safe for the moment, his folboat had been discovered by the Japanese and taken away. But while he had food and water, Stewart was stranded, and soon after he was captured.

Having made their escape, Davidson and Campbell somehow managed to paddle to Tapai, but Warne and Huston, no doubt hearing the sound of the firefight and figuring no one would be joining them, set off for Merapas after sinking the rubber supply boat. Now alone with one pistol and no ammunition, and just one hand grenade, they knew they had little chance of either escape or of fighting off any further attack. They also knew the Japanese would brutally torture them and had been warned not to allow themselves to fall into Japanese hands. Taking the small glass vials of potassium cyanide from their packs, they crushed them between their teeth and within seconds were dead, sitting upright side by side where they were found by the Japanese the following day.

Four of the Rimau party were dead – Lyon, Davidson, Campbell and Ross – and Stewart was soon to be captured. Huston and Warne were making their way to Merapas, where 16 others were waiting for the return of the submarine. Unbeknown to the Rimau men, the Kempeitai were quietly closing the net. The Japanese had found a list of the party and other incriminating details on the bodies of the fallen operatives, which would be enough to ensure the capture and fate of them.

On around 20 October, Able Seaman Huston and Private Warne arrived at Merapas, bringing the total number there to 19 men. While they expected the Japanese would be continuing their search, they felt some comfort being about 80 miles (130 kilometres) from Singapore on a remote, uninhabited island and away from inquisitive locals. If they could remain undiscovered, they needed to only await the return of the submarine on 7 November for their extraction and return to Australia. But it wasn't to be.

A Japanese aircraft, flying over the general area of Merapas and the larger nearby island of Mapur en route to Singapore, developed engine trouble, which was found to be a drop in oil pressure. On further investigation it was discovered that perhaps a bullet had ruptured the line to create the emergency. To begin the search for the origin of the bullet, two wooden barges containing 50 Japanese arrived at Mapur early on the morning of 4 November and, after questioning the headman, who knew nothing of the Allies' presence in the area, continued on to Merapas, just six miles (ten kilometres) away.

Upon landing, the Japanese officer, Captain Fujimura, intercepted a fisherman, but after questioning then beating him was unable to get information on sightings of the Rimau party. However, keen to make a thorough search of the island, he landed his troops in Kolek Bay on the western coast and pushed inland through the coconut plantation. The SRD operatives were in two groups, one on the high ground on Wild Cat Hill about 400 yards from the beach, and the other in the Cache Swamp about 220 yards from the beach. As the Japanese slowly advanced inland, the tension among the operatives increased until one of them discharged his silenced Sten gun, killing Fujimura and wounding his batman.

Initially the Japanese troops were surprised, but as silent bullets started ricocheting off rocks, they dived for cover. The second-in-command, Lieutenant Orzawa, quickly took command, sending one of the barges back to the nearby Japanese base at Kidjang with the body of Fujimura and his wounded batman, and assembling his men in a defensive perimeter on the beach to await reinforcements. To prevent the operatives from escaping, he sent his remaining barge to patrol the coast of the island, a circular journey of about three miles. But the slow, chugging barge took two and a half hours to make one transit of the coast, which gave the wily operatives, now keen to distance themselves from Merapas, time to get away.

At midday on the following day, about 100 Japanese troops, mainly Kempeitai and *heiho* troops, joined the search for the troublesome white men. Breaking the large party in two, one group travelled north along the coast then turned east and began to climb Wild Cat Hill, while a second group moved into the coconut plantation to storm the hill from the south-west.

Defending the northern side of the hill were just two men, Sergeant Colin Cameron and Sub-Lieutenant Grigor Riggs, who had dug shallow trenches and built them up with stones collected from the shore to form one-man sangers, small, defensive emplacements built above ground of stones and sandbags. They did not stand a chance. As the Japanese swarmed up the hill towards them, their short-range Sten guns and then their pistols could not halt the advance. Cameron was wounded, and as the Japanese stormed over his position he was shot dead through the back of the head, the bullet passing out his mouth and knocking out some teeth.

Riggs took to his legs. Realising he had no chance of surviving the mass of Japanese chasing him on this tiny island, and with no way off, his best tactic was to draw Japanese forces away to the southern end of the island and allow his mates the chance to paddle away. Perhaps this was a plan discussed the previous night, but it worked. Six operatives – Lieutenant Albert 'Blondie' Sargent, Lieutenant Bruno Reymond, WO Jeff Willersdorf, Corporal Colin Craft, Lance Corporal Hugo Pace and Private Warne – took to sea on two native koleks (Malayan canoes) and headed south. With the seas rough and the Japanese landing barges unsuitable for pursuit, the operatives disappeared from view, their traditional outrigger sailing craft blending with the native vessels that dotted these island waterways.

The casualties were mounting, as six of the Rimau party were dead. With Lyon and Davidson lost, Captain Page was now in command, not only of his small group on the neighbouring island of Mapur, six miles (ten kilometres) to the north-west of Merapas, but also of those fleeing south in the two koleks. The contingency plan, should the submarine pick-up at Merapas not happen, was for the group to meet up on Pompong Island, where they proposed to hijack a junk and sail it back to Australia. Though the plan was somewhat farfetched and bold, the men had few options, and with the intelligent and skilled operatives in the party, it was their only chance.

Meanwhile in Perth, the original submarine, the HMS *Porpoise* which had captured the *Mustika* and dropped the Rimau party off, needed urgent repairs. It was replaced by HMS *Tantalus* under Captain Hugh Mackenzie, a successful and aggressive hunter with an enviable record in sinking enemy vessels. Mackenzie had been disappointed on recent missions in the South China Sea, because of the lack of suitable targets and 'kills' – by this time in the war, the Japanese had very few ships, so convoys were rare and suitable targets scarce – and because he seemed to be continually diverted to pick up downed pilots and service special operations. Now he was tasked to collect the Rimau party rather than sink Japanese ships, and he was not impressed.

On 16 October, *Tantalus* left Fremantle for the rendezvous, the very day Lyon and Ross were killed on Soreh Island. After being distracted by operational opportunities, including the sinking of a small Japanese freighter, the submarine missed the planned first pick-up date at Merapas of 7 November and did not return on the following two nights. Mackenzie later justified this action by stating that as he had both fuel and torpedoes, and his primary mission was to sink ships, the operatives could in effect wait and he would collect them on his way back to Perth.

Apart from Mackenzie's lack of interest, other factors were conspiring to further jeopardise the extraction of the operatives. By late October, the Japanese were well aware of the existence of the operation and had found the bodies, notebooks, cameras, weapons, supplies and lists of personnel, so they knew who and what they were dealing with. The coded reports sent by the Japanese at the time about this incident were not given a high priority and so, when they were intercepted in Australia, they were also not given a high priority for their decoding. As a result, Japanese messages about the growing debacle went unnoticed. Had the Japanese provided an urgent or priority classification to these signals, they would have been prioritised more highly in Australia and perhaps SRD would have been provided with details about the seriously compromised position the operatives were now in.

Mackenzie had continued his patrol but, finding no suitable targets, and with the 15 torpedoes still aboard, decided to return to Merapas to reluctantly undertake what he called 'lifeguard duty'.[18] He was now over two weeks late, arriving at the island and undertaking a periscope reconnaissance which showed no sign of the Rimau party.

At 1 am on 22 November, *Tantalus* surfaced 450 yards off the north shore and two men, Major Walter Chapman and Corporal Ron Croton, paddled ashore from the submarine. Over the following day, they searched the island for the SRD men, and while they found evidence of their occupation none of the party remained, leading to various, often preposterous stories about their possible fate. On the following night, Chapman radioed the submarine and the two were picked up by an anxious and furious Mackenzie. He had spent the day submerged after a depth charge attack by a Japanese warship and having been sighted by a patrolling Japanese float plane.

Bob Page had been sending a nightly two-man patrol to await the submarine at the agreed spot on Merapas Island, but now realised the date for their extraction had long passed and reluctantly decided he must begin to move south as there seemed little hope of rescue. The idea was to meet at Pompong Island, about 115 miles (185 kilometres) to the south-west, after setting out in two separate groups about two weeks apart. The first group under Lieutenant Sargent comprised six other men: Lieutenant Reymond, WO Willersdorf, Corporals Stewart and Craft, Lance-Corporal Pace and Private Warne. As they would need to island-hop and get lost from the Japanese in the islands along the northern coast of Sumatra, they first headed south-west across the Riau Straits then across some 25 miles (40 kilometres) of open water to Pompong, where the *Krait* had spent a night during Jaywick.

After the two groups meet at Pompong, on 16 December 1944, the plan was to then move into the coastal trade routes, where they might commandeer a junk and sail back to Australia. Although Sargent's group had been fortunate not to be reported by the local people they came across and had somehow been lost to Japanese searchers, they now attracted suspicion as they sailed along the south-western coast of Lingga Island, about 125 miles (200 kilometres) south of Singapore. They were reported to the Kempeitai, who chased and caught up with them. In the ensuing firefight, the folboat of Fred Marsh and Andrew Huston, both Jaywick veterans, was sunk and Marsh was wounded and captured. Huston was swept away by the fast-flowing tide and drowned, his body washed ashore and discovered by the Japanese the following day.

Two days later, more Rimau men were rounded up. First, Major Ron Ingleton and Jack Hardy were caught on a nearby island. Bob Page, by now exhausted and dispirited, was also captured, hiding in a native hut. Wally Falls, another Jaywick veteran, had been wounded and taken, and the following day Sergeant Gooley and Corporal Fletcher were also captured. Then, on 27 December, the Japanese, after finding the operatives' supply dump on Pompong Island, captured the last three in this group: Lieutenant Walter Carey, WO Alf Warren and the wounded Fred Marsh. The whole of Page's group of ten men were now in the hands of the dreaded Kempeitai and, after a time, were taken to Singapore. It was not long before Marsh died an agonising death from a bayonet wound, the Japanese attributing his demise to malaria.

There were now nine Rimau men in Japanese hands, eight had been killed and seven were still on the run, with the Japanese hard on their heels. After the death of Lyon and Ross on Soreh Island, Corporal Stewart had been betrayed by a local native and brought to Singapore on 18 October. He was relentlessly tortured by the Kempeitai but refused to talk, knowing any details of the operation would compromise his mates' escape. But with the arrival of the other captured operatives, and despite their attempts to provide false cover stories and misinformation, the Kempeitai had Davidson's diary, a camera and various other documents, and were able to piece together not only the Rimau plan but also the secret locations of the submersible boats that had been included in the operation.

The failure of the submarine extraction had of course raised concerns at SRD headquarters in Australia. In late December, a plan was formulated, codenamed Rimexit, to undertake a submarine rescue mission. It was proposed to return to Merapas and abduct locals to interrogate them about the Rimau party and gain information on Japanese shipping in Singapore Harbour and any general intelligence on Japanese naval activity in the Rhio Archipelago.

If no information was obtained about the Rimau party on Merapas, it was also proposed to undertake a ground recce of Penjantan Island in the hope they had found sanctuary there. There was to be no contact with the enemy unless absolutely necessary, and details of the voyage were not to be shared with the submarine crew. So keen were SRD to hear any good news of the Rimau men that the captain of the submarine was told to 'break radio silence as early as possible if sortie results in firm information being obtained as to the whereabouts of RIMAU party'.[19]

However, after further Japanese signal traffic was decoded mentioning the capture and extermination of Allied operatives who they had found to be using rubber boats, SRD realised the party had been compromised and were probably wiped out. They had not been aware of this, working as they did on the high priority and most secret decoding, hence missing the information already at hand about the predicament of the Rimau operatives. As a result, the Rimexit mission was cancelled.

Unbeknown to SRD, seven of their men were still at large: the party under Lieutenant Sargent who had left Merapas, called at Pompong and then headed south along the coast of Sumatra in search of a junk to commandeer. It took the party three weeks, but they were able to capture a junk and head east towards Pelapis Island, 300 miles (480 kilometres) to the east, just off the Borneo coast where the Dutch NEFIS (Netherlands East Indies Intelligence Section) had established a collection point for downed Allied airmen.

However, as the junk closed in on the island, the Chinese crewmen attacked the Rimau party, killing Lieutenant Reymond and Corporal Craft, both of whom disappeared over the side of the junk. Sargent leapt into the sea and, after spending ten hours in the water and a further 24 hours exhausted on a fish trap, was found by native fishermen and handed over to the Japanese.

This left three men at large: WO Willersdorf, Lance Corporal Pace and Private Warne. After the attempt by the Chinese crewmen to retake their vessel, the crew were overpowered and thrown overboard by the three surviving operatives, who then sailed the junk to the south-east, to the south of Borneo and on towards Timor. On the voyage Warne became very sick with malaria, and in the hope of getting him medical attention he was dropped at a village on the island of Kadapongan, off the southern tip of Borneo. A tough man, Warne recovered, and taking to the kolek left for him by his mates, set off alone, island-hopping eastwards. Without navigational equipment or maps, Warne spent a number of weeks slowly paddling eastwards until he too was betrayed and handed over to the Japanese, who took him to Surabaya before flying him to Singapore.

It was now early January. Willersdorf and Pace meanwhile continued their journey eastwards, a monsoonal breeze pushing them along and on course for tiny Nila Island, a speck in the Banda Sea, just 400 miles (640 kilometres) north of Darwin. After island-hopping, they arrived on Romang Island, 50 miles (80 kilometres) north of Timor and now just 150 miles (230 kilometres) from safety on Nila Island. Coming ashore in a village on Romang, they probably felt secure, as they remained two days resting and regaining their strength after an amazing, voyage of about 1850 miles (3000 kilometres). Here their luck ran out, as the local headman, who they trusted, reported their arrival to the Japanese. The Japanese suddenly swooped, capturing the last two operatives on 19 January 1945.

Flown to Dili, Willersdorf and Pace were beaten and tortured, and over a two-day period of severe ill-treatment and neglect, gave up details of their mission and their long journey of escape south. Meanwhile, in Singapore, the decision had been made to put the remaining ten Rimau survivors on trial, but the harsh treatment meted out to Willersdorf and Pace meant these two would never make it. Within a few weeks of their arrival in Dili, Willersdorf died from his fly-blown wounds left untreated by his captors. Pace would struggle on until June, when he too would die, from starvation, disease and the results of his torture.

The ten men being held in Singapore awaited trial. Initially, the Rimau operatives were treated reasonably well, but the Japanese were confronted with a number of problems, not the least being how they would justify the execution of a large number of Allied soldiers. Should it become known that Allied operatives had undertaken the attacks on shipping in Singapore Harbour, how could the Japanese justify the massacre of thousands of the local population, some only a few weeks before? Also, the fact that the Japanese had been completely hoodwinked and effectively humiliated by a few brave men coming all the way from Australia was difficult for Japanese pride and 'face' to deal with.

In the end, the trial of the ten Rimau survivors was a legal charade. Suffice to say, it followed an inconsistent and flawed legal process to arrive at the predetermined conclusion that the operatives were guilty as spies and saboteurs under the Hague Convention of 1907. The court sentenced them to death, stating they were heroes and as such deserved to die a hero's death.

On the morning of 7 July 1945, just five weeks before Japan surrendered, the ten Rimau men were taken to a desolate, scrubby area near Reformatory Road and beheaded, their dismembered bodies toppling into three pre-prepared graves. Soon after, realising the war was all but over and the Allies would soon be asking questions, the Japanese erected Christian crosses above the graves. The Kempeitai also ensured their files and the court judgement were rewritten to respect international obligations, and this they did very well, deceiving and misleading Allied investigators into Japanese war crimes.

Today, 16 of those brave Rimau men lie in marked graves in Kranji Commonwealth War Graves Commission Cemetery in Singapore, including Ivan Lyon, Harold Ross, Donald Davidson, Pat Campbell, Grigor Riggs and Colin Cameron, plus the ten men executed in July 1945: Ronald Ingleton, Bob Page, Albert Sargent, Walter Carey, Alf Warren, David Gooley, Clair Stewart, Ron Fletcher, Wally Falls and Jack Hardy. Those without a known grave are today remembered on the Kranji Memorial to the Missing: Jeff Willersdorf, Hugo Pace, Colin Craft and Doug Warne. Three others, Bruno Reymond, Andrew Huston and Fred Marsh, are commemorated on the Naval Memorial in Plymouth, England.

Of all the SRD operations, some 81 in total, this raid, while probably the most ambitious and audacious, was also the most deadly, with every man in the party losing his life.

When asked about the Rimau operation, Keith Stringfellow, a captain and party leader on the Raven and Finch operations in 1945, said the following:

> It shouldn't have happened. I wasn't briefed exactly on the operation, but I was told enough and asked if I wanted to go, but the fact is that they were going back to Singapore and they were using a new type of equipment and the party was getting too big. So I said, I don't think I'll accept this one, I don't think it's on, so if you'll excuse me, I'll drop out. Others did too as they could see it was dangerous and not very well planned. You could refuse any

operation even if you'd been briefed. There was no slur on your name if you said you would not take part in that one. Bob Page didn't want to go. He thought it was too dangerous. It was mostly Lyon's idea . . . he wanted to get back to his wife and punish the Japanese – that was what was behind it. It was badly planned and the equipment they had was not properly proven. It was never going to work, never. I'm sorry, as Bob Page was a particularly nice guy, I shared a tent with him, I met his wife. I think it was very foolhardy to go back again.[20]

SIXTEEN

The Last Raids

During the period SRD operated to the north of Australia between 1942 and late 1945, they were reliant in most cases on aircraft – flying boats or modified bombers to allow parachute drops – or British and American submarines. Without this support, operations could not go ahead, and SRD often found that operations were delayed or cancelled as transport could not be secured to insert or evacuate operatives and provide their supply needs. A similar situation occurred in England, where Bomber Command were reluctant to divert available aircraft from the offensive bombing of Germany to sorties for the insertion of SOE personnel or the delivery of supplies and weapons. For SRD operations, aircraft and submarines also often needed modification – for example, the changes to the British submarine *Porpoise* to store and launch submersible boats and kayaks for Operation Rimau – and crews needed to be trained and exercises carried out to prepare.

As the war moved further north from Australia after mid-1944, and the distances to prospective targets increased, there was more pressure applied by SRD on the services, in particular the British and US Navy, for access to and cooperation from their submarines. But submarines could now range further to meet these new targets, and it was believed that the addition of trained operatives to submarine crews would allow attacks on shipping and other targets in protected ports or waterways, or shore installations like radio and radar stations, that would not be otherwise accessible.

The Americans were not initially interested in responding to SRD requests, having been involved in three unsuccessful attempts to extract the Python party from British North Borneo after its insertion in September 1943. In a subsequent inquiry by Major Bill Jinkins of SRD, it was found 'that the submarine crews lacked local knowledge, were not specially trained for such work and did not possess suitable equipment'.[1]

To overcome this problem, the US Navy agreed to try again to work with SRD and to allow the inclusion of two SRD operatives on a war patrol of the US submarine USS *Harder* in May and June 1944. The mission resulted in the successful extraction of the Python party and their return to Perth.

This success opened the way for an agreement between the US Navy (Commander Task Force 71) in Perth and Australian GHQ to attach SRD personnel to US submarines on war patrols. Initially it was proposed that six SRD operatives should be attached to CTF-71 for future operational duties aboard US submarines, and this was later expanded to 12. The initial six operatives commenced a specialist training program at Careening Bay Camp under the operational codename Politician.

A number of valuable lessons had been learnt with respect to SRD–Navy operations, so specialist submarine training was provided to the selected operatives, in particular 'in communications between party and submarine, rendezvous procedure and equipment'.[2] Then, in January 1945, SRD were able to secure the support of the Royal Navy to allow another six operatives to be attached to RN submarines for similar offensive operations. This was codenamed Optician.

In all, 11 operations under the codename Politician were undertaken by SRD operatives on US submarines between May 1944 and June 1945. The first of these two-man missions, as mentioned above, was led by Major Jinkins and Lieutenant S. W. Dodds, who left Perth on USS *Harder* on 26 May 1944. During the mission, a number of attempts were made to attack Japanese shipping in Bongao Harbour in British North Borneo, but the continued presence of patrolling Japanese seaplanes made surfacing within ten miles (16 kilometres) of the harbour too dangerous. This put it outside the operational range of the two-man folboats, hence the plans were shelved. But the submarine was able to recover and extract the Python party on 8 June 1944 and return them to Perth.

The second operation was also led by Major Jinkins, this time with Lieutenant Tom Barnes, aboard USS *Redfin*. The operational plans for this trip included attacks by SRD operatives on shipping in Kuching Harbour and at Labuan Island off Borneo, but both plans were abandoned when the submarine was directed to Palawan Island in the Philippines to rescue survivors from an American submarine. After eight survivors were picked up and transferred to Darwin, *Redfin* resumed operations in the Flores Sea, where intelligence and topographical information was collected before the submarine returned to Perth after 60 days on station.

On 18 December 1944, the third mission left Perth with two operatives, Lieutenant John Sachs and Lieutenant Alexander Hawkins, this time aboard USS *Bream*. Sachs was a 31-year-old veteran who had been recommended for the Victoria Cross for his actions in Greece: in the retreat due to the German advance there, he had held up the Germans alone, killed many of the enemy and then, with the assistance of a New Zealander, collected a number of prisoners. He had been badly wounded and captured, escaped and was captured again, but escaped a second time and, after attempting to steal a German aircraft and fly out, instead stole a boat and sailed it back to Cairo, where he rejoined his unit.

He had been awarded a Military Medal after he returned to Greece to assist with the extraction of Allied military personnel threatened with capture by the Germans. Sachs came back to Australia in August 1942 and went on to fight in Papua New Guinea, where he again showed his valour and independence, and came to the attention of SRD. After training at Canungra, Queensland, he was attached to Operation Politician, where he embarked on a raid with Lieutenant Hawkins.

In a report by Sachs after this mission, he writes that he and Lieutenant Hawkins 'were ordered aboard for the purpose of striking targets of opportunity along the way',[3] including the tiny island of Itu Aba, 375 miles (600 kilometres) to the east of the Indochina coast towards the Philippines. The intended raid would see the two operatives land on Itu Aba and destroy the oil storage facility there, along with other enemy installations on the island.

After an uneventful journey, the *Bream* arrived at Itu Aba and a periscope recce was carried out in daylight on 7 January 1945 on the north, south and west sides of the island. Due to the northerly wind and the presence of a sea wall on the south-western corner of the island, it was decided that the operatives would approach the island from the south. At 1950 hours, the folboat was assembled on the deck of the submarine and loaded with stores, weapons, explosives and an ATR4 portable radio, an Australian-built transceiver weighing 20 pounds (about nine kilograms). At 2035, the folboat with Sachs and Hawkins was launched 'approximately 10,000 to 12,000 yards from the target',[4] and shortly after, a radio check was made a short distance from the submarine. Quietly the men paddled ashore into a northerly breeze, the sea calm with a slight swell and above them a clear, starry sky.

At 2230 the sky became overcast, making it difficult to sight the shoreline, which finally came into view at 2340. Searching for a gap in the surf, the men landed just after 0100 on a sandy beach, having slightly damaged the hull on the reef. They carried the folboat across the narrow beach, concealed it in the scrub and set out, moving north-east along the spine of the small island. Soon after, they came across what was thought to be oil tanks that had been seen from the submarine, but this was found to be an abandoned water tank. They moved north, hampered by thick scrub and the darkness of the night, past dilapidated, collapsing buildings and scattered rubbish, but finding nothing worth destroying. After passing the first water tank, radio masts could be seen on the western end of the island 'silhouetted against the sky, and since the oil tanks were the main objective, the masts were disregarded'.[5]

Creeping north, the operatives discovered a second tank that had been seen during the periscope recce the previous day, but this too turned out to be for water rather than oil. As they were now near the north-eastern corner of the island, the men changed direction and came upon a third tank, but since they expected it to also be a water tank, they did not investigate it.

They now followed a track and thought they saw a movement ahead of them, so slipped into the bush and waited. Hearing no more and fearing they were making noise themselves in the thick scrub, the men crossed the track and continued on a westerly course. It was now 0200. Concerned they had little time before they needed to return to the submarine, they headed back by a different approach route to their hidden folboat location, which they reached at 0235.

The two men launched their folboat and tried to radio the submarine, but received no reply. At 0315, they used a prearranged light signal. This was replied to by the submarine, which was at the time moving slowly towards their agreed rendezvous point. Fifteen minutes later, they came aboard the submarine, but a sudden wave washed the folboat and Lieutenant Sachs off the deck. Quickly two crewmen dived into the water and pulled him aboard, but the folboat and the stores were lost. Just before 0400, the operatives and the crew were safely below and the submarine proceeded on its mission.

In a subsequent war patrol by USS *Bluegill*, two operatives, Lieutenants Dodds and Cecil Anderson, proposed an attack on facilities on Itu Aba Island, but permission was refused and the patrol confined itself to gathering intelligence on Japanese shipping movements and boarding locals' craft to interrogate their crews, before returning to Perth.

On 7 January 1945, the fifth Politician operation sailed from Perth aboard USS *Flounder* under Major Jinkins with the operative WO Alec Chew. Initially plans were drawn up for the patrol to do a reconnaissance on potential railway targets close to the Indochina coast between Saigon (now Ho Chi Minh City) and Tourane (now Danang), but they did not eventuate. Orders were instead received to check on some French nationals resident on Woody and Paracel Islands, and to undertake a reconnaissance while there. The two operatives were transferred to USS *Pargo* on the night of 1–2 February along with their stores, and from there proceeded to the islands.

Woody and Paracel Islands were part of a tiny group of atolls far out into the South China Sea, some 225 miles (365 kilometres) from the Indochina coast at Danang, and were separated by about 40 miles (64 kilometres) of open sea. Upon the party's arrival at

Woody Island, a periscope reconnaissance revealed many buildings and storage facilities, a radio mast, and on the shore many serviceable boats. The decision was made to put Jinkins and Chew ashore, but the weather remained rough and the surf breaking 600 yards out from the shore prevented a safe insertion.

After a wait of several days, and after charging her batteries, USS *Pargo* launched the two-man party 3600 yards from the shore just after 0400. They were instructed to make immediate radio contact on landing, and in case they needed covering fire to assist a fast extraction, they were provided with a Very pistol and a red flare to signal the submarine of their predicament. After an anxious paddle through a six-foot surf, the operatives landed and the folboat was hidden and camouflaged.

Safely ashore, the two operatives made radio communication and a radio schedule was confirmed for 0600, 0900, 1200 and 1900. At 0620 they quietly moved off, but came upon footprints in the sand that looked like those left by the familiar split-toe shoes popular with Japanese troops and also dog footprints. Hidden in the undergrowth along the beach edge and some 200 yards from a wooden jetty, the operatives saw a large dog, 'a cross between an Alsatian and an Airedale',[6] run out onto the beach and proceed in their direction. As the dog came towards them, a man walked out onto the jetty to attend to some fishing lines. Through their binoculars, Jinkins and Chew identified him as a Japanese marine.

Given the dog was sniffing around their hiding place and the Japanese marine was just 200 yards away, their position looked precarious. The men realised that a considerable number of Japanese troops were on the island, and that it would be difficult during the day to remain undetected, so they decided to 'launch the canoe, paddle out beyond the reef while the opportunity presented, and remain at sea until radio contact was established'.[7]

Quickly they navigated the breaking surf and paddled directly out to sea, hoping that no one on shore would see their seaward flight and begin firing. Fortunately all was quiet, and at 0820 the periscope of the submarine was sighted. By 0900 they and their folboat were back on board and below deck. Hearing of the Japanese presence on the island, the submarine captain decided to shell the island facilities, and a number of targets were damaged.

Following this action, orders were received that the SRD party were to transfer back to USS *Flounder*, but on the way to Subic Bay, the gigantic American naval port in the Philippines, *Flounder* was rammed by a submerged submarine while travelling at periscope depth, which forced it into Subic Bay for repairs. The operatives also found themselves far from Australia, and it took them some time to get a flight back. A number of valuable items had been lost and damaged during the mission, including one folboat, three radio transceivers, demolition charges, photographs and escape money.

In a report by Major Jinkins dated 10 March 1945 under the subject 'Possible Activities', he suggested 'that Woody Island and Pattle Island be occupied by Army personnel. Primarily to supply weather information for all operations in area.'[8] He went on to suggest that these islands might be a suitable base for operations by country craft – the replica junks to be built in Victoria and used by SRD in clandestine operations around Malaya and Indochina – and could be taken 'in a co-ordinated night attack by SRD personnel. This attack should be made as soon as possible to be of material use. Suggest within one month.'[9]

Jinkins explained that many of the buildings on the islands had been recently damaged by Allied air strikes and the area was lightly held by about 60 Japanese troops, who 'do not appear to have any defence preparations'.[10] Jinkins made the point that the islands could be easily resupplied by surface vessels, and that it would not be 'considered feasible nor does it appear profitable for the Japs to attempt to retake these islands when once occupied by Allied Forces owing to the air superiority held by Allied Forces'.[11]

In early March 1945, a combined operation between the US Task Force 71 and SRD, codenamed Gunnard – the sixth operation under Politician – began. This saw the submarine USS *Gurnard* ordered to tranship an SRD operative, Lieutenant A. S. Hawkins (AIF), along with a Malay local, Abdul Madjid, to the USS *Brill*, at that time on her first war patrol, and insert them onto Sakala Island, 100 miles (160 kilometres) north-east of Bali.

As the orders stated, they were to 'pick up five friendly natives from the island and transport same back to submarine'. No reason is given why these five were to be collected or who they were, but they were subsequently flown to Melbourne, so they must have had valuable intelligence for the US Navy and SRD to undertake this operation. So, following the transhipment the two-man patrol were taken to Sakala and, after a daylight periscope reconnaissance of the island on 25 March, were sent ashore in a rubber boat.

This was considered a simple, safe operation. The operational order had included a line under 'Enemy' which stated, 'From latest information it is reported that there are no enemy troops or enemy defences on Sakala Island.'[12] After arriving on the beach, the two men walked to a village 500 yards inland, where Hawkins reported, 'I handed over the money and the cloth to the Kapala Kampong [village] and made arrangement for the five natives to collect for return to the submarine. Two of the natives were apparently in a village at the eastern end of the island and there was some delay waiting for their arrival.'[13]

After Hawkins and Madjid had assembled the five locals, the group returned to the beach and loaded their seven-man inflatable boat and, with the aid of a 3.5-horsepower Mercury outboard, returned to the submarine. As the evacuation had successfully been carried out, the *Brill* returned with the SRD party and the locals to Fremantle. At the end of the official report, there is a chilling inclusion: 'It is of interest to note that had the landing been made twenty-four hours earlier, the party would have been met by a detachment of thirty Japs.'[14] These Japanese troops had arrived unexpectedly from a powered patrol boat armed with a medium machine gun and two submachine guns, and each man carried a rifle and a sword. After inspecting the island they had left the same night, without either taking anything or harming the locals, who were very anti-Japanese.

Before the *Brill* had returned to Perth, another operation, the seventh patrol, had set out on the USS *Bream*. Again it was a two-man SRD operation, led by Lieutenant John Sachs along with Lieutenant Cliff Perske.

Following the Itu Aba raid with Lieutenant Hawkins, Sachs came up with a bizarre scheme to attack Japanese shipping and check whether those masquerading as hospital ships were what they seemed. This involved boarding suspect vessels from a submarine and, after confirming their bona fides, signalling the submarine to determine the ship's fate. Sachs' plan was rejected, but the idea of attacking enemy shipping at anchor from a submarine remained with him. The time aboard USS *Bream* gave him just that chance.

After departing their base in Perth, *Bream* made for their patrol area in the South China Sea. On the way, they interdicted a Japanese convoy bound for Surabaya and sank one ship in the vicinity of the Masalembo Islands, between Borneo and East Java. Fearing further attack, the Japanese convoy took refuge in the lee of Great Masalembo Island, much to the delight of

Lieutenant Sachs, who sought permission to put in a folboat attack. It was a wet, dark and rainy night and with a calm sea, so conditions were ideal. With permission granted, he and Lieutenant Perske set off on a paddle of 4200 yards, with instructions that, after attaching limpet mines to the sides of the Japanese vessels, they were to continue paddling in a north-westerly direction for 6000 yards, after which they would be picked up by the submarine.

Unknown to the operatives and the captain of the *Bream*, this same convoy had been attacked by a British submarine that day and the Japanese crews were on heightened alert. Sachs and Perske were never seen again and the *Official History* states, 'They were posted "missing believe killed" but their ultimate fate was not established.'[15]

The *Bream* made every effort to collect the Australian operatives, remaining in the area for an extra two days, despite being depth-charged and damaged by the Japanese as they continued their search. Finally, they picked up a radio message purportedly from the operatives, but the all-important authenticator code was missing at the beginning of the transmission and the *Bream*'s captain rightly surmised the Australians were now captured and that the radio transmission, forced upon them by the Japanese, was intended to lure them into a trap. The following day, the *Bream* was damaged after being attacked and heavily depth-charged by a Japanese 'hunter-killer' anti-submarine pack.

Research has concluded that Sachs and Perske were captured by a Japanese naval patrol boat and transferred to Gubeng Prison in Surabaya City, East Java. Here both the Australians were subjected to torture and long sessions of interrogation, but Sachs would only reveal he had come to the island by submarine from Perth with the intention of sinking Japanese shipping with limpet mines. Unable to extract anything further from the two, the

Japanese sent them to join other Allied prisoners, including ship-wrecked merchant seamen, American airmen and Chinese and Indonesians, all of whom had been secretly sentenced to death.

A Japanese naval captain by the name of Dr Nakamura had been trying to produce an anti-tetanus serum to inoculate Japanese military personnel who were dying from the disease in vast numbers. Although experiments had been conducted on monkeys, human trails were urgent, and Nakamura obtained permission to use the condemned group in Gubeng Prison in a human experiment to ascertain the dosage to be given. A number of the prisoners were given the serum and others a placebo, and in the days after, many died, including Doug Warne, the Rimau operative who had been captured and sent to Surabaya.

As Sachs and Perske were both given the placebo, and were immune to the disease from their inoculations in Australia, they survived this barbarous experiment, but they had little time to live. Nor did the two American airmen in the prison who had survived the downing of their B-24 Liberator bomber in an attack on Sandakan. After the Doolittle raid on Tokyo on 18 April 1942, the Japanese had declared that captured American airmen would be executed, and that command was extended to Australian airmen, in particular those captured in the Papua New Guinea campaign, where many, like Flight Lieutenant Bill Newton VC, were tortured and executed.

On 30 March 1945, the survivors of the serum experiment were taken from their cells for the 30-minute drive to the execution ground at the Eastern Fort. After being held in a small hut for an hour while their burial pits were dug, the prisoners were taken forth blindfolded, then forced to kneel and beheaded, sometimes in a botched and inhumane way, with three or more sword blows necessary to complete the beheading.

In her book *Deadly Secrets: The Singapore Raids 1942–43*, historian Lynette Ramsay Silver tells an eerie story that took place at the moment of Lieutenant Sachs' execution:

> Thousands of kilometres away at the Sachs family home in the
> [Sydney] harbourside suburb of Double Bay, at approximately
> 2.30 pm local time on the afternoon of Good Friday, 30 March
> 1945, Lieutenant John Sachs' framed Army Commission crashed
> to the floor. While Fritz Sachs, who had no idea his son was
> even missing, stared at the shattered glass with a feeling of great
> foreboding, the officer in charge of the execution glared at Sachs'
> lifeless body in absolute fury.[16]

While the *Official History*, Volume II, numbers the Politician missions I–XI, in fact the mission by Sachs and Perske (number 7) came after another mission (number 8) which had departed Perth three days earlier. This was the war patrol of USS *Bluegill*, which included the two SRD operatives, Lieutenants Cecil Anderson and Cliff Owens. The submarine departed Fremantle on 7 March 1945 and was to arrive at Subic Bay in the Philippines on 18 April upon completion of the mission. While they had a number of tasks, including destroying a beached Japanese ship on the Indochina coast, reporting on locals' craft and Japanese shipping movements, their main objective was to destroy a section of railway line running along the coast at Vung Ro, some 225 miles (360 kilometres) north-east of Saigon.

The two-man party left *Bluegill* at midnight on 5 April and landed two hours later, when they signalled the submarine of their safe arrival. They had arrived on a rocky section of coastline, but the operatives dragged their folboat into a secure hiding place among the large rocks and spent the day waiting for a chance to undertake a reconnaissance of the railway line. At dawn the nearby bay filled with small fishing craft, some within 20 yards of their hiding place, so they were prevented from moving out until 1330, when they took the chance to sneak away. For the next two hours they climbed a steep hill, rising 880 feet (270 metres) in the hope of getting a good vantage point, but the sea haze and the dense jungle limited their view across the water to the western shore. They could see a section of railway line and two girder bridges, but observed no trains or traffic in the area.

Just after 1600 hours, Anderson and Owens returned to their hidden folboat and stores, but found that the small fishing boats were still close by. Even by 2045, there were still five boats just 100 yards away, but given the fishermen had probably settled in for the night, the operatives decided to move. At 2130 they quietly climbed into their folboat and, remaining close to the rocky shore, silently paddled for the western shore, avoiding the numerous fishing boats along the shoreline, lit with small lamps and naked flames. Arriving again upon a rocky shoreline about two miles away, they found movement 'extremely difficult, but quickly moved into the treeline, carrying only explosive, pistols and Welrods [pistols]'.[17]

The railway track, just 50 yards inland from this point, appeared well constructed and maintained. After a quick inspection the two men turned north and after 400 yards came across a narrow railway cutting some 150 yards long. After hearing some noise, they retreated 900 yards south down the line, to where they believed another bridge was located. It was now just after midnight. They had begun to place their charges when three men were seen approaching, two believed to be armed and one carrying a light, slowly inspecting the track as they advanced towards them. The three men found the first charge and halted, just as Lieutenant

Owens was placing the final charge at the northern end of the cutting and Lieutenant Anderson was working on preparing a Fog signal igniter (a small fuse which was fixed to the railway track to set off the charge) just 75 yards from the railway patrol.

Realising the objective was lost and needing to prevent discovery, Anderson and Owens quickly and silently moved up the line and turned off into thick elephant grass, then came out on the shoreline 500 yards from the landing point, where the boats were hidden. The rocky shoreline made movement difficult and in the pitch black night they had a number of falls, many down six to eight feet. At one point Anderson fell 25 feet (7.5 metres) into the water and was forced to swim, hugging the cliff edge until he finally reached the folboat 200 yards away. The two operatives slipped into the folboat and again negotiated their way among the now-sleeping fishermen back to the eastern shore, where they immediately made contact with *Bluegill*. With little time before first light, they set out for the paddle back to the waiting submarine, which they boarded at just after 0400. While their mission had failed and they were forced to leave behind explosives and other stores, they were fortunate to be back and relatively safe in the body of the submarine.

But the operatives' work was not yet over. Fifteen miles (24 kilometres) to the south, at the most easterly point of Indochina, was a small island named Hon Doi, where the damaged and burnt-out remains of a Japanese ship were beached and being salvaged by local people. The task was to further damage the ship, determine its name, its cargo, the extent of the damage and the salvage work, and to collect any charts, papers or equipment that might be worth collecting. The two operatives set out by folboat at 2215 on the night of 14–15 April 1945, paddling 1500 yards to the north-west of the island, and arrived at 2245. An inspection of the vessel confirmed it was a Fox Baker class, converted to carry bulk fuel, and it was identified as the *Hokki Maru*, weighing at 5600 tons.

The operatives attached six limpets and destroyed the undamaged hold and forecastle. After collecting a number of documents and a Browning machine gun that was found mounted to the deck, they returned to the submarine and departed the area. At 0341 the first explosion was heard and the second at 0350, which set the ship alight. Bright explosions and flames could be seen, and a heavy pall of black smoke rose into the sky from the combustible remnants of fuel in the hull. By 0630, the hull had sunk further into the water and the fire had reduced to a glow, the wooden parts of the ship completely destroyed. From here, the USS *Bluegill* returned to Subic Bay, and Lieutenants Anderson and Owens took the mandatory 14 days' rest before preparing for their next mission.

Three days after the departure of the *Bluegill* to Subic Bay on 11 March, the ninth war patrol departed Perth on USS *Boarfish* under Lieutenant Bill Chaffey and Sergeant Lloyd Campbell. The opportunity to hit Japanese lines of communication, in particular unprotected railway infrastructure in Indochina, was too tempting a target to pass up. The orders stated that a daylight reconnaissance of Tourane Bay (now known as Danang Bay) on the coast of Indochina be undertaken, with the 'order of priority of targets as follows: submarines, large transports, small transports, seaplanes, the railway line'.[18]

On the way north the submarine slipped through the Sunda Strait, but was chased by some Japanese patrol boats. Sergeant Campbell recalled of that experience:

Coming through the Strait, I was on watch on the top deck when the man next to me saw smoke on the horizon. The submarine commander decided to get up in front of this convoy and take one of the ships out. The convoy turned out to be several small destroyer types with a derelict tanker. This of course was a trap, a killer pack, and all the commander could see on the leading destroyer were lookouts, so we dived and as we did we were attacked. We got to 120 feet and were blown back to 90. We got 15 depth charges at that stage and it was frightening for me, never having been depth-charged before. This went on for quite a while, spasmodic depth-charging, destroyers running over the top, screws thrashing in the water like a cauldron and coming back for more. Fortunately we were able to get into 'heavy water', where the ASDIC could not penetrate, a bit like clouds, and that's how we escaped from the depth-charging. But it made quite a mess of the submarine.[19]

Arriving off Danang on the night of 14–15 April 1945, the two operatives set out at 2215, but the outboard motor would not start so they were delayed while repairs were undertaken. At midnight they slipped away from the submarine and headed for the shore under the power of the outboard. Campbell recalled:

But we were 15 miles [24 kilometres] off the harbour, not five, so we went flat out until we cut the motor. I thought I could hear birds so we started paddling cautiously around this island, and suddenly a Japanese patrol boat shot out from the island to the mainland. We still kept paddling slowly, and fortunately it was dark. We got through to the end of this passage and here was another fishing fleet, and so for the next hour we tried to find a way through it. Eventually, with me sitting holding a silenced machine gun and Bill paddling, we finally came out the other side.[20]

Continuing their silent paddle, Chaffey and Campbell turned into Tourane Bay and landed half a mile inside the entrance. While the sea was calm, the surge across the rocky shelf that lined the shore made the landing difficult, and the fine coral at water level damaged the canvas shell of the folboat. The operatives dragged their boat across the rocks and into the scrubby thicket 15 yards above them, and it took 45 minutes for them to conceal themselves in the lantana while giving themselves a good field of observation across the bay. From here they were able to watch the railway line, visible on the far shore some 2.5 miles (four kilometres) across the bay. Based on their observations of train movements, they decided to attack the line that night.

At 2230, the night dark and with the calm sea lapping on the rocks, they set out for the far coastline. Landing again on a rocky shore, they dragged their folboat above the waterline and into a concealed spot, covered it with branches and strode out for the railway line. Campbell recalled, 'Bill had the detonators in his back pocket and I'm of course following him up the hill with my head fairly close to his backside, and I thought, if he falls, I'm going to get my head blown off here.'[21]

They pushed through 500 yards of low scrub for half an hour then climbed 600 feet (180 metres) to the railway line that followed the coast north to Hue, arriving scratched and with their hearts pumping from the arduous climb. Noting that the last train had passed travelling north at 0900 the previous day, they assumed the next train would be travelling south on the single line, so they decided to lay a double charge at the southern end of a shallow cutting in the hope that any train derailed by their charges would roll down the hill towards the sea.

Lloyd Campbell remembered this part of their operation, 'We got up to the rail line. There were no sentries, and [we] proceeded with our individual work: Bill putting the device under the line, I was doing the explosives. Partway through this I saw a light to my left, so we lay low and watched a Japanese patrol boat come along the cliffs with its searchlight. We hesitated for a bit then got down and started back on our work.'[22]

By 0130 they had finished laying and checking their charges. All was eerily silent and still, apart from the twinkling lights of a few fishing boats along the shoreline below them. They retreated down the hill back through the scrub to their hidden folboat, which they soon launched, pushing it out into the open bay at 0215. Almost immediately they heard the sound of an approaching northbound train and, looking up, saw the slow-moving locomotive and a number of carriages, heading towards their recently laid charges. As Campbell remembered, 'At that point, a train came, not from the north as we'd intended it to go over the cliff, but from the south, from Tourane. There was panic as we were fairly close to the shore.'[23]

Five minutes later, an enormous explosion was heard. The two operatives saw the locomotive and two carriages topple off the line. Campbell recalled, 'When it blew . . . there were rocks pelting on us on the seashore. The searchlight on the front of the train was still alight. There were Japanese running everywhere and then they started coming down the hill, probably looking for saboteurs. We spent no time trying to ascertain the damage.'[24]

As the post-operation report stated, 'The only activity observed from the scene of the explosion was a light moving about, which at one stage appeared to start off down the slope as if following the party's tracks. The light eventually concentrated on the train – probably assessing the damage, and commencing repairs.'[25]

Fearing immediate discovery, the two operatives paddled hard along the coast to the north-east, opening the distance between them and the confusion along the railway line. Hugging the northern shore and avoiding the bobbing fishing boats whose crews of locals were awake and staring at the far hillside, they arrived back at their landing point at 0415. Campbell recalled the end of the operation:

> When we got back to the cache, we decided to ditch everything because the dawn was coming. With the motor working, we headed out through the centre of the harbour this time. We were spoken to by some natives, but they wouldn't understand who we were as we were all blacked up and they probably thought we were Japanese. I got a message out at 6 am on a walkie-talkie the Americans had loaned us. Out through the harbour and the next minute Bill said, 'The *Boarfish* is coming to pick us up,' and had taken the risk of coming through this minefield. We confirmed it was them with the infra-red ray, and at 6.30 am they pulled us on board and it [the folboat] broke in half. So it was a pretty close thing.[26]

With the operatives loaded, the submarine immediately put to sea. In Lieutenant Chaffey's post-operation report, under the heading 'Estimate of Damage', the following was noted:

> As the train was on an up-grade and travelling very slowly, the engine on being derailed would probably run into the embankment, preventing any possibility of it going down the slope and dragging the carriages (or trucks) with it. The damage done is estimated at:
> a) One engine derailed and partially wrecked.
> b) Probably two leading carriages derailed.
> c) Damage to line as a result of engine running off; this in addition to one rail cut by demolition.

d) Rear carriages would have to be towed back to Tourane to enable repair gang to get through.

e) Line out of commission for probably 24 hours.

f) Faced with the possibility of a repetition, the enemy may cancel night train schedule.[27]

The report went on to state, 'No enemy counter action was observed, such as aircraft, patrol boats searching the bay, or use of searchlights.'[28]

From the Indochina coast, they sailed to Subic Bay for repairs. From there Lloyd Campbell hitched a ride to Morotai, but his aircraft crash-landed when one of the wheels did not come down. He stated, 'I understand [this operation] was one of the most successful sabotage missions carried out by Z Unit in the Pacific. As a result, Bill was awarded the American Bronze Medal and both of us were Mentioned in Despatches.'[29]

Having returned to Subic Bay from their war patrol on USS *Bluegill*, Lieutenants Cecil Anderson and Cliff Owens were sent to the Submarine Rest Camp to await further orders. But the war still needed to go on, and instructions were received that *Bluegill* would depart on its third war patrol on 4 May. This was to become the tenth US submarine patrol under Politician and the penultimate one for this operation.

The islands of Pratas lie far out in the South China Sea, about 200 miles (320 kilometres) south-east of Hong Kong. On 14 May, the American submarine USS *Blenny* shelled the island, at which time an aircraft that was spotting for the submarine is claimed to have been fired upon. The *Bluegill* was tasked to investigate and gather intelligence on enemy forces on the island, should they still be there, to land a party to destroy enemy installations and equipment, and to gather documents of intelligence value.

On 27 May, *Bluegill* completed a periscope reconnaissance of the island, which is only one and a half miles long and half a mile wide. This, along with recent aerial reports, 'revealed no signs of life on the island'.[30] To confirm this, Lieutenants Anderson and Owens disembarked from the submarine on the night of 28–29 May and paddled the 6000 yards to the beach, landing without incident at 0100 in the vicinity of the south-western headland. They moved south-east, came upon the jetty and then moved ashore and searched the various houses, but found no sign of any remaining Japanese. They retraced their steps back to the location of their folboat and radioed the submarine the results of their recce.

The submarine captain, Captain E. L. Barr Jr, decided to send a search party from the submarine to further explore the island. With the assistance of the two operatives, the party landed at 0945 and proceeded to undertake a further search of the island, discovering a cache of ammunition and food as well as 2000 gallons of fuel oil. Also found were weapons pits and a defensive trench system to cover the jetty, along with clothes and Japanese insignia, identified as Japanese naval badges. After the operatives laid charges on the food, ammunition and fuel caches, these were destroyed and the party returned to the submarine late in the afternoon without casualties. The report finishes by stating, 'The co-operation of the Comdr., E. L. Barr Jr. and the officers and crew of the USS *Bluegill* was as usual 100%.'[31] On 21 June, *Bluegill* berthed in Pearl Harbor and arrangements were made to fly the two operatives to Melbourne for 'refit and further duty'.[32] Together they departed Pearl Harbor by air on 26 June and arrived in Melbourne on 2 July 1945.

As the war drew to a close there had been one more war patrol for USS *Boarfish*, with the Australian operatives Lieutenant Chaffey and Sergeant Campbell, between 16 May and 6 June. However, from the start they were hampered by a lack of equipment, aerial photographs and other necessary stores, and as Chaffey later noted in his report, 'We feel entitled to all the material that will help to make our jobs successful as there are too many doubtful factors involved without having to cope with faulty equipment which should NOT be if someone would only try.'[33] There were by this time very few opportunities for attack on Japanese shipping, and the patrol returned to Perth.

So ended a long and successful association between the Australians of SRD and the US Navy. As the *Official History* notes, 'The operatives were treated by the US Navy staff and officers and crew of each submarine as full members of the crew, receiving every facility to members of the US Navy. During each patrol, the operatives stood watch [and] performed normal duties as officers of submarines.'[34]

After the war, as a result of the successful cooperation between SRD and the US Navy the operatives of Politician were asked to share the Presidential Unit Citation Ribbon awarded to USS *Harder*, but because the Australians were not US personnel the citation could not be rewarded. In another case, Lieutenant Rowan Waddy, who planned the cancelled operation Crocodile with Major Bill Jinkins, was informed he would receive the US Submarine Combat Insignia, but although he was allowed to accept the honour, he was not allowed to wear it. As Waddy said in his book, *On Operations with Z Special Unit*, 'Finally, mainly due to Jinkins' persistence, approval was granted and I eventually received the Submarine Combat Pin in 1987, over forty years after the event.'[35]

SEVENTEEN

War's End

While the detonation of the two atomic bombs on Hiroshima and Nagasaki in early August 1945 formally ended the war with Japan, the war was far from over for the operatives of SRD. Unlike the German surrender, which had led to the immediate cessation of hostilities by the German armed forces, it was going to be a challenge to locate, notify and neutralise Japanese forces to enforce the conditions of the surrender. Germany had been reduced to rubble, and Berlin and the open landscape of that country had been captured, while most Japanese forces were hiding out in jungles and on islands from northern China south to Timor and New Britain, and west to Malaya, Indochina and Burma. Simply notifying isolated and distant Japanese units that the war was over was one thing, but having them believe what they considered propaganda was another. They also thought of themselves as the warriors of the Emperor, with surrender an unthinkable prospect after this long and draining war, so many were determined to fight on to the death.

These conditions did not bode well for any Allied troops given the task to round up remaining Japanese garrisons to enforce the surrender. For those held in captivity by the Japanese, their release was not guaranteed, and their fate remained at the direction of local commanders who were now themselves cut off from control by their higher command. To further complicate the situation, within Japan the disgrace of defeat was driving the military and political leadership further apart, and there was an attempted coup d'état in the days before the pre-recorded speech of the Emperor announcing the war was over was broadcast, to prevent the nation from hearing it. The surrender brought out mixed emotions in the Japanese – anger, hatred and the loss of face – which Allied forces would have to deal with before completely defeating Japan.

The Japanese had become increasingly concerned about the course of the war. In July 1944, the long-serving militarist prime minister, General Hideki Tojo, was replaced by General Kuniaki Koiso, who, after the loss of the Philippines, was replaced by Admiral Kantaro Suzuki. While the Japanese troops spread south to Rabaul, all knew of the shortages of food, ammunition and reinforcements. Japanese leaders realised they were now cut off from urgent raw materials, in particular oil, iron, rubber and coal, due to the American submarine blockade and the extensive mining of Japanese ports.

US submarines based now in Guam and Saipan ensured that few Japanese ships entering home waters were not sunk or badly damaged and the Japanese Navy ceased to be a factor in the final outcome of the war. American bombers flew daily from bases in Okinawa to destroy war industry, ports and vast suburban areas as the American armed forces prepared for Operation Downfall, the Allied invasion of the Japanese mainland. With Germany's defeat, Japan was alone, and given there were 40 Russian divisions poised along the Manchurian border, few options remained.

While the Emperor was the great leader, it was the Supreme Council for the Direction of the War, made up of six leading ministers including the Navy and Army ministers under Prime Minister Suzuki, that effectively ran the war. In 1945, as Japan's fortunes changed, the council became divided between continuing the prosecution of the war and pursuing peace. Japan had never lost a war, though it had fought few, and the thought of surrender was to many Japanese leaders unthinkable. On one side the military hardliners in the council believed that a decisive battle, once the Americans had landed on Japan resulting in massive Allied casualties, would sway American public opinion and a negotiated peace would follow. The moderates suggested an approach to the Russians to find a diplomatic solution whereby Japan would not face invasion, the Emperor would remain and Japanese war criminals would not be prosecuted.

This political and diplomatic positioning in faraway Japan had little impact on the SRD personnel in the field. As the *Official History* states, 'By the end of 1944 the situation in which SRD was first formed was largely reversed. There was no question of leaving underground parties to disrupt enemy communications in areas evacuated by Allied forces. Instead, the whole organisation of SRD could now be used in support of Allied advances and conquests.'[1] As a result, by 1945 SRD became 'entirely paramilitary',[2] but this saw a clash of personalities after the departure of the SRD commanding officer, Colonel Chapman-Walker, and his return from Morotai to SRD Rear HQ in Melbourne.

By June, SRD operations were confined mainly to Borneo and the Celebes and Moluccas, with excursions to French Indochina, Malaya and the Chinese coast. SRD had supported Oblivion, a Canadian operation, to insert a party of Chinese Canadians under a British officer, into the area around Hong Kong and along the coast between Hainan and Swatow, but this was cancelled due to political concerns by the Americans, concerned about dealing with the Chinese communists.

In November 1944, operations had been divided into five groups, each according to a geographical area. Group C, which had operated in Papua New Guinea, New Britain and the Solomons, was now closed down, with a new group formed under Captain Stringfellow to control Dutch Borneo.

This was confirmed at a meeting of senior personnel in July, where it was decided that SRD was 'dissipating its efforts in maintaining five operational groups' and was ordered 'to abandon all targets or areas which had become strategically unimportant and to concentrate the whole strength of the organisation on Group A (China Seas, British North Borneo, Sarawak) and Group B (Dutch Borneo, Western coast of Celebes, Java)'.[3] SRD was also ordered to discontinue training and technical developments, and 'to concentrate every effort on operations connected with the Allied advance'.[4]

In mid-August 1945, there were SRD parties active in Timor, Papua New Guinea, Borneo, Sarawak, the Celebes and Moluccas, in Malaya and the South China Sea. A draft document dated 20 August 1945 and headed 'Notes on SRD Policy – Post Surrender'[5] captures the confusion of this time:

> It is not yet possible to define SRD's post-surrender policy until such time as GHQ finally lay down the overall surrender plan. This is now being decided in Manila. It is understood that in all probability it will be on the following lines: (a) 9 Div to take over British Borneo and Sarawak. (b) 7 Div to cover Timor and Lesser Sundas Group. (c) 93 US Div to cover Celebes and Moluccas including Ceram and Buru.[6]

Given the location of SRD units, the tentative policy was for them to consolidate and secure their current operational areas and not undertake 'additional operational commitments'[7] except in the case of POWs. It was confirmed that SRD would provide the same support to these units until they were to be officially taken over by either the local military commander or by a civil administration unit. Due to concern about intertribal fighting, field units were to seek the return of issued weapons and ammunition, leaving weapons only with those kampongs (villages) that required them for self-defence. Included in these instructions was a provision stating, 'Danger money [an additional payment made to SRD personnel] will continue to be paid until the situation is such that no threat from the enemy can reasonably be expected.'[8]

While Allied offensive operations were ongoing, SRD was called upon for information on Japanese escape routes and troop concentrations, on POWs, and on the situation regarding locals in the area: their food and medical needs, and their attitude to the return of both the British and Dutch administrations into Borneo. For example, the Semut I party in Sarawak, while encountering very few Japanese in the interior, needed to assist with managing the considerable numbers of armed Japanese still roaming around on the coast. Due to the refusal of the Japanese to surrender, offensive actions continued in this area until October 1945, as was the case in a number of areas.

At the far southern end of the Japanese front was Timor. Initially the Japanese garrison there had three lines of communication north: one through the Moluccas and Ambon, another through the Macassar Strait to Java and a third via the South China Sea to Singapore. By April 1945, these lines were virtually cut off and the Japanese began withdrawing their forces. But as the Japanese lacked suitable shipping, and troop movements were confined to barges, prahus and small craft, their troops were easy targets for Allied air attack from intelligence supplied by SRD operatives and Coastwatchers. Since it was important for the Allies to protect their left flank as they drove towards the Philippines, it was crucial to gather intelligence on the movement of Japanese forces, something SRD were tasked to undertake.

SRD operations in Timor, right from the start, had been a disaster. To investigate missing SRD operatives, an operation codenamed Groper was despatched after the cessation of hostilities to determine the fate and ideally the graves of the following parties: Lagarto with seven men, Cobra with five men, Adder with five men, Sunbaker with four men, Sergeant Marshall from Salmon III, Sunable with four men, Suncob and two men and the crew of the Liberator A72-159, with nine RAAF crew members and the Sunbaker party.[9] The operatives of Groper were to also investigate possible survivors from Rimau, who it was believed could have found their way to Timor and been captured there.

The Groper party, under Captain A. D. Stevenson, was transported from Darwin to Kupang in Timor by ship as part of the Allied Occupying Force (Timforce), which had arrived to accept the Japanese surrender, disembarking on 11 September. To ensure they were self-sufficient, the party were equipped with stores for one month plus two jeeps with trailers and two B-2 wireless sets for use within Timor. The party travelled to Dili, where the Japanese-installed Governor of Portuguese Timor refused them permission to undertake their investigation as they did not have valid visas. They simply ignored him, making their way 25 miles (40 kilometres) south of Dili to the wreckage of an aircraft which they soon determined was the missing Liberator from 200 Flight with the Sunbaker team on board. The party were able to determine that three of the crew parachuted from the aircraft after it had mechanical trouble, but had been captured and killed.

With the return of most of the Groper party to Darwin on 19 October, Captain Stevenson with Sergeant Dooland as interpreter continued their work, including enquiring into reported Japanese atrocities and the disappearance of a British national, which resulted in the capture of eight Japanese troops. After interviewing some Malay and Indian members of Japanese labour units, they were able to ascertain the fate of two members of the Starfish party, Lieutenants Crofton-Moss and M. V. Gillies, and further details were extracted from the interrogation of Japanese officers who claimed one had been shot while trying to escape and the other shot 'when he offered resistance to capture'.[10] Following this work, Stevenson went on to command 'Steveforce', an Australian Army unit formed to transport Japanese troops and their supplies to Soembawa, north-west of Timor, ascertain the availability of Japanese shipping and determine the sympathies or otherwise of the local population.

Another unusual mission for SRD was the despatch of Lieutenant L. S. Black to Browse Island in the Indian Ocean to recover buried SRD caches from Mugger of arms, food and petrol, as the island was to be leased for phosphate mining. After a delay getting transport, Lieutenant Black flew to Truscott airfield in the north of Western Australia and then by launch to Hornet Base at Cape Voltaire on the Kimberley coast. The *Official History* notes:

> The stores cache near the camp site at Hornet Base had been
> disturbed, possibly by natives, and all food and camp utensils were
> missing. Two .38 Smith and Wesson pistols and one 9mm Austen
> SMG were also missing. All other arms comprising one Bren,
> two .303 rifles, two Austens and four pistols were found to be in
> unserviceable condition due to rust and were returned to SRD
> Darwin. Water cans and tins containing webbing were rotted
> and dumped in the bay.[11]

Further north, in British North Borneo, the end of the war saw even greater support from the local inhabitants. In a report headed, 'Application of Propaganda Labuan-Brunei Areas', it states that the Japanese 'had adopted a general plan of withdrawing to the hinterland, and unlike the situation generally prevalent in other Pacific theatres, had not shown the usual aggressive spirit in the holding of fixed lines. It was reasonable to assume then that the Japanese realised Allied superiority in men and material and sought the means of withdrawal and possible escape, rather than the typical suicidal stand'.[12]

This intelligence of the withdrawal of the Japanese had been sourced by SRD, who had been active in support of the AIF Borneo operations, in particular at Tarakan and Balikpapan and in attempts to rescue Allied POWs in Japanese camps around Sandakan. In British North Borneo, the series of Agas operations had begun in February 1945 and consisted of five separate operations (known as Agas I–V), and a parallel series of operations codenamed Semut (Semut I–IV) began the following month. Both of these large parties remained in the field until well after the end of the war and unlike many previous SRD operations worked in close cooperation with the Australian 9th Division (Oboe I), at Labuan and in Brunei (Oboe VI) and in support of the Australian 7th Division at Balikpapan (Oboe II).

Due to the remote nature of the Semut groups, it took some time to pass on the details of the Japanese surrender and the work that isolated units were expected to now do. Jack Tredrea, the radio operator who had been involved in Operation Semut in Sarawak, stated:

When I got orders from Harrisson [Major Tom Harrisson, the CO of the Semut operation] that the war was over, it was the third week in October and he then told me to get out the best way I could. I paid off my boys, but went against Harrisson's orders that all the weapons issued to my boys had to be destroyed. I did destroy perhaps 95 per cent, but no way was I going to let my guerrillas travel back to their areas without protection. So I did leave them with a few 303s and bullets. The rest all went in the river.[13]

By the end of hostilities, Agas I had been in the field for six months, sending back intelligence, training an effective local guerrilla force and on occasion ambushing and killing Japanese troops. In early August, the party split: one group was under Captain D. S. Sutcliffe and the other under Lieutenant D. K. L. Harlem. Harlem had planned four short, sharp raids, and to assist him Lieutenant Jock Hollingworth cut a secret jungle track to enable the party to operate and escape. During this time, a local informed Harlem that a large Japanese party of 60 troops were in a number of prahus and heading in his direction to wipe out his camp. This information was relayed to Morotai, which quickly ordered an air strike in which 16 prahus were destroyed and about 50 Japanese were killed or drowned.

On 14 August, Lieutenants Harlem and Hollingworth met to plan raids on Japanese in the Paitan area in the far north of Borneo, but 'received orders that day to cease all military activities except in self-defence'.[14] The Australians split into three parties to return to Bongaya, but one ran into Japanese troops who immediately fired on them. Harlem, acting on a hunch, quickly moved through a village called Basai, where on the following night the Japanese laid a major ambush for the Australian party. All three parties returned safely to Keniogan Island and were extracted, except for Harlem, Sergeant D. Roberts (signaller) and Corporal

W. A. C. Russell, plus a few locals who remained behind to keep watch on the Japanese and guard their base.

Just before the surrender, Des Foster, an operative on Semut III, was inserted by Catalina in the Philippines, about 50 miles (80 kilometres) up a river with instructions to return to Cebu and report on the Japanese. He recalled of this operation:

> . . . we took up a position about 300–400 yards from the Japs. We tested them out and we were there when the war ended. [As I was] a cadet journalist, we had a radio and listened to the BBC, and I took down the announcement that Japan had surrendered. So I wrote a letter to the Japanese commander telling him of these events and calling on him to surrender and I signed myself 'Major'. We found a brave Chinese man who was prepared to carry it into Cebu and we waited and waited, and later that day he came back. He'd been roughed up a bit, but he had an answer addressed to me asking me by what authority I acted. In the next day or two, [Major] Bill Sochon accepted the surrender on the bridge at Cebu.[15]

Beginning on 20 September 1945, now well over a month after the cessation of hostilities, Lieutenant Harlem led a ten-day patrol of 180 miles (290 kilometres) with Sergeant Roberts and Corporal Russell to report on Japanese troop movements and their organisational status, and to find any remaining POWs. He soon found that the remaining Japanese forces were without food and medical supplies, and were suffering from various diseases. Harlem also located abandoned Japanese camps, some showing signs of strafing, along with the sites of various unoccupied bivouacs. They found evidence that 75 POWs had been killed by Japanese troops in June 'and that cannibalism was practised'.[16] Along the way they also came upon a Japanese commander who, aware that the war was over, was prepared to lead his troops to Sandakan. A following reconnaissance of the village of Khamansie 'revealed the presence of 42 armed Japanese, 47 Javanese Police, 150 Chinese Japanese Coy Employees and 4 Japanese prostitutes'.[17]

A crucial part of SRD's work at this time was trying to find and return Allied POWs. On 8 August, SRD had received information that two Australian POWs were hiding in the jungle, having escaped from their camp at Ranau, and immediately set out to locate them. On 10 August, they found WO Bill Sticpewich,[18] who was in a very weak condition and who informed them that his mate, Driver Herman Reither, had died two days earlier of dysentery. He also reported that four other Australians, Privates Bill Moxham, Nelson Short, Keith Botterill and Gunner Francis 'Andy' Anderson, had also escaped, but he did not know where they were at that time. (These men were discovered soon afterwards, and returned to Australia.)

On 18 August, the party under Flight Lieutenant Geoffrey Ripley (RAAF), Sergeant Amos Hywood (AIF signaller) and some native police were reinforced by a medical team under Major J. A. Forster and six men to search for and extract any remaining POWs in British Northern Borneo inland from Sandakan. A local by the name of Gimbahan attempted to sneak food into the 110-mile camp (this was 110 miles from Sandakan (176 kilometres) and about five miles (eight kilometres) south of the end of the march route at Ranau), where about 20 Australian prisoners were under guard by 80 Japanese soldiers. At the time, there were still about 2000 Japanese in the area, and though many were seriously debilitated through sickness and starvation, some were still searching for WO Sticpewich and collaborators had been sent to return him.

After Sticpewich was found, messages began arriving from other Australian POWs, all in a very grave condition, by local people. These men were flown back to Labuan, but not before one of the small Auster aircraft carrying Private Bill Moxham crashed on take-off and he suffered head injuries.

The idea of rescue missions to save Allied prisoners had long been debated and planned. There were up to 20,000 Australian POWs in Japanese hands, those who were captured after the fall of Singapore and the survivors of Sparrow, Gull and Lark Forces. Allied intelligence was that some 2750 Allied prisoners had been sent from Singapore to work on Japanese airfields at Sandakan. Here they suffered at the hands of the camp commandant, Captain Susumi Hoshijima, from overwork, starvation, torture and untreated diseases including malaria, dysentery, beri-beri and tuberculosis.

In mid-1944, a rescue mission involving an Australian paratrooper drop had been planned and training had begun. This never went ahead, and the reasons for the delay and then abandonment of the plan have been debated ever since. At the time, General Blamey said MacArthur had refused to supply C-47 aircraft (Douglas Dakotas) as transport, but this seems odd given he had over 600 at his disposal and the Australians had about 80 aircraft also available.

Others blamed SRD for not providing the necessary intelligence and the RAAF for not providing aerial photographs of the camps. There was also a genuine concern that any attempt by the Allies to rescue POWs would result in mass executions of both prisoners and civilian internees, if for no other reason than to cover for war crimes.

Whatever was the case, it seems in retrospect that the rescue mission was not given the priority it should have been given. Even in SRD operational orders for Agas and Semut, the finding and reporting on POWs, while noted, is not given high priority. As a result, SRD found themselves a scapegoat for Blamey's lack of concern about POWs, as did MacArthur. Winning the war was Blamey's main goal, and a POW rescue mission was not on his list of priorities.

Putting aside the possible failure of SRD with respect to the rescue of POWs, the work of the unit in Borneo, from the insertion of Python in October 1943 through to the Agas, Semut and Platypus operations, was a major contribution to the success of AIF operations during mid-1945, in particular at Tarakan, Brunei Bay and Labuan and in the landing at Balikpapan. In the case of Agas I, in a short time they were able to establish a rapport with the local people and build an extensive network of intelligence-gathering agents.

While the information was at times overstated and unreliable, it provided details for Allied air operations including the bombing of land-based facilities, camps and defensive positions, and the strafing of supply vessels and river craft. The Agas operatives were also able to train and arm local guerrilla units, who contained Japanese movement inland. Also invaluable was the establishment of radio links to various points, the identification of potential drop zones and Catalina landing points and the provision of medical help through the building of hospitals for the local people.

The Allied position in Borneo was aided by the continued dropping of leaflets and propaganda. As the Japanese retreated inland, hungry and with very low morale, leaflets were dropped along their lines of retreat 'harping on reverses on the home front, the lack of planes, ammunition, and the hopelessness of reinforcements arriving, the difficulty of the terrain through which he [the Japanese soldier] was retreating and the ability of native ambush, and finally stressing allied successes and advances in Borneo'.[19]

It was reported that, due to the constant bombardment and strafing, the enemy were confused as to where to flee, and were discarding their arms and equipment so as to carry any food and supplies they could obtain. Leaflets were also dropped to the locals informing them of the defeats of the Japanese to the north and the bombing of Tokyo, stressing that the locals must avoid the Japanese, provide no food or assistance, report the lines of Japanese retreat to the Allies and if possible provide assistance to downed Allied airmen.

It was also important for SRD to determine the morale and health of the remaining Japanese, as ill, demoralised troops are likely to put up less resistance. It was widely reported that Japanese morale was very low, and that

> many of their guns had been spiked and those not blown up
> had been abandoned. They have very few machine guns and are
> poorly armed. Each Japanese officer is reputed to have a white
> surrender flag with him as well as a Union Jack. (note quite
> possibly souvenirs but it has been suggested might be for eventual
> surrender usage). The officers are reputed to be particularly
> nervous during air raids.[20]

This intelligence work regarding the enemy was carried on by Agas II and the Semut missions. While some argue the Agas operations had little military success, they were politically successful. By contacting guerrilla units and coordinating the harassment of the Japanese, the training and arming of local people, the building of hospitals and the provision of medical attention and food, the Agas operatives gave the local people hope and a future.

After the defeat of the enemy, the Allies were able to provide the familiar administrative structure which existed prewar to allow for the postwar resumption of the British and Dutch administrations. By also including an active role for locals in the new administration, the Allies dramatically reduced the potential of anarchy, civil disorder and tribal clashes in the administrative vacuum that often exists after the end of hostilities, as happened in French Indochina.

To manage the immediate postwar administration of Borneo and to establish a stable administration, the 1st Australian Corps, which then had control of this territory, created the British Borneo Civil Affairs Unit, known as BBCAU. After various discussions between Brigadier C. F. C. Macaskie and Lieutenant Colonel Chapman-Walker of SRD, guidelines for the implementation of BBCAU were drawn up. SRD personnel were to assist BBCAU officers to take over areas once under SRD control, which provided a convenient overlap between the wartime administration and the ongoing task of SRD to report on and address the remaining Japanese forces dispersed across Borneo. This cooperation continued until the disbandment of the BBCAU in December 1945.

On 12 October 1945, SRD officially handed over command of the area then under its responsibility to BBCAU.[21] This handover to BBCAU included responsibility for the continued payment for supplies, local police and the costs of civil administration in areas occupied by SRD, both within British North Borneo and Sarawak, and included reimbursement of SRD for expenditure after 1 September. After which time, all financial responsibility would be assumed by BBCAU. It also stated in the meeting notes to confirm the verbal arrangements, dated 17 September, that, 'All SRD personnel not attached to BBCAU must be withdrawn from the field by 7 Oct 1945 so that the complete evacuation of SRD from British Borneo should be complete by 16 November 1945'.[22] It was signed by Lieutenant Colonel G. B. Courtney OC Group 'A' SRD.

SRD also handed over all stores, including weapons, vessels of various kinds, medical stores, food, clothing and radio equipment. The handover also allowed for those personnel from SRD wishing to remain for the period of military occupation to stay in Borneo, 'together with those who wish to be considered for post-war employment in the country'.[23] The collection of issued weapons was another concern. In Sarawak, unlike in Malaya, as Semut had kept a precise record of rifle and bolt numbers and who they had been issued to, they were able to account for every weapon issued.

The operational details of this handover, and the overall control imposed by HQ 9th Australian Division, did see issues arise. As a result, Lieutenant Colonel Courtney, the officer in command of the handover, wrote, 'The withdrawal of white control in the interior will inevitably result in a Dyak rising in Sarawak and inter-tribal strife in parts of BNB [British North Borneo], and the rehabilitation of the country will be retarded. British prestige, already difficult to maintain owing to the apparent inaction of 9 Aust. Division, and the freedom from molestation, will suffer a severe decline.'[24]

Yet, in some places, the locals did not even know the war was over. A report dated 3 September 1945 noted, 'The natives are unaware of the surrender of Japan. They are intensely pro-allied and hate the Japanese. It is stated that if the Japanese runaway to the villages, they will be killed by the inhabitants.'[25]

At this time, SRD was also providing intelligence reports on Singapore and Bali. An example is a report dated 13 August, indicating possible minefields and safe passages through the western approaches to Tanjong Pagar near Singapore, details of black-market prices for rice, the location of Japanese-occupied buildings and the 'coolie' work being done by white POWs loading and unloading barges 'in the area where Havelock Rd runs adjacent to the Singapore River'.[26]

Similarly detailed reports arrived from Bali on Japanese troop numbers and movements; the placement of defences, in particular anti-aircraft defences; and details about Japanese stores, fuel supplies and food stashes. The movement of ships, down to small wind-power sailing craft, were logged, and often their cargo identified. One report on a village on Bali stated, 'About 500 Army personnel were stationed there, many of them carrying wooden weapons only',[27] while in another, 'Living conditions . . . were bad. Women and children dressed in gunny bags and many suffered from malaria and skin diseases.'[28] There were even reports on education, with one stating, 'There were 98 children and two teachers in the school. Japanese study books were confiscated on instruction of the NEFIS III Party and the teachers were instructed to continue teaching on the pre-war basis. They were very agreeable to this instruction.'[29]

Another report from Bali notes that the 3000 Japanese on the island were 'more or less equally divided between Navy and Army personnel',[30] with their headquarters in the Bali Hotel, and that due to the recent shelling of the harbour, the Japanese had installed a six-inch gun, though this had not been mounted by 8 June 1945. The same reports indicated the location of underground shelters, tank traps, anti-aircraft guns, fox holes and the existence of dummy aircraft made of bamboo. Details of the chief of the Kempeitai are also provided. The man was 'named Kawa Seka (known to the inhabitants as the 'Yellow Tiger'). He lives in

Denpasar and his office is in the Dutch Administrative Offices. He is a ruthless man. His age is between 32 and 35 years. He is about 5'5" tall and very stocky and thickset. His face is slightly pock-marked. No visible gold teeth.'[31]

In the same report, there is mention of 'one Dutchman and one Eurasian, both of the military forces, [who] have been at large since the Japanese occupation and are cared for by certain Chinese and Balinese. They have a hut in the jungle. The Japanese are not aware of their presence. Both men are in a pitiful condition.'[32] It continues, 'At Boeleleng, apart from the brothels of the Indonesian women, there is one containing a Dutch girl, blonde, name not known, aged 20 plus and one Dutch girl, blonde, name unknown, aged 7–8 years. There were also three Eurasian girls aged about 20. They were for the use of special officers. It is not known whether the little girl has been used for immoral purposes, but it is assumed not.'[33]

While all this intelligence-gathering back-and-forth went on, the men of SRD, in particular the operatives from the Z Special Unit, had one wish: to go home. As in the First World War, a priority system was introduced whereby married men with families went first, and 'It depended how long you had served overseas but it was several weeks before we came home on a troop ship, which took about ten days.'[34]

Roland Griffiths-Marsh estimated that of the 2098 days he served in the AIF, he spent just 91 days in a bed,[35] and as he had been just 16 when he enlisted, on his return from the war he had little education, no professional training, and no useful or influential contacts back in 'Civvy Street'. His hardships didn't end there. As he recalled:

For five years and seven months I had been a frontline soldier.
I had fought in four campaigns around the world, consisting

of seven major battles, several operations, one major rear-guard action, innumerable patrols, ambushes and firefights. I had been sunk at sea, strafed and bombed from the air. I had been wounded, injured many times and had malaria, dengue, sand-fly fever, amoebic dysentery and God knows what else.[36]

After the war I suffered from amoebic dysentery and my bowel extruded and I was dying. I had operations as a result. It took me about five years to return to civilian life. I was unemployable, I was completely shattered, my nerves had gone, I'd knock a person down for the slightest provocation. But I was very lucky. I met a marvellous lady and slowly my sanity came back.[37]

There were many men like him, dedicated volunteers into the AIF who found themselves, through bad luck or bad management, in a unit like Z Special. While it was 'Boys Own' stuff, it was deadly serious, unbelievably frightening and fraught with danger and the possibility of an agonising death. Yet these men had volunteered, trained and stepped out of an aircraft into the cold jet stream of a lumbering Liberator over a green carpet of hostile jungle or paddled their frail, canvas folboats into a darkened shore, not knowing what awaited them. While some question the military value of SRD's operational successes, the men involved in its operations were truly brave men and their exploits were accomplishments. Today, so many seem to forget what so few men did to help win the war.

While the intention was to have all SRD personnel out of Labuan by 15 October, some units and men remained, for example Major Tom Harrisson, who, with Lieutenant W. T. Thomas, two ORs and a Japanese envoy, were attempting to contact Japanese troops between the Bawang valley and the Borneo coast to complete their surrender and disarming. It was not until early

December 1945 that the last of the SRD operatives and their headquarters staff returned to Australia.

By the time of SRD's disbandment, the unit had a strength of 205 officers and 996 other ranks. It had at its disposal Flight 200, a total of eight modified Liberators for its own use with nine air crews, each of 11 men, plus a ground staff of 450. It also had a fleet of vessels plus access to US and British submarines. As at August 1945, the controller of AIB, the organisation of which SRD was part, 'reported that the several Intelligence and guerrilla organisations co-ordinated by the bureau had, during the course of the war, killed 7,061 Japanese, taken 141 prisoners and rescued 1,054 servicemen and civilians from enemy occupied territory'.[38] SRD's stated casualties were 18 killed, 11 executed, two died while POWs, 36 missing believed killed and four drowned.[39]

The *Official History* concludes of these missions, 'The operations of the AIB as a whole undoubtedly justified the expenditure of blood and effort, but that is not to say that each of its components justified itself or that every type of project it undertook was wise.'[40] As an operative on Magpie I and Semut III operations, Des Foster, reflected, 'I've often asked myself what was achieved in strategic or tactical terms, but it is about the futility of war in many ways.'[41] Remembering so many of his mates who had been killed, it is no wonder he saw the futility of war. When asked about remembering the work of Z Special and SRD, he went on to say, 'I'd like to see some recognition for the guys who lost their lives doing what they did. And they were volunteers twice; they volunteered to serve and they volunteered again to take on difficult jobs.'[42]

After the war, many of the unit's records were destroyed, and the remainder went into storage with the proviso they were not to be released for 30 years, until 1976. While this policy existed to protect the sensitive nature of the operations, it set the precedent for the retention of documents under what is known as 'the closed period' in the case of files from ASIO and probably ASIS and the Australian Signals Directorate. However, the 30-year rule did not seem to apply at the time I requested files for research in 1989–90, when I was denied access on the grounds that material contained in these files was sensitive and still relevant for national security.

And so the gallant, dangerous and lonely world of SRD slipped into historical oblivion, its operatives left to hide behind their AIF enlistment units, unable to tell their stories, particularly to their families, and in many cases these men died without their deeds being rightfully acknowledged. Fortunately some committed their wartime experience to books, often privately published and not widely distributed. But their commitment to the war effort and their gallantry must never be forgotten.

Acknowledgements

Research for this book came principally from SOA, AIB and SRD files held in the National Archives of Australia in Canberra and made available to researchers and writers online. I want to thank the NAA for their great contribution to our history with the massive task they have undertaken to digitise files and make these available online to researchers and authors. They do a superb job making all Commonwealth Government documents available to the people of Australia, not only via their online resources, but also through exhibitions and the presentation of documents at their offices in Canberra. When in Canberra, take the time to visit their exhibition space in Kings Avenue, a stone's throw from Old Parliament House.

Of course the other great repository of Australian military history is the Australian War Memorial. While most of the files I accessed were from the NAA, research was also undertaken at the AWM, and I thank members of the AWM staff at the Research Centre, in particular Dr Roger Lee, an old mate. Over the hill is another source of research information at the Australian Defence Force Academy, a Canberra-based faculty of the University of New South Wales, where again the staff have always been helpful. I used material from their massive oral history collection and give my thanks for their work in this area and their permission to reproduce this material.

Acknowledgements

Individually I would also like to thank various people who have assisted with the research for this book. First, Lionel Aitken, Tony Turner and Ben King, for providing access to the filmed interviews they have shot over many years of men from SRD and Z Special and the supportive services. I am most grateful for their generosity and assistance in getting access to these interviews and being able to extract quotes from these men and include them in my manuscript.

Prior to beginning this book, I was fortunate to meet and interview Roland Griffiths-Marsh and Edgar 'Mick' Dennis. What wonderful Australians and unbelievably brave, resourceful and true gentlemen, gracious and happy to pass on their experiences and the details of their terrible war. Both have sadly passed away, but their memory remains in the hearts of all who knew and had the privilege to meet them. In this regard, I would like to mention Roland's wonderful partner in life, Maayken Griffiths-Marsh, who also passed away recently, on 28 April 2020, and who assisted Roland with his book, *I Was Only Sixteen* and looked after him to the end. Thanks also to Geoff Black, who wrote up Mick Dennis's story in his book *Against All Odds*, and my thanks for the introduction to Roland and Maayken by Jennifer Ballard, the founder and patron of the Under Sixteens organisation.

I also thank Lynette Ramsay Silver for her invaluable assistance and insight in answering my queries and providing original research and details as presented in her book, *Deadly Secrets: The Singapore Raid 1942–45*. Lynette was responsible, along with others, for the recovery of the story of missing operatives from the ill-fated Operation Rimau and in making this history available to a wider audience. In this regard, thanks also to my old mate Rob Macklin, who provided details of the operation in his book *Kill the Tiger: The Truth About Operation Rimau*.

Others who assisted and who I would like to thank are Caroline Terode for assistance with oral history, Ian McPhedran for access to his book *The Mighty Krait*, General Steve Gower for answering my odd questions, Professor David Horner for information from his definitive history, *SAS: Phantoms of War*, and to Dr Antony Lighten for the loan of Tom Harrisson's book *World Within: A Borneo Story* and Paul Ham for details on Sandakan.

Thanks to my publisher at Penguin Random House Australia, Meredith Curnow, for her patience and gracious help, to my editors Tom Langshaw and Patrick Mangan and to all at Penguin Random House Australia for supporting, assisting and promoting Australian writers and their important contribution to our history and culture.

Thanks to my wife Heather and my family for allowing me time and space to work, to travel to Canberra and get lost in research and early-morning writing sessions.

And my sincere thanks to all who cheered me along, encouraged me and raised my spirits through some dark times with droughts, fires and pandemic.

I hope my small contribution to our history and to the memory of these wonderful souls may fill a gap in popular history and ensure their deeds and their contribution is never forgotten.

Lest We Forget.

Notes

Introduction

1 Herodotus, *The Persian Wars*, VI, p. 106.

1: Return to War

1 *Report of Admiral of the Fleet Viscount Jellicoe of Scapa on the Naval Mission to the Commonwealth of Australia*, p. 163.
2 *Sydney Morning Herald*, 22 October 1919, p. 11.
3 *The Official History of Special Operations Australia*, Volume I, Chapter 1, 'Between the Wars', pp. 4–5.
4 Horner, D. M. *High Command: Australia and Allied Strategy 1939–1945*, pp. 1–2.
5 Shedden, F. 'An Outline of the Principles of Imperial Defence with Special References to Australian Defence'.
6 Day, D. *The Great Betrayal: Britain, Australia and the Onset of the Pacific War 1939–42*, p 3.
7 *Official History*, Volume I, Chapter 1, 'Between the Wars', p. 23.
8 Ibid., p. 24.
9 *House of Commons Debates*, Volume 299, p. 1062, quoted in *Official History*, Volume I, Chapter 1, p. 22.
10 *Official History*, Volume I, Chapter 1, p. 21.
11 Hasluck, P. *The Government and the People 1939–1941*, Chapter 2, p. 104.
12 *Official History*, Volume I, Chapter 1, p. 31.

2: 'Now Set Europe Ablaze'

1 Mentioned in a speech in the Commons by Churchill, 28 May 1940, reporting on the capitulation of Belgium.
2 Statement by Hitler, 5 June 1940, after the Dunkirk evacuation.
3 Churchill, speech to the House of Commons on 4 June 1940.
4 Lett, B. *The Small Scale Raiding Force*, p. 4.
5 Churchill, speech to the House of Commons, 4 June 1940.
6 Churchill, speech to the war cabinet, 28 May 1940.
7 Dalton, H. *The Second World War Diary of Hugh Dalton 1940–45*, p. 62.
8 Simpson, P. *The Spy: Modern Spying from the Cold War to the War on Terror*, p. 5.
9 Foot, M. R. D. *SOE in France*, p. 153.
10 Captain Selwyn Jepson in an interview by the sound archive section of the Imperial War Museum, London.
11 Foot, M. R. D. *SOE in France*, pp. 35–6.

3: A Fourth Fighting Force

1 Brown, G. and Anderson, D. *Invasion 1942? Australia and the Japanese Threat*, Background Paper No. 6, 1992, Department of the Parliamentary Library, Canberra.
2 *Official History*, Volume I, p. 3; National Archives of Australia (NAA), A3269:235324, p. 16.
3 Ibid.
4 Ibid., p. 17.
5 Ibid.
6 Ibid., p. 18.
7 Ibid.
8 Ibid., p. 21.
9 Ibid., p. 23.
10 Ibid., p. 24.
11 Ibid.
12 Ibid., p. 14.
13 Ibid., p. 15.
14 FELO Section 1 – Organisation, NAA, A3269:235384, p. 4.
15 Ibid.
16 Ibid., p. 6.
17 There is a naval message which states: 'Aeroplane with F/O Keogh and ashes overdue feared lost. Believed not to have reached Lae. Suggest send more ashes and leaflets'. A3269:235423, p. 44.
18 FELO document, NAA, A3269:235423, p. 14.
19 *The Official History*, Volume II, Part 3, Semet I, p. 28; NAA, A3269:235326, p. 160.
20 Ibid., p. 31.

4: 'We're Going to Singapore'

1 McPhedran, I. *The Mighty Krait*, p. 15.
2 The author of *The Jungle Is Neutral*.
3 McPhedran, I. *The Mighty Krait*, pp. 18–19.
4 Ramsay Silver, L. *Deadly Secrets: The Singapore Raids 1942–45*, p. 118.
5 Ibid., p. 22.
6 Notes and Observations on training: NAA, A3962:235232, p. 49.
7 *Log book relating to Operation Jaywick* compiled by Lieutenant D. M. N. Davidson (RNVR), NAA, A3269:235233, p. 15.
8 All descriptions from *Log book relating to Operation Jaywick* compiled by Lieutenant D. M. N. Davidson (RNVR), NAA, A3269:235233, pp. 6–12.
9 Oral history interview of Horace Young, ADFA Australians at War Archive, 1815.
10 Ibid.
11 Secret Report dated 24 March 1943. NAA, A3269:235232, p. 85.
12 Oral history interview of Arthur Jones, ADFA Australians at War Archive, 1010.
13 Davidson, D. *Report from Exmouth Gulf*. NAA, A3269:235232, pp. 34–6.
14 Ibid., p. 35.
15 Narrative Account, NAA, A3269:235331, p. 9.
16 Oral history interview of Horace Young, ADFA Australians at War Archive, 1815.
17 Oral history interview of Arthur Jones, ADFA Australians at War Archive, 1010.
18 Oral history interview of Horace Young, ADFA Australians at War Archive, 1815.

19 Oral history interview of Arthur Jones, ADFA Australians at War Archive, 1010.

20 Report, Part III, Navigational Log, NAA, A3269:235231, p. 22.

21 Report, NAA, A3269:235232, p. 95.

22 Ibid., p. 22.

23 NAA, A3269:235232, p. 96.

24 Ibid.

25 Contained in secret report, 24 March 1943: Ref: 1940919, 12/61.

26 Oral history interview of Horrie Young, ADFA Australians at War Archive, 1815.

27 Contained in secret report, 24 March 1943: Ref: 1940919, 12/61.

28 Oral history interview of Horrie Young, ADFA Australians at War Archive, 1815.

29 Narrative Account, NAA, A3269:235231, p. 12.

30 Oral history interview of Arthur Jones, ADFA Australians at War Archive, 1010.

31 Ibid.

32 Narrative Account, NAA, A3269:235231, p. 13.

33 Ibid., p. 13.

34 Oral history interview of Arthur Jones, ADFA Australians at War Archive, 1010.

35 Ibid.

36 Ibid.

37 NAA, A3269:235231, p. 14.

38 Oral history interview of Arthur Jones, ADFA Australians at War Archive, 1010.

39 Ibid.

40 Ibid.

41 Ibid.

42 NAA, A3269:35231, p. 14.

43 Ibid.

44 Oral history interview of Arthur Jones, ADFA Australians at War Archive, 1010.

45 Ibid.

46 Ibid.

47 Ibid.

48 NAA, A3269:235231, p. 15.

49 Ibid.

50 NAA, A3269: 235231, p. 18.

51 Oral history interview of Arthur Jones, ADFA Australians at War Archive, 1010.

52 Ibid.

53 Ibid.

54 Narrative Account, NAA, A3269:235231, p. 16.

55 Oral history interview of Arthur Jones, ADFA Australians at War Archive, 1010.

56 NAA, A3269:235231, p. 18.

57 Oral history interview of Horrie Young, ADFA Australians at War Archive, 1815.

58 NAA, A3269:235231, p. 16.

59 Oral history interview of Arthur Jones, ADFA Australians at War Archive, 1010.

60 Oral history interview of Horrie Young, ADFA Australians at War Archive, 1815.

61 Ibid.

62 Ibid.

63 Oral history interview of Horrie Young, ADFA Australians at War Archive, 1815.

64 Oral history interview of Arthur Jones, ADFA Australians at War Archive, 1010.

65 Oral history interview of Horrie Young, ADFA Australians at War Archive, 1815.

5: The Early Days – Operations in Timor

1 *Official History*, Volume V, Appendix 2, Timor, p. 606.
2 *Official History*, Volume II, Operations, NAA, A3269:235326, p. 12.
3 Report on Lizard II, *Official History*, Volume II, NAA, A3269:235326, p. 27.
4 Ibid., p. 28.
5 Report on Lizard III, *Official History*, Volume II, NAA, A3269:235326, p. 29.
6 NAA, A3269:235186, p. 27.
7 Ibid.
8 Ibid., p. 29.
9 Ibid.
10 Ibid.
11 Ibid., p. 33.
12
13 Report on Portolizard. NAA, A3269:235326, p. 32.

6: The Great Tragedy of Lagarto

1 *Official History*, Volume II, NAA, A3269:235326, p. 21.
2 Lagarto Report, NAA, A3269:235326, p. 37.
3 Ibid.
4 Ibid., p. 38.
5 Ibid.
6 Ibid.
7 Ibid., p. 39.
8 Ibid.
9 Ibid.
10 Ibid.
11 Ibid., p. 27.
12 Ibid., p. 28.
13 *Official History*, Volume II, Report on Operation Cobra, NAA, A3269:235326, p. 48.
14 The Japanese text mentions ACB but this is probably a typo as they would most likely be referring to AIB.
15 *Official History*, Volume II, NAA, A3269:235326, p. 37.
16 Laffin, J. *Special and Secret*, p. 100.
17 From an oral history interview with Captain Keith Stringfellow.

7: The Insect and Fish Operations – Papua New Guinea

1 NAA, A3269:235134, p. 4.
2 NAA, A3269:235140, p. 290.
3 Ibid., p. 293.
4 NAA, A3269:235140, p. 294.
5 Ibid., pp. 38–9.

8: Increasing the Pressure and Pushing West

1 Kwai, Anna Annie. *Solomon Islanders in World War II: An Indigenous Perspective.* Introduction, p. 3.
2 Quoted in The Coastwatchers website, RAN Gun Plot.
3 Report Captain N. Blood, NAA, A3269:235119, p. 37.

4 *SRD Official History*, Volume II, p. 78, NAA, A3269:235326, p. 78.
5 *Official History*, Volume II, p. 81.
6 *Official History*, Volume II, A3269:235326, p. 116.

9: The Ill-Fated Operation Copper

1 Black, G. *Against All Odds*, pp. 99–100.
2 Oral history interview with Mick Dennis.
3 Black, G. *Against All Odds*, pp. 99–104.
4 Oral history interview with Mick Dennis.
5 Ibid.
6 Black, G. *Against All Odds*, p. 111.
7 Ibid.
8 Ibid., p. 114.
9 Ibid., p. 115.
10 Oral history interview with Mick Dennis.
11 Black, G. *Against All Odds*, p. 116.
12 Ibid., p 117.
13 Ibid., p. 119.
14 Ibid., pp. 120–1.
15 Oral history interview with Mick Dennis.
16 Black, G. *Against All Odds*, p. 127.
17 Ibid., p. 129.
18 Oral history interview with Mick Dennis.
19 Black, G. *Against All Odds*, p. 136.
20 Ibid., p. 139.
21 Ibid.
22 Ibid., p. 146.
23 Ibid.
24 Oral history interview with Mick Dennis.
25 Black, G. *Against All Odds*, p. 149.

10: The Bite of the Sand-fly – the Agas Operations

1 *Official History*, Volume II, p. 94, NAA, A3269: 235326.
2 Oral history interview with Graham Greenwood.
3 Ibid.
4 Oral history interview with Lindsay Cottee.
5 Ibid.
6 Ibid.
7 Ibid.
8 Ibid.
9 Ibid.
10 Ibid.
11 Ibid.
12 NAA, A3269:235015, p. 44.
13 *Official History*, Volume II, NAA, A3269:235326, p. 98.
14 NAA, A3269:235015, p. 49.
15 NAA, A3269:235015, p. 53.

16 *Official History*, Volume II, p. 104.
17 *Official History*, Volume II, NAA, A3269: 235326, p. 105.
18 Ibid., p. 106.
19 Ibid., p. 108.
20 Ibid., p. 109.
21 Ibid., p. 112.

11: The Bite of the Ant – the Semut Operations

1 Ibid., p. 157.
2 Ibid.
3 Ibid., p. 158.
4 Ibid.
5 Ibid., p. 159.
6 Ibid., p. 161.
7 Ibid.
8 Oral history interview with Jack Tredrea.
9 Ibid.
10 Untitled Intelligence Report, NAA, A3269:235039, p. 18.
11 Ibid.
12 Ibid., p. 19.
13 Oral history interview with Roland Griffiths-Marsh.
14 Oral history interview with Jack Tredrea.
15 Ibid.
16 Unnamed report, NAA, A3269:235039, p. 20.
17 Ibid., p. 21.
18 Oral history interview with Roland Griffiths-Marsh.
19 Oral history interview with Jack Tredrea.
20 Ibid.
21 Ibid.
22 Ibid.
23 A cosh is a handheld weapon like a small club, often a metal bar encased in leather for striking an opponent.
24 Oral history interview with Jack Tredrea.
25 American fighter aircraft, P-38 Lightning.
26 Oral history interview with Jack Tredrea.
27 Oboe operations III (Banjarmasin), IV (Surabaya) and V (NE Dutch Borneo) did not go ahead.
28 *Official History*, Volume II, p. 128.
29 Ibid.
30 Oral history interview with Jack Tredrea.
31 Oral history interview with Roland Griffiths-Marsh.
32 Heimann, J. M. *The Most Offending Soul Alive: Tom Harrisson and His Remarkable Life*, p. 212.
33 Oral history interview with Jack Tredrea.
34 NAA, A3269:235039, p. 23.
35 Ibid. *Official History*, Volume II, A3269:235326, p. 163.
36 NAA, A3269:235042, p. 86.
37 Ibid.

38 Account on Operation Semut III, AWM 2017.7.192, Collection Number 3DRL/6502, p. 1.
39 *Official History*, Volume II, p. 176.
40 Ibid., p. 178.
41 Ibid.
42 Ibid.
43 Account on Operation Semut III, AWM 2017.7.192, Collection number 3DRL/6502, p. 15.
44 Ibid.
45 *Official History*, Volume II, NAA, A3269:235326, p. 181.
46 Ibid., p. 184.
47 Ibid.
48 Ibid., p. 185.
49 Ibid., p. 186.
50 Ibid., p. 193.
51 Ibid., p. 195.
52 Oral history interview with Roland Griffiths-Marsh.
53 Oral history interview with Jack Tredrea.

12: The Secret War in the Spice Islands

1 It was during this landing, on 17 September, that cameraman Damien Parer was killed while filming US Marines.
2 Ibid.
3 *Official History*, Volume II, p. 190.
4 'Report of the Operation', NAA, A3269:235087, p. 16.
5 Special Report by Captain K. Stringfellow. NAA, A3269:235085, p. 20.
6 NAA, A3269:235085, p. 13.
7 Ibid., p. 8.
8 Oral history recording of Henry Fawkes.
9 Oral history recording of Des Foster.
10 Oral history recording of Henry Fawkes.
11 Ibid.
12 Raven, NAA, A3269:235093, p. 7. See report on Operation Raven, pp. 17–21 and pp. 26–28.
13 NAA, A3269:235093, p. 85.
14 Ibid., p. 17.
15 Ibid., p. 18.
16 Oral history interview with Gordon Philpott.
17 NAA, A3269:235093, p. 19.
18 *Official History*, Volume II, p. 199.
19 Oral history recording of Henry Fawkes.
20 Operational Report, Raven, NAA, A3269:235093, p. 20.
21 Oral history recording of Henry Fawkes.
22 NAA, A3269:235093, p. 20.
23 Oral history recording of Henry Fawkes.
24 Ibid.
25 Oral history recording of Keith Stringfellow.
26 Oral history recording of Henry Fawkes.
27 A3269:235093, p. 21.

13: In Support of Oboe II – Balikpapan

1 *Official History*, Volume II, p. 170.
2 Ibid., p. 172.
3 Ibid.
4 Ibid., p. 176.
5 Ibid., p. 179.
6 Ibid.
7 Ibid., p. 180.
8 Ibid.
9 Ibid., p. 181.
10 Ibid., p. 183.
11 Ibid., p. 184.

14: The Rescue of the Sultan

1 NAA, Report on Operation Opossum, A3269:235091, p. 36.
2 Ibid.
3 NAA, A3269:235092, p. 27.
4 Ibid.
5 Ibid., p. 34.
6 Ibid., p. 53.
7 Ibid.
8 NAA, A3269:235091, p. 32.
9 Ibid.
10 Oral history interview with Gordon Philpott.
11 Ibid.
12 NAA, A3269:235091, p. 30.
13 NAA, A3269:235107, p. 5.
14 Ibid., p. 8.
15 Oral history interview with Gordon Philpott.
16 Odgers, G. *Air War Against Japan*, p. 450.
17 *Official History*, Volume II, NAA, A3269:235326, p. 258.

15: The Audacious Disaster of Rimau

1 Operation Hornbill – Situation to Date. NAA, A3269:235244, p. 20.
2 Letter from Director SRD to the Controller of AIB on 24 April 1944. NAA, A3269:235244, p. 140.
3 NAA, A3269:235241, p. 4.
4 Ibid., p. 6.
5 Ibid.
6 NAA, A3269:235244, p. 19.
7 Ibid., p. 33.
8 Ibid., p. 34.
9 Ibid.
10 Memo from Director SRD to Controller AIB, 19 Sept 1944, NAA, A3269:235244, p. 6.
11 Q Plan Rimau Operation, NAA, A3269:235241, p. 9.
12 Ibid.
13 Ibid.

14 Lt-Comdr Davidson's Diary, p. 1, NAA, A3269:235236, p. 11.

15 Ibid., p. 2, ibid., p. 13.

16 Report by Major W. W. Chapman, NAA, A3269:235236, p. 27.

17 See NAA, A3269:235236, p. 32.

18 Ramsay Silver, L. *Deadly Secrets*, p. 265.

19 Planning orders, Operation Rimexit, NAA, A3269:235242, p. 3.

20 From an oral history interview with Keith Stringfellow.

16: The Last Raids

1 *Official History*, Volume II, p. 220.

2 Ibid., p. 221.

3 Report dated 10 February 1945. NAA, A3269:235247, p. 15.

4 Ibid., p. 19.

5 Ibid.

6 Report by Major W. Jinkins, NAA, A3269:235247, p. 28.

7 Ibid., p. 29.

8 Major Jinkins to Director SRD, NAA, A3269:235247, p. 88.

9 Ibid.

10 Ibid.

11 Ibid.

12 'Gunard' Operational Order, March 1945, NAA, A3269:235214, p. 6.

13 Report by Lieutenant Alex Hawkins, 4 April 1945, NAA, A3269:235214, p. 9.

14 Report from Captain USS *Brill*, NAA, A3269:235215, p. 9.

15 *Official History*, Volume II, p. 223.

16 Ramsay Silver, L. *Deadly Secrets*, p. 292.

17 Report by Lieutenant Anderson, 8 April 1945, NAA, A3269:235247, p. 44.

18 Operation Politician, Section IV – Report No 2, NAA, A3269:235247, p. 4.

19 Oral history interview of Lloyd Campbell.

20 Ibid.

21 Ibid.

22 Ibid.

23 Oral history interview of Lloyd Campbell.

24 Ibid.

25 Operational Report, NAA, A3269:235247, p. 5–6.

26 Oral history interview of Lloyd Campbell.

27 Operational Report, NAA, A3269:235247, p. 6.

28 Oral history interview of Lloyd Campbell.

29 Ibid.

30 Ibid., p. 69.

31 NAA, A3269:235247, p. 68.

32 Ibid., p. 65.

33 Ibid., p. 79.

34 *Official History*, Volume II, p. 224.

35 Waddy, Rowan. *On Operations with Z Special Unit*, Part 2, p. 19.

17: War's End

1 *Official History*, Operations and Administration, Volume I, NAA, A3269:235324, p. 34.

2 Ibid.
3 Final Reorganisation, NAA, A3269:235324, p. 34.
4 Ibid., p. 35.
5 NAA, A3269:235309, p. 22.
6 Ibid.
7 Ibid.
8 Ibid., p. 23.
9 *Official History*, Volume II, pp. 65–6.
10 Ibid., p. 67.
11 Ibid., p. 68.
12 Application of Propaganda, NAA, A3269:235077, p. 22.
13 Oral history interview with Jack Tredrea.
14 Ibid., p. 102.
15 Oral history interview of Des Foster.
16 Ibid., p. 103.
17 Ibid., p. 104.
18 Later investigations found WO Sticpewich may have collaborated with the Japanese, but this was inconclusive.
19 Application of Propaganda Labuan-Brunei areas – N. Borneo, NAA, A3269:235077, p. 22.
20 Extract from Diary Reports of Flight Lieutenant Elam, NAA, A3269:235077, p. 32.
21 Certificate of Hand Over From SRD to BBCAU, A3269:235065, p. 3.
22 Meeting notes from OC Group 'A' SRD to HQ 9 Aust. Div., 17 September 1945, A3269:235065, p. 14.
23 Summary of the position regarding control of BNB and Sarawak at 12 September 1945, A3269:235065, p. 16.
24 NAA, A3269:235065, p. 16.
25 Information Report No (AIB) 560, NAA, A3269:235227, p. 4.
26 Information Report No (AIB) 520, NAA, A3269:235227, p. 10.
27 NEFIS III Intelligence Report, NAA, A3269:235225, p. 11.
28 Ibid., p. 13.
29 Ibid.
30 Information Report No (AIB) 519, NAA, A3269:235227, p. 12.
31 Ibid., p. 15.
32 Ibid.
33 Information Report No (AIB) 519, NAA, A3269:235227, p. 16.
34 Oral history recording of Des Foster.
35 Griffiths-Marsh, R. *I Was Only Sixteen*, p. 362.
36 Ibid., p. 361.
37 Ibid.
38 *Second World War Official History*, Volume VII, The Final Campaigns, Appendix 4, p. 621.
39 Ibid.
40 Ibid., p. 622.
41 Oral history recording of Des Foster.
42 Ibid. Des Foster went on to manage radio station 2GB from 1960 to 1970.

Index

371

Index

Index